T0140437

Human–Computer Interaction Series

Editors-in-chief

Desney Tan
Microsoft Research, USA

Jean Vanderdonckt
Université catholique de Louvain, Belgium

More information about this series at http://www.springer.com/series/6033

Phil Turner

A Psychology of User Experience

Involvement, Affect and Aesthetics

 Springer

Phil Turner
School of Computing
Edinburgh Napier University
Edinburgh
UK

ISSN 1571-5035
Human–Computer Interaction Series
ISBN 978-3-319-88974-0   ISBN 978-3-319-70653-5   (eBook)
https://doi.org/10.1007/978-3-319-70653-5

Printed on acid-free paper

This Springer imprint is published by Springer Nature
The registered company is Springer International Publishing AG
The registered company address is: Gewerbestrasse 11, 6330 Cham, Switzerland

Preface

This book is about why we care about digital technology.

Origins

Human–computer interaction (HCI) is the study and development of interactive technology and has witnessed significant changes in brief history. While we continue to use these technologies to complete tasks—everything from managing a company's finances to killing make-believe aliens and, more recently, a whole raft of activities on our smart phones—our understanding is changing. This change centres on the move from the instrumental use of technology to the use of technology as an end in itself.

From the beginnings of HCI, psychology has been called upon in the service of better design, and rather less markedly, in the understanding of users. Changes in the use and application of interactive technology have also changed the scope of the underlying psychology of interaction. Where once "plain vanilla" cognitive psychology could be relied upon to make sense of how we use these technologies, it is now no longer sufficient. In thinking about how this has come about, we should recognise that a number of factors have been in play.

From HCI to UX

As a start, we briefly introduce three different ways in which the origins and development of HCI have been described by researchers. We begin with Grudin (2005) who offers a detailed, traditional, US-centric account; then we consider Harrison et al. (2007) who describe much the same developments but in terms of paradigms and changing metaphors; finally, Bødker, who prefers to characterise this in terms of "waves".

Grudin traces the roots of human–computer interaction to the work of a host of American visionaries including Vannevar Bush, JCR Licklider and Douglas Engelbart and, of course, to innovations such as ENIAC, the first American electronic computer. Inspired by their work, three threads of research differentiated themselves, namely human factors (and ergonomics), "HCI in MIS" (or information systems) and computer–human interaction which is described as the discretionary use of interactive technology. These three forms can still, more or less, be recognised.

Ergonomics is concerned with human factors and might be thought of as "fitting the machine to the person" and is where Grudin locates the psychology of HCI (as cognitive ergonomics perhaps). Ergonomics has witnessed renewed interest stimulated by the advent and widespread adoption of smaller, portable devices such as the smartphone and tablet. HCI in MIS includes user-centred and participatory design and the various technology acceptance models, while computer–human interaction (CHI) includes, for example, such things as Norman's emotional design proposal. Grudin notes that historically the human factors/ergonomic and the IS threads arose before CHI which he distinguishes by virtue of its focus on discretionary use. Grudin's history ends in 2005, and although he has identified much of the detailed historical development of the discipline, we should recognise that much has changed since then.

A complementary review appeared in 2007 in which Harrison, Tatar and Sengers told a different story using much the same evidence. They begin by observing that HCI rests on three different intellectual traditions. The first is human factors with its focus on man–machine fit; the second is "Classical Cognitivism/Information Processing" which emphasises theories and models of the relationship between computer and the human mind; while the third concerns the phenomenologically situated, experiential nature of interaction. It is argued that while the first two paradigms had dominated the (then) last twenty-five years of HCI, the emergence of the third saw the rise of approaches which did not fit these schools of thought. The authors identify such approaches as "participatory design, activity theory, user experience design, ethnomethodology, interaction analysis and critical design", adding that while the results of more traditional work would typically be a set of design implications, research in the third paradigm would be more likely to have a descriptive output which might not directly link to design. The epistemological and methodological assumptions are very different.

Finally, Bødker (2006) offers a distinctly European, or more specifically, Scandinavian, perspective. Her discussion identifies a "second wave[1]" of HCI which is characterised by "groups working with a collection of applications", with the emphasis on work tasks and significant participation of users (Bannon's 1991

---

[1]The characteristics of a first-wave HCI remain implicit in Bødker's argument, but may be assumed to be centred on task-based single user interaction.

human actors) in the design process. The second wave is informed by the theo-retical perspectives of situated action, distributed cognition and activity theory, and strongly grounded in context. She adds to this a third-wave HCI as the current paradigm, that is not only concerned with non-purposeful, often consumerist, home and leisure use, but ad hoc constellations of technology, together with the factors of emotion, culture and user experience. Bødker's critique observes that that some third-wave approaches partition home and work contexts too strongly and may also pay insufficient attention to user needs. The discussion closes with a call for gen-uine user participation in reflexive technological experiments and for research into tailoring not only of applications, but of configurations of technologies.

Since these reviews were published in the first decade of this century, aspects of Harrison et al.'s third paradigm and Bødker's third wave have become indeed become firmly established as the zeitgeist, with a focus on ever more capable technology, context—and of course the near-tautologous user experience (UX).

Scattered usages of "user experience" in its current sense[2] can be found in the HCI research literature as far back as the early 1990s—and arguably in Wixon and Whiteside's insightful 1987 paper which identifies the dialectic tension between user experience and engineering. However, the popular adoption of the concept may have been triggered—as with many other memes in HCI—by Donald Norman. In 1995, Norman and his colleagues Jim Miller and Austin Henderson presented an overview of their work at Apple, noting that their preferred alternative to "human interface research and application" was "user experience". The new term was reflected in the titles of Apple's "User Experience Architect's Office", which worked across research and design divisions, and the newly introduced "User Experience Requirements Document". The published summary of this organisa-tional overview (Norman et al., 1995) is silent on the rationale for the adoption of the term, although we may speculate that it reflects an intention to broaden the focus of research and development beyond the interface and its usability.

We can see very similar thinking underlying Alben's (1996) article for the ACM's *interactions* magazine, entitled "Quality of experience". Here Alben writes that "experiences, as [people] use a range of products, from off the shelf software to websites, from electronic games to medical diagnostic equipment, are what effective interaction design is all about" and that experience encompasses "all the aspects of how people use a product: the way it feels in their hands, how well they understand how it works, how they feel about it while they're using it, how well it serves their purposes, and how well it fits into the entire context in which they are using it. If these experiences are engaging and productive, then people value them." In these two statements, we find some of the enduring aspects of what is now "user" experience—it is concerned with products, with application areas beyond the functional, with feelings and with context, and further development of the argument later in Alben's article adds aesthetics to the mix.

---

[2]Rather as a synonym for the user familiarity with the use of technology.

Technological Developments

Such movements in HCI thinking cannot be detached from technological and design-led advances. From technology as a means to an (work-related) end, interactive technology became ubiquitous and design for the ordinary person became an issue. Then, technology ceased to be just a means to an end but became an end in itself, used for non-productive purposes and became about all about me. The personal computer that sat–and still sits—on the desk of many an office worker was anything but personal. A personal computer was distinguished from other technology of the time in that it had its own processor, hard disk and local applications. It was personal only in as much as it was not shared. The first personal computers worthy of the name were laptop computers, jealously owned by the office manager or junior executive: they were more of a status symbol than they were portable computing power.

Some 10 years after the appearance of the first personal computer (PC), the journal Personal Technology appeared in 1997. It is fascinating to see what constituted "personal" then. The first, defining issues of the journal focussed on wearables. Indeed, what could be more personal than something one wore. Subsequent issues, however, rapidly become broader in scope. Discussion of the design and use of agents was followed by reports on location-aware systems and home/domestic technologies. A further 10 years saw the journal add the word ubiquitous to its title. In its new incarnation, Personal and Ubiquitous Computing began to publish work on sharing and supporting memory and life recording. Then, applications designed to invoke enchantment and attachment appeared. Around 20 years after its first publication, the latest volume of the journal includes treatments of mobile device applications for e-coaching, ubiquitous intelligence, activity recognition, digital cultural heritage (a remarkably constant element), "intergenerational philosophical play" and cross-device media.[3]

---

[3]Desktop or laptop personal computers are unlikely to be able to compete with the sense of ownership that an Apple iPod brought. When they first appeared, they rode about with us in a jacket or shirt pocket and were recognised as such because of their distinctive white earbuds and cable. The iPod was both personal and personalised as it had a copy of one's own playlist of music (and a little later, audiobooks, TV shows and movies). The Apple iPod appeared in October 2001 and was to herald a whole series of products whose names became with an "I" prefix. A prefix which was not explained. It could plausibly stand for information or Internet or, of course, for the personal pronoun and, it might be argued, offered a fresh view of what was meant by personal computing. So, could the I in iPod, iPad, iPhone, iMac suggest an identification between person and technology? Anecdotally, the origins lie in the iMac, "We returned with five names, one of which we all loved: iMac. Each option came with a presentation board briefly describing why it was a good name. For iMac, it was obviously all about the i. Most important, it stood for Internet. But it also stood for other valuable i things, like individual, imagination, i as in me, etc. It also did a pretty good job of laying a solid foundation for future product naming." www.quora.com/History-of-Apple-Inc/How-did-Apple-choose-the-i-naming-convention-iMac-iPod.

This Book

This book is a first attempt at presenting a psychology of user experience (UX). This book's complementary text—HCI Redux—sought to revisit the role of cognition in how we use interactive technology, but we quickly found that cognitive psychology per se was no longer sufficient in itself. This form of psychology has been replaced in HCI by a much broader theoretical base that mirrors the breadth of use and experience of current digital products.

This book attempts to capture what is meant by user experience from a psychological perspective. This psychology of user experience goes beyond cognition, computation or the computer metaphor and includes perspectives from social psychology, evolutionary psychology, folk psychology, neuroaesthetics, neuropsychology, the philosophy of technology, design and the fine arts. Our thesis is that user experience consists of three core, inter-related elements: involvement, affect and aesthetics.

Chapter 1 considers the nature of experience, and the user experience of digital products in particular, offering a new, broader definition of the term.

Chapters 2 and 3 make the case for the pre-eminent place of involvement in user experience. Chapter 2 introduces concepts of involvement, and its manifestations as shared sense making, familiarity, appropriation and dwelling with technologies. A major theme is how we are thrown ineluctably into treating digital products as social beings. Chapter 3 is a further development of this argument in the context of relational technologies, examining the contribution of anthropomorphism and discussing how far relations with digital products may be considered to be authentic.

Chapter 4 discusses the role of affect and more specifically distinguishes emotions, feelings, impressions and moods as part of user experience. It brings together material from diverse fields of study where researchers have worked in parallel, but not mutually cognisant, endeavours.

Chapter 5 proposes a psychology of aesthetics for user experience and again integrates previously scattered findings from other cognate disciplines including neuroaesthetics and anthropology.

Finally, Chap. 6, as well as summarising the discussion thus far, provides new insight into how and why much of our current use of digital products is simply idling, or killing time.

Edinburgh, UK   Phil Turner

References

Alben L (1996) Defining the criteria for effective interaction design. interactions 3(3): 11–15

Bannon L (1991) From human factors to human actors: The role of psychology and human-computer interaction studies in system design. In: Design at work: Cooperative design of computer systems, pp 25, 44

Bødker S (2006) When second wave HCI meets third wave challenges. In: Proceedings of the 4th Nordic conference on Human-computer interaction: changing roles. ACM, pp 1–8

Grudin J (2005) Three faces of human-computer interaction. IEEE Annals of the History of Computing 27(4): 46–62

Harrison S, Tatar D, Sengers P The three paradigms of HCI. In Alt. Chi. Session at the SIGCHI Conference on Human Factors in Computing Systems San Jose, California, USA, April 2007, pp 1–18

Norman D, Miller J, Henderson A (1995) What you see, some of what's in the future, and how we go about doing it: HI at Apple Computer. In Conference companion, CHI 1995. ACM, p 155

Acknowledgements

Thanks to Susan, again.

Contents

Chapter 1
Experience

Over the next twenty years computers will inhabit the most trivial things: clothes labels (to track washing), coffee cups (to alert cleaning staff to moldy cups), light switches (to save energy if no one is in the room), and pencils (to digitize everything we draw). In such a world, we must dwell with computers, not just interact with them.

Weiser (1996, p. 3)

1.1 Origins

Interest in user experience (UX) became apparent in the mid-1990s when its advocates proposed that the design and evaluation of digital technology should be extended beyond the purely instrumental to include the broader range of experiences which it offers. Blythe and his colleagues noted that there had been a, "… move in human-computer interaction studies from standard usability concerns towards a wider set of problems to do with fun, enjoyment, aesthetics and the experience of use" (Blythe et al. 2003). So, rather than being solely concerned with the ease of use of a particular technology, the focus has shifted to include whether it is aesthetically pleasing, engaging and so forth. We add that there is no reason to suppose that users might not demand whatever new and exciting experiences that happen to be fashionable at any particular time.

At the time of writing, UX exists in two overlapping forms (some authors have described finer divisions, but two are enough to make the point). There is UX as the object of design, which is sometimes described as user experience design (UXD) and this has proved popular (irrespective of whether it is possible) with the newest generation of design consultants, web designers and app peddlers. The other form of UX, which is the subject of this book, focuses on understanding the range of experiences we might have with digital technology with explanatory discussions drawn from philosophy, psychology and the cognitive sciences. As this form of UX

© Springer International Publishing AG 2017
P. Turner, *A Psychology of User Experience*, Human–Computer Interaction Series,
https://doi.org/10.1007/978-3-319-70653-5_1

emphasises the subjective, evaluative and primarily psychological nature of the domain, we simply describe it as "the psychology of UX". One other change of language we should note is that we will henceforth largely try to refer to digital technology and interactive technology as *digital products* which is more in keeping with the spirit of UX.

So, this is a psychology of our experience of digital products. Our approach to this has been to begin with what has been written of theoretical side of UX, of which there is surprisingly little. In try to understand this, what can be observed is that, overwhelmingly, designers and computer scientists want to create digital products which might be a source of aesthetic pleasure or unrestrained joy without worrying too much (if at all) about what is meant by these psychological states. Further, there is also a striking asymmetry to this as there is an understandable bias towards to the good, the positive and the lucrative. Thus, there are no (deliberately) ugly or ungainly products nor are there designs which produce frustration or anger. It is important to stress the word, deliberately. Designers do seem to be only interested in designing for what has been called our "inner chimp" (Haldane 2015) with its reliance on emotion rather than rationality and a fondness for the bright and shiny. This might be seen as a simplistic treatment of the complexities of human psychology.

Further, the various attempts to define UX have not been particularly helpful either. What is noteworthy are the number of researchers who are quite content to avoid defining what is meant by experience or user for that matter. It might have been expected that a new discipline such as UX might have come complete with a set of initial but extensible objectives and aims. UX has not. Instead researchers have reflected on its appearance and then set out to understand it and perhaps direct it.

Finally, and this cannot be stressed enough, psychology and computer science were never designed to work together. They have different aims, vocabularies, and (unspoken) assumptions. The assumptions are probably the most problematic. In human-computer interaction (HCI) this is difficult, in UX it is, as I have learned, harder. HCI was created as a conjunction of cognition and computing but both are instrumental. We use our cognition, mediated by technology to serve our ends. Not simple, perhaps but it is a statement with a simple validity. In UX, the equivalent might read, we use technology to meet our aims while having fun or meeting our ends elegantly or while projecting an aura of superiority. In HCI, psychology, usually in the form of cognition, and technology are more or less be congruent. In UX, psychology, which might take any number of forms, and technology are all too often tangential.

So, this resulting psychology of UX may surprise.

This chapter
This chapter has five sections after this introduction. In the first section is our appeal to philosophy since in many ways, philosophy is the most natural place to begin any discussion of experience. We draw upon the work of a number of 20th century philosophers, including Heidegger, Merleau-Ponty and Dewey to help us to shed a light on the nature of experience. While we have endeavoured to keep this brief and

relevant and to minimise the use of specialist language, it nonetheless provides the basis for our treatment of UX.

Next, we consider definitions of user experience. Here we consider how UX has been treated from three different perspectives. We begin with the evidence that UX as "usability for the new millennium", this is familiar ground but with a "few bells and whistles", then from the view that any discussion of experience encounters the problem of it being ineffable (that is, personal and unknowable). More usually, however, UX is treated as an open list, for example, UX includes ease of use, and fun, and pleasure, and aesthetics, and immersive and engaging and on goes the list.

Then we consider how experience changes over time. At its most approachable, experiences begin before the digital product is encountered and this progresses through first impressions, and then momentary and episodic use. In time, experience becomes accumulated and is subject to recall.

The next section outlines our new definition of UX. UX comprises three elements namely, involvement, affect and aesthetics. Affect and aesthetics are familiar enough to need no further immediate description but involvement needs a word or two. We propose involvement as a replacement for use or interaction as it embraces being-with technology, treating it as though it were a person, appropriating it, enjoying its vicarious use and, of course, interaction. The final section of this chapter notes that user experience is still largely treated as though it were disembodied—the way HCI used to be thought of.

1.2 A Basis for Experience

As we have already noted, understanding experience is classically a philosophical problem or at least one which many philosophers have seized upon. There are contributions from Kant, Kierkegaard, Husserl, Heidegger, Dewey and Peirce (among others), all of whom have offered their own definitions and own prejudices and which are of value here. We draw upon philosophy primarily to provide a framework (though skeleton might be a better description) upon which we might arrange our empirical findings from psychology and the cognitive sciences. In keeping with the nature of a skeleton, we have done our best to keep as much as we can out of sight.

Of the more or less contemporary writers we consider, Martin Heidegger is probably the most familiar to HCI researchers while remaining one of the least well understood. We introduce a little of his work before we consider Merleau-Ponty's writings through the contemporary lens of Svanæs (2013) who has done much to make his (their) work relevant to HCI. Then we consider Dewey in some detail. Dewey has been the subject of a book directly linking his treatment of experience to technology. McCarthy and Wright's (2004) *Technology as Experience* is an excellent example of mapping the philosophy of experience to technology. However, and this is not always made clear, Dewey was a Pragmatist and this school of thought is concerned with ends not means. Dewey does not offer explanations of the experiences but he describes their effects which is consistent with Pragmatic thought. So, Dewey's work, we suggest, is of particular value to those engaged in "designing for experience" but is less directly useful for those of us seeking to offer explanations. We begin with Heidegger who sought to both describe and explain what it means to be in the world.

Heidegger/being-in-the-world

Winograd and Flores were responsible for bringing the work of the philosopher Martin Heidegger to the attention of the HCI community in their Understanding Computers and Cognition (1986). Heidegger is famous for his obscurity and paradoxically for his treatment of our experience of the everyday. In many respects, his work is a natural choice for the student of user experience except for his use of language (which even for a philosopher is difficult), secondly, he did not really approve of "technology" much less "modern technology" and thirdly, he showed, if not contempt for psychology, a fairly open frustration with it. However, his work is brilliant and surprisingly relevant.

Heidegger's major work, Being and Time (1927/1962) is concerned with the question, "what does it mean to exist?" and his reply is an appeal to the practical and everyday. He avoids the abstract and theoretical, arguing that we have placed too much emphasis on these while our real focus should be on the mundane, everyday and concrete. So, to exist, is to be in the world—nothing to do with trusting or questioning our cognition, just being-in-the-world (the hyphens indicating that there is nothing standing between us and the world).

However, of the concepts Winograd and Flores introduced to HCI from Heidegger, the most important are undoubtedly ready-to-hand and present-at-hand which are his descriptions of how we experience technology.

Before we go any further we need to introduce hammers. Imagine we have reached into our toolbox to pull out a hammer which we then use to fix a hook to hang a picture. We pick up the hammer without a thought, and skilfully fix the hook. This "not having to think about it" means that the hammer is experienced as ready-to-hand. Now imagine a variation on this scenario whereby we dislodge some plaster from the wall while hammering. An expletive to two later and we think about repairing the damage. The hammer is unsuitable for this and ceases to be ready-to-hand becoming experienced as present-at-hand.

Instead, after a moment or two of reflection, we reach for a tube of filler and a palette knife with which to apply it. This takes a moment or two as it is relatively unfamiliar. So, a tool is experienced while hammering as proximal, familiar and immediately useful (ready-to-hand) but when we have stopped hammering it becomes an object of detached interest. This readiness-to-hand/present-at-hand distinction can be applied to digital products. And our routine use of these technologies we have described elsewhere as coping (Turner 2013). Coping simply means engaging with a digital product effectively and I am happy to say, for example, that I personally cope with Microsoft Word® every day (sic). I am not in any sense disparaging this product, to cope with MS Word is to engage with it smoothly and effectively which in turn means that I am frequently not aware of using it—in short, it has disappeared and having disappeared, I am left to focus on the text I am composing. Phenomenologically, I (the user) and the technology have effectively disappeared as separate entities and this will occur when people cope. We should recognise that this apparent union of person and product is sought after as it is symptomatic of a highly usable digital product.

In general, this is as far into the Heidegger corpus as many HCI/UX readers will have managed. However, there are two further points worth considering. The first of these is that he tells us that each item of equipment is available for a specific task which he describes as in-order-to, for example, a chair is something which is (used or experienced as) in-order-to sit on, a hammer is experienced as something which is used in-order-to hammer-with and so. He is essentially talking about their affordances without mentioning the concept. While this all appears rather functional, tools for enjoying ourselves and for having fun are no different as these too are encountered as ready-to-hand and in-order-to.

The second point we would identify is that, it is not meaningful to describe a tool or an in-order-to, in isolation. All tools exist with respect to each other as equipment in an holistic whole. Back to hammering for a moment, we hammer because we are maintaining our house. So, we repair a loose roofing tile by hammering a new nail to fasten it; in-order-to ensure that the roof does not leak in-order-to keep the house safe and dry in-order-to (and on it goes) for-the-sake-of keeping the family safe and dry. Every for-the-sake-of-which provides the base structure of all (subsequent and dependent) involvements and offers a possible way for us to be, to be an academic, to be an amateur repairman, a parent, or whatever (Wheeler 2005). Thus, I help keep house (fix roofs, look after my family or whatever), if and only if, I understand myself as a husband or repairman, and I engage in acts for-the-sake-of my being a husband. If this sounds a little circular and self-referential then this is very much a consequence of Heidegger's holistic thinking.

So, what does Heidegger bring to HCI and UX? Coyne (1995) helps here by identifying issues such as identity, proximity, and embodiment (p. 338). He writes that our interest should shift from "the abstract, technological concern to the everyday" and that we should focus on "care, being-with, corporality, praxis, disclosure and the not-yet". These ambitions remain largely unfulfilled.

Merleau-Ponty/the corporeal basis of experience
Merleau-Ponty, another advocate of the fact of our being in the world, has argued that this is a consequence of our lived bodies which give us access to the "primary world" (this is in sharp contrast with Heidegger who never mentions the body). Indeed, without our bodies there could be no world. The world and the lived body together form what Merleau-Ponty calls an intentional arc which is said to bind the body to the world, for example, the movement of the body creates lived (existential) space. It is not, however, the 'objective' movement of the body as such, instead it is the experience of this movement, "Far from my body's being for me no more than a fragment of space, there would be no space at all for me if I had no body". To feel our body (kinaesthesia) feeling its surroundings is not merely an exercise in

self-reflection but the means by which we 'prehend' the world. This kinaesthetic feedback is the means by which we both objectify the world and orient ourselves within it.

However, Merleau-Ponty also recognised the role of the world when he wrote, "To move one's body is to aim at things through it; it is to allow oneself to respond to their call". This 'intentional arc' is then the knowledge of how to act in a way that coheres with one's environment bringing body and world together. This is more than just being physically present in the world: "the life of consciousness—cognitive life, the life of desire or perceptual life—is subtended by an intentional arc which projects round about us our past, our future, our human setting, our physical, ideological and moral situation". Thus, the concept of the lived body is central to his account of corporeal intentionality and necessarily the basis of our experience of the world.

Perhaps Merleau-Ponty is best known for making tools disappear. He tells us that we are able extend the scope of the body to include external tools and devices [Botvinick and Cohen's (1998) rubber hand illusion is a good example of this]. However, a more usual illustration of this is the blind person's white stick. Initially provided with a white stick, the blind person will struggle to use it. However, once the skill is acquired, the stick effectively ceases to exist as an external artefact for that person, and (according to current thinking) It has become part of the person's body schema (a representation of the body we maintain). Merleau-Ponty (1962, p. 152) describes this as follows: "Once the stick has become a familiar instrument, the world of feel-able things recedes and now begins, not at the outer skin of the hand, but at the end of the stick … The pressures on the hand and the stick are no longer given; the stick is no longer an object perceived by the blind man, but an instrument with which he perceives. It is a bodily auxiliary, an extension of the bodily synthesis." The stick has become an extension of his sensory apparatus and a source of experience. This and related ideas have more recently been extended to a wide range of artefacts including rubber hands. If this work were to be unified and extended, we might imagine that it could be applied to, for example, the study of the experience of wearable technologies.

However, more immediately, Svanæs has reported his work in using Merleau-Ponty's phenomenology to the direct experimental investigation of user experience. He writes that this work has given rise to three new concepts, namely, the "feel dimension", "interaction Gestalts", and "kinaesthetic thinking" and of these the "feel" of the user experience is the most relevant and interesting here. He has identified a number of the properties of this felt dimension which he illustrates in the following example of an imagined work of abstract interactive art, which is part of an imagined art exhibition called "Touch me". This is quite a simple exhibit. The canvas is white when first viewed, but it toggles black when touched by the gallery visitor. A second touch toggles its initial white appearance. Svanæs then asks whether Merleau-Ponty's work can account for the user experience here. He begins by noting that Merleau-Ponty tells us that perception is shaped by the phenomenal field. In "touch me" example, the phenomenal field that all his interactions take place in. Part of this phenomenal field is the habit of touching and clicking things to learn more, which originates from our life with all digital products. Next, we should recognise that perception is also directed. The direction here comes from the contained in the name of the exhibit ("Touch me") thus the artwork will present itself as something to be touched and not primarily viewed. The next two features of perception are that it is active and that it involves the whole body. The resulting user experience is the integrated sum of its visual appearance and its behaviour. Without action, or interaction we would not have witnessed the change in appearance. Finally, experiencing the interactive artwork requires not only visual perception, but also an arm and a hand. Arm, hand, and eye movements are integrated parts of the perceptual process that leads to perception of the artwork's behaviour. The interactive experience is thus both created by and mediated through the body.

Using Merleau-Ponty's ideas, it becomes meaningless to talk about interaction purely as stimuli reception leading to actions. Certain aspects of interaction are better described as perception. The gallery visitor perceives the behaviour of the artwork through interaction. This perception involves arm, hand, and eyes in an integrated manner. This kind of embodied perception is immediate and "close to the world".

Dewey/a pragmatic analysis of experience
While Dewey was not the first philosopher to be appropriated by the HCI community in the pursuit of a definition and explication of experience, he has proved to be one of the most accessible. His Art as Experience (1934) has been borrowed and updated by McCarthy and Wright in their own Technology as Experience (2004) to good effect. These texts, as their titles indicate, aim to explore the nature of our experiences of art and technology respectively, from the perspective of Pragmatism. Thus, we can begin with Dewey's definition of experience which is, "… the result, the sign, and the reward of that interaction of organism and environment which, when it is carried to the full, is a transformation of interaction into participation and communication" (Dewey 1934, p. 22). However, Dewey has also more practically told us that experience can be understood by means of four "threads" and multiple processes. He emphasizes that experiences are not composed of these threads but that they can be used to reason about experience itself.

The sensual thread of experience is concerned with our sensory engagement with a situation, "which orients us to the concrete, palpable and visceral character of experience" (McCarthy and Wright ibid, p. 80). More than this, it draws us to experience the world pre-reflectively or intuitively. The authors explicitly link the importance of this thread of experience to children playing with "cyberpets" or on a more contemporary basis their tablet computers, teenagers with their latest app and the rest of humanity with their smart phones.

The second thread is the emotional. As McCarthy and Wright put it, "[emotions] are the color shot through the experience that holds all aspects of the experience together and make it different from other experiences" (2004, p. 83). They go on to give quite a nice example of this from their own earlier research. McCarthy and O'Conner (1999) have reported on the different ways individuals in a hospital setting construe and use patient information. They contrast how nurses, managers and clinicians see their work. For example, nurses see patient care in terms of "a personal relationship" between themselves and the patient; managers see this in terms of the effective treatment of numbers of patients; and for doctors it is a matter of medical treatment. As for the emotional thread, emotions are seen as qualities which colour particular experiences rather than being independent of them which is how we typically think of joy, anger or fear. The third and fourth threads are distinctly less compelling and are less well developed. The third thread is the compositional. Imagine we have been invited to look at a painting and in doing so to reflect on the relationships being depicted therein and to ask the questions, "what is this about?" and "where am I?". In essence, this is a reference to aesthetic experience and from a careful reading of McCarthy and Wright's analysis, it seems to prefigure some aspects of embodied or enactive aesthetics. The fourth and final thread is the spatio-temporal. All experiences are said to have a spatio-temporal component. An intense engagement can affect our sense of time. Sitting in the dentist's chair time seems to drag; in contrast, an exciting movie is finished quickly. In addition to time, awareness of this component might also allow us to distinguish between public and private space, and the boundaries between self and others. While each thread is distinct, there is also a great deal of overlap and inter-dependency. In addition to these four threads, Dewey proposed that there are the six sense-making processes. These are anticipating, connecting, interpreting, reflecting, appropriating and recounting. In turn, anticipating refers to the expectations we might have prior to an experience; connecting refers to the "immediate, pre-conceptual and pre-linguistic sense of a situation encountered"; and interpreting means discerning the narrative structure of an experience—what has happened and what is likely to happen. The remaining three processes are reflecting; appropriating and recounting. Reflecting, which occurs in parallel with interpreting, is concerned with making judgements of the experience. Appropriating is the process by which we make the experience relevant to the self. Finally, recounting is concerned with telling others about the experience. In all, this appears to be a fairly comprehensive account of experience, though the interaction between the threads and processes is not clear as McCarthy and Wright note, "the relationship between experience with technology and the sense we make of it is clearly not straightforward" (ibid, p. 127). However, it is interesting that the social and personal dimensions of experience are recognised but are treated merely as aspects of sense-making (and merit a correspondingly small discussion).

1.3 Definitions of UX

Before we begin to consider the nature of user experience, we have identified a troublesome point which may have stalled the development of theoretical UX in recent years. This issue is that we are still largely treating technology instrumentally. Despite introducing fun, pleasure and aesthetics along with "getting the job done" in our treatment of digital products, it is still fundamentally a matter of interaction. However, if we were to appreciate that our relationship with digital technology has changed then we would recognise that we now, for example, live alongside technology just as Negroponte foresaw 40 years ago when he described computing "as living". In our homes, for example, we ask for medical advice from our digital assistants, with queries such as, "Alexa, my wife is having an asthma attack, what should I do?" which can now be handled with a first-aid app. In our cars (assuming that we are still driving them) we use our smart phones as a "sat-nav" which again tells us, in natural language, to turn right at the next junction. Gone or going are the road atlases and the skill to use them. We encounter, robots working in a 24 h coffee franchise. In short, we live with it and, all too often, we treat it as though it were another person. This is missing from most definitions of UX.

Varieties of experience

As user experience is a particular example or form of experience, we need a clear understanding of experience itself. This is no small matter, for example, Forlizzie and Battarbee (2004) have distinguished among three forms of experience, namely, experience (per se), an experience and co-experience. They describe experience as a constant stream of "self-talk" which emerges when we interact with a product and propose examples of these including "light housekeeping" (from the context we can imagining "washing the dishes), or using a messaging system. Experiences are subjective, appearing in our consciousness as a flow of perceptions which might be accompanied by interpretations and emotional responses. This is a classical phe-nomenological description of experience. Secondly, an experience has a beginning, and an end, so, watching a movie would be an example of this. The final type is co-experience which is the co-creation of meaning (and emotion) from the use of the product with others. Battarbee (2003) defines it as a form of user experience, which is created in social interaction. Specifically, "Co-experience is the seamless blend of user experience of products and social interaction. The experience, while essentially created by the users, would not be the same or even possible without the presence of the product and the possibilities for experience that it provides" (p. 109). Arguably this is the most important form of UX but has received little attention.

An absence of theory

This absence of a strong theoretical underpinning is troublesome as Forlizzie and Battarbee (ibid) tell us that not only is the term user experience associated with a wide range of meanings, but also "no cohesive theory of experience exists for the design community". Law and her colleagues (2009) have also reported the results of their own surveys of academics and practitioners which indicate that while the term user experience is widely used, "it is not clearly defined nor well understood" (p. 719). They go on to note that UX is also "associated with a broad range of fuzzy and dynamic concepts". Bargas-Avila and Hornbæk (2011) broadly agree and have reported from their own analysis of studies of UX, confirming that there has been a shift from "desktop computing" towards consumer products and art. They also found that affect, enjoyment and aesthetics were the most reported attributes, while context of use and anticipated use were the least reported.

In their survey of academics and industrial designers, Law and her colleagues, gave no fewer than five sample definitions of UX and found that the most popular definition was "The consequence of a user's internal state (predispositions, expectations, needs, motivations, mood, etc.), the characteristics of the designed system (e.g., complexity, purpose, usability, functionality, etc.) and the context (or the environment) within which the interaction occurs (e.g., organizational/social setting)". In second place was a definition which emphasized the effect and affect produced by aesthetic experience, the meaning we attach to the product, and the feelings and emotions produced (Law et al. 2009).

On the basis of this initial evidence, it is clear that UX has witnessed the successive postings of a research agenda (Hassenzahl and Tractinsky 2006), a manifesto (Law et al. 2007), and most recently a white paper (Roto et al. 2011), all of which are united in their aim to seek clarification.

Three perspectives

So, how has the UX been defined? The answer, simply, is in quite a number of different ways. Forlizzi and Battarbee (2004) have, for example, sought to make sense of this by grouping these definitions into product-centred, user-centred, and interaction-centred but perhaps the most striking thing about them is that most authors ignore what it is to experience. While UX is a sub-category of experience, it is, all too often, treated as something resembling an engineering problem.

However, we have adopted our own three perspectives to group UX definitions, namely,

1. UX is basically a "new millennial usability". It includes usability, which is still the most important attribute, but also includes accessibility, and fun and aesthetics (and so on) depending on context. Arguably the most persuasive proponent of this is Sutcliffe (2009) who rejects the notion of UX per se in favour of engagement and tells us that aesthetics is simply "good design" for particular contexts. Quite simply, Sutcliffe prefers the expression user engagement rather than user experience.
2. UX is ineffable and, more or less, it is all but impossible to define adequately in words. As experiences are personal, of the moment, and cannot be repeated, all we can do is to recognise that they exist.
3. UX is a fresh way of thinking about digital products and any definition should not only recognise that they are a source of fun, aesthetics and so forth but should also reflect the complexity of human psychology and the context of use too. These definitions inevitably give rise to unbounded, rather elastic definitions.

We now examine each of these in a little more detail, beginning with "UX is usability with frills".

Usability+

Even in the early usability checklists there was a wild card, namely, subjective satisfaction (e.g., Nielsen 1994). So, while objective measures were proposed to establish the usability of the digital product, there was always a option for the user to tell us whether or not they actually liked using it or thought it was well designed.

This was to take form in one of the earliest definitions of UX, such as that offered by Alben (1996) who defines it as, "the way a [device/system] feels in the hands, how well they understand how it works, how they feel about it while they are using it, how well it serves its purpose and how well it fits the entire context in which they are using it". Alben identified, along with usability and usefulness, affect and aesthetics (hand-feel) which have now established themselves as UX staples.

We see elements of this again in the ISO definition (below), in Kuniavsky's (2010) thoughts on UX and in Norman's Emotional Design as "the totality of end users' perceptions as they interact with a product or service. These perceptions include effectiveness (how good is the result), efficiency (how fast or cheap is it?), emotional satisfaction (how good does it feel?), the quality of the relationship with the entity that created the product or service (what expectations does it create for subsequent interactions?)".

At this point, we need to return to Sutcliffe's case against UX which he describes in his *Designing For User Engagement* (2009). In this we find an approach to designing for what might be described as a good experience without having to use that "diffuse" and "much over-used term" (Sutcliffe, *ibid*). He proposes the expression "user engagement" (UE) to describe how people are attracted to use interactive products. Although this book is concerned with design, he begins it by critiquing Norman's writing on *Emotional Design* which, he claims, are based on only a partial understanding of UX. Sutcliffe tells us that emotions are reactions to events, objects and are a component in our understanding UX but are not enough in themselves.

He then considers the work of Tractinsky and of Hassenzahl. The former, he tells us has developed questionnaires for measuring user judgments about the quality of interactive products, producing measures for aesthetics, traditional usability and pleasure. However, when the determinants of classic aesthetics are inspected, many relate to traditional usability concepts such as consistency and structural layout. Hassenzahl apparently has done something similar as his questionnaire-based approach to understanding the relationship between hedonic and pragmatic design qualities has revealed that hedonic qualities are more closely associated with aesthetics, while pragmatics is closer to traditional usability. However, most tellingly, these studies tend to ignore the fact that user judgement is context-dependent. Specifically, whatever the underlying constructs by which we judge products, our judgement depends on the context of use.

Sutcliffe based these conclusions on a series of studies wherein he compared interactive tech which shared the same functionality and content but differed in aesthetic and interaction design. He found that user judgement can be biased by the tasks given (serious v. less serious use), by their background, and by the order in which design information (positive/negative) is presented. Clearly, he writes, beauty is in the eye of the beholder, but it depends on who the beholder is and what they are doing.

The ineffable

Quale is a term used to refer to individual instances of subjective, conscious experience. The term derives from the Latin for "what sort" or "what kind" and examples of qualia are the taste of wine, or the feel of silk and probably most famously quoted example is the redness of an apple. Dennett (1988) writes of qualia as follows (they are): ineffable; that is, they cannot be communicated, or apprehended by any other means than direct experience; and are intrinsic; that is, they are non-relational properties, which do not change depending on the experience's relation to other things. They are also private; that is, all interpersonal comparisons of qualia are systematically impossible and directly or immediately apprehensible in consciousness; that is, to experience a quale is to know one experiences a quale, and to know all there is to know about that quale.

Davis (2003), in a very similar vein, has highlighted some of the problems encountered in making sense of experience. He writes that an experience is not an object (or even a collection of objects), but a process and an intangible one at that which involves an interaction among humans and the world. Experience has its existence in human minds and as such cannot be archived or transmitted. Unhappily, while Davis' paper has been frequently cited, its allusions to the ineffable nature of experience are all too frequently ignored—and here, we are guilty too.

An open list of attributes

Finally, the most popular approach to defining UX is the list. Usually a long list. Hassenzahl and Tractinsky (2006), for example, have proposed that UX, "is about technology that fulfils more than just instrumental needs in a way that acknowledges its use as a subjective, situated, complex and dynamic encounter. UX is a consequence of a user's internal state (predispositions, expectations, needs, motivation, mood, etc.), the characteristics of the designed system (e.g., complexity, purpose, usability, functionality, etc.) and the context (or the environment) within which the interaction occurs (e.g., organisational/social setting, meaningfulness of the activity, voluntariness of use, etc.)" An immediate question that come to mind here is the nature of the etcetera's in this definition.

The appearance of Hassenzahl initial work was to signal the beginning of interest in the pragmatic—hedonic treatment of UX. The pragmatic aspects of a digital product enable the user to get the job done (they are the usability and effectiveness aspects), while the hedonic aspects are a source of arousal and identification, that is whether we like or identify with it.

A couple of years later Hassenzahl (2008) offered another definition of UX claiming that it comprises a "momentary, primarily evaluative feeling (good-bad) while interacting with a product or service" and "Good UX is the consequence of fulfilling the human needs for autonomy, competency, stimulation (self-oriented), relatedness, and popularity (others-oriented) through interacting with the product or service (i.e., hedonic quality). Pragmatic quality facilitates the potential fulfilment of be-goals".

Hassenzahl is not alone in favouring detailed definitions as Robert and Lesage (2010) have suggested that UX is both multi-dimensional and holistic. Their proposed dimensions are: functional, physical, perceptual, cognitive, social, and psychological. They also suggest two meta-levels being sense making and aesthetics. They add, each experience has a unique and coherent set of dimensions meeting together according to variable ratios. They also add that UX is dynamic, situated. The most telling thing about these definitions is that they are not complete.

ISO's contribution

The formal definition of UX as issued by the International Standards Organisation is a "person's perceptions and responses that result from the use and/or anticipated use of a system, product or service". The description of UX as "perceptions and responses" makes this definition appear predominantly psychological but the reference to "anticipated use" suggests something more than simple psychology. Anticipated use may refer to making-believe the use of the digital product or imagining oneself using it (in the broadest sense) in one's "mind's eye". Here there is no readymade psychology of make-believe or imagination (with respect to technology anyway) to call upon. This standard, being ISO 9241-210, has also been amplified for clarification and comes with the following notes:

Note 1: User experience includes the user's emotions, beliefs, preferences, perceptions, physical and psychological responses, behaviours and accomplishments that occur before, during and after use.

Note 2: User experience is a consequence of brand image, presentation, functionality, system performance, interactive behaviour, and assistive capabilities of a system, product or service. It also results from the user's internal and physical state resulting from prior experiences, attitudes, skills and personality; and from the context of use.

Note 3: Usability, when interpreted from the perspective of the users' personal goals, can include the kind of perceptual and emotional aspects typically associated with user experience. Usability criteria can be established so as to assess aspects of user experience.

This is a primarily psychological definition. UX is described as the result of perceptions and responses to and of the use of digital products. Footnotes 1 and 3 are only an amplification of the initial statement. In contrast, footnote 2 introduces a huge amount of additional details including such things as prior exposure and context. This is another open-ended list.

1.4 Experience Over Time

UX's "white paper" (Roto et al. 2011) is aimed at "Bringing clarity to the concept of user experience", and is worth considering as it principally introduces the notion of time. The white paper has two points of interest for the current discussion.

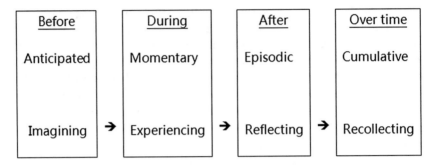

Fig. 1.1 Adapted and simplified from Roto et al. (2011), p. 8

The paper begins by telling us a number of familiar things about UX in that it is "a subset of experience as a general concept" thus UX is more specific, since it is related to the experiences of using a system. These encounters are recognised to be not only active, personal use, but also include encountering a digital product in a more passive way, for example, observing someone else using it. The authors also recognise that UX is influenced by prior experiences and expectations based on those experiences and UX is rooted in a social and cultural context. Then they introduce a timeline (see Fig. 1.1). They divide "time" into four categories or types, the first is anticipated UX may relate to the period before first use, or any of the three other time spans of UX, since a person may imagine a specific moment during interaction, a usage episode, or life after taking a system into use. Then comes momentary UX, followed by UX arising from a specific usage episode (episodic UX), and finally the UX which is a consequence of having used the system as a whole (cumulative UX) (Fig. 1.1).

The white paper also focussed on the use of digital products, with the word use cited repeatedly. As for its properties, the authors tell us that UX is personal, and then use a number of expressions which are more usually associated with cognition. UX is situated and it is embedded. Use appears again a little later, when we find that, "While the core of user experience will be the actual experience of usage, this does not cover all relevant UX concerns. People can have indirect experience before their first encounter through expectations formed from existing experience of related technologies, brand, advertisements, presentations, demonstrations, or others' opinions". So, there we have it—*core user experiences arise from direct use.* Although there is no definition of "core" we can reasonably read it as the majority situation from which user experiences arise. We shall further assume that by direct use they mean the ordinary, routine use of interactive, digital technology, but this presents a problem. The ordinary, routine use of products is typically automatic and unconscious and given these circumstances it is difficult to see user experiences occur. Without a thorough definition of use this is inadequate.

1.5 A New Definition of UX

Our definition of UX does not start with usability, nor that fact that we get pleasure from the appearance of technology, instead we begin with (an admittedly) philosophical perspective that we involved with it. We are involved with it because it is everywhere and we loved or hated it and we cannot live without it. It is a fact of our everyday life and "user experience" is the result of being involved with it. We have relationships with it: we are involved with it by caring about its appearance, and how it makes us feel. So, our definition of UX is based on our practical, everyday involvement with it rather than as a result of a factor analysis.

Further, UX cannot be confined to individual digital products such as phones or tablets because we are surrounded with a network of them. This might turn out to be the "Internet of Things", time will tell, but however it turns out, we are enfolded and involved with digital technologies.

User experience is also the result of making sense of digital products. It is not limited to the fun or pleasure or engagement we may have with them. Instead, we try to make sense of digital products, consciously and unconsciously, by appreciating their appearance, how we feel about it and how it makes us feel, how we make it our own and the many other things which we discuss in this book. What brings together these very different experiences are that they all contribute to making sense of technology.

UX is an ad hoc category
User experience arises both from our direct use of digital products, from its anticipated or imagined use and from vicarious use (e.g., by watching other people use their technology). These experiences are also coloured by internal dispositions (of all kinds) and by the environment (including the product itself). Add to this, definitions of UX are frequently loosely phrased or appear as a simple list of plausible attributes littered with a surprising number of "for examples" and "so ons". This presents UX as an open-ended concept and with each new attribute the definition grows, and correspondingly when last year's tired old ideas gutter and fade it shrinks again.

We propose that we can best think of UX is an ad hoc category. Barsalou originated the idea from observing that people form and use highly specialised and unusual sets of things as a matter of their everyday coping. These he calls ad hoc categories (1983) or goal-derived categories (1985) and for the purpose of this discussion they can be treated in much the same way. He found that people create such categories to achieve particular goals (e.g., Luciarello and Nelson 1985; Ross and Murphy 1999; Medin et al. 2006; Chrysikou 2006). These categories begin life as simple lists but they help achieve a relevant goal by organizing the current situation in a way that supports the current goal. For example, the first time that someone packs an over-night bag, the category is "things to pack in a bag" is ad hoc. However, subsequent trips leave a memory of bag-packing. Barsalou has proposed that both conceptual and linguistic mechanisms have a role in forming ad hoc categories: from a conceptual perspective, people combine existing concepts from objects, mental states, properties, and so forth to form new conceptual structures; while linguistically, people combine words in novel ways to index these concepts. The conceptual and linguistic mechanisms that formulate ad hoc categories are very flexible, as that components of these categories can be replaced with alternative values. He also notes that the instantiations of an ad hoc category are held in memory and become increasingly well-established through frequent use (Barsalou 1991). Overall, it is fair to say that ad hoc categories are ubiquitous in everyday cognition.

A familiar ad hoc category is the package holiday. We are all aware that it is possible to purchase a package holiday of the form, "Experience Egypt" or "Experience New York" and we all generally understand what the vendors have in mind. An experience of kind is not just a matter of flying there but would normally including sampling the local cuisine, enjoying the culture, the music, the history, the people and on the list, goes depending on the extensiveness of the package and the enthusiasm of the holiday-maker. Despite the variety, we would expect the holiday to include core attributes such as transportation, accommodation and food. Here we have a holiday as an ad hoc category, comprising a class (or list) of things. We can also note that not all members of this category are equal, and that some are more representative than others. This degree of membership reflects the category's graded structure which seems to be a universal property of categories.[1] We recognise that UX is an ad hoc category with a small number of strong attributes (members) and a host of other attributes which have a lesser degree of membership.

Three key attributes

Having proposed that UX can be thought of as an ad hoc category, we now argue that category is organised around a number of what define as core attributes. We propose that UX has three core attributes, namely, involvement, affect and aesthetics. We do not foreground engagement, enchantment, bewilderment, attachment or any of the very many attributes which have been or may become associated with UX. This is not to suggest that they are not potential members of the category but membership of this category, as we have already discussed, is graded.

Involvement

We should note that our involvement with digital technology is a concept we have adopted from the work of Martin Heidegger about which we now say a little more as it provides an undercurrent to the entire book.[2] Heidegger's major work—Being and Time (1927/1962) is primarily concerned with the question of being. This is the unanswered question which Descartes posed in his famous dictum, "I think therefore I am". Having established that all he could be certain of was that he was thinking, Descartes fails to discuss the consequence, namely, that he was (the "I

---

[1]The graded structure of a concept refers to the evidence that some examples are better than others. For example, if we consider birds, clearly robins are better members of this category than penguins.

[2]To the alarmed reader, don't worry—beyond this chapter there is relatively little Heidegger.

am" in his question). Heidegger's reply to this question is to tells us that we-are-in-the-world, not separate from it, not separable from it (hence the use of hyphens) and to-be-in-the-world is to be involved with it and all it comprises by definition. This, then, is an holistic account as it necessarily abandons any subject-object dualism.

By addressing the nature of being from this perspective, Heidegger shifts the focus of attention from the theoretical to the practical; from the reflective to the phenomenological; from abstract knowledge to the practical and every day. So, despite the fact that the current discussion is philosophical in character, it is squarely based in the real, everyday world experiences of people using digital technology.

So, having established that we are in-the-world, what of involvement? In short, to-be-in-the-world is to be involved: they are effectively synonyms. We are involved with the world in the sense we cannot escape it. As we have already seen, for Heidegger, all human activity is located in a holistic "web of significance" comprising inter-related items of technology which are perceived as being useful in order to complete tasks. From this reading, involvement with technology is an inevitable, unavoidable consequence of being-in-the-world. Thus, most of us have not adopted a theoretical stance with respect to technology because we are (already) involved with it. To phrase this differently, our involvement with technology provides the context for our other involvements with technology.

Our first encounter with technology is likely to be that we find it *available*. Dreyfus and Wrathall (2005, p. 4) tell us, "we first encounter worldly things as available. Something is available when (1) it is defined in terms of its place in a context of equipment, typical activities in which it is used, and typical purposes and goals for which it is used, and (2) it lends itself to such use readily and easily without need for reflection. The core case of availability is an item of equipment that we know how to use and that transparently lends itself to use". Having encountered technology as available (a term we introduced a little earlier in this chapter) we also recognise that it can be used in-order-to do practical stuff. An in-order-to is equivalent to what Gibson described as an affordance (Gibson 1986) thus when we make use of an in-order-to, it is equivalent to engaging with a task. All of this activity is also set against a background of affect and aesthetics which orients us towards the technology, of which we will say more below.

However, our use of technology has (at least) one further consequence as it also serves to define who we are. Heidegger regarded the "self" as being indeterminate and contingent, so much so that he described us as *Dasein* (which is not usually translated). The self is grounded in what we do and in the variety of tools we use to do what we do, as these change, so does our identity—from husband, to teacher, to cricket fan, to surgeon. These relationships are, of course, self-referential for example, a scalpel is that tool used by a surgeon and a surgeon is someone (*Dasein*) who uses a scalpel.

We are involved in the world and all it comprises and this involvement is evidenced by a variety of psychological and bodily states including, flow, a self of presence, engagement, enchantment, attachment and so forth. Involvement is a primordial state in that it cannot be reduced to simpler or component states, but is one from which these psychological states emerge.

In this book, we treat involvement in two ways. The first addresses the various ways in which our involvement manifests with respect to our everyday use of digital products (Chap. 2). We discuss our social relationship and familiarity with them, our appropriation of digital products to better suit us and in Chap. 3 where we are concerned with how we experience relational artefacts examples of which are social robots and digital assistants. This again is primarily social but we also discuss anthropomorphism.

Affect

We have been interested in the many manifestations of affect for millennia, and indeed, we introduce Chap. 3 with an introductory survey of past and current thinking on how emotion worrks. Our stance on affect is quite simple. Firstly, our primary interest is in emotion (as distinguished from feelings, mood and so forth) as we see a mapping between digital product and emotion ("I love my new phone") and we do not regard it (following Dewey) as being separate from experience. Dewey writes that affect colours experience, and we find this a meaningful way to regard it in this context. Affect is not, however, as many of these accounts of emotion imply confined to the brain. There are compelling arguments that affect as emotion, feelings and mood is the sense by which we make sense of the world. Affect is cognitive but not intellectual.

Aesthetics

If we were to exchange the word "like" for "love" with regard to our new phone, have we moved from affect to aesthetics? What is clear is that much of the time affect and aesthetics overlap considerably, and to tease them apart may not be entirely meaningful. However, what has emerged is that aesthetics may have a role not very different from the way we discuss affordances. Add to this the recent appearance of neuro-aesthetics and we may have the means of distinguishing feelings from appearance.

1.6 Conclusions

Perhaps the most surprising thing about UX, after these many years of speculation and research, is that no one agrees on how to define it without invoking a fairly arbitrary open-ended list of attributes. A plausible reason for this is the clear absence of theoretical background. It is also interesting to note that while the instrumental treatments of HCI have happily embraced notions that cognition is not laboratory-bound but situated (e.g., Suchman 1987), distributed (e.g., Hutchins 1995), embodied (e.g., Metzinger 2004), and even enactive (Valera et al. 1991). There is no such enthusiasm in the UX community. Indeed, judging by the definition of UX and the instruments which have been created to capture or measure it, thinking appears rather dated. It is worth remembering that the word 'experience' is from the same root as the word 'experiment' and is about trying out things and learning from them. Thus, experience is the result of doing stuff with things (digital products) in the world, which points at experience is not something which only happens in an individual's head. Thus, we can recognise the truth of people having a "gut reaction" or commenting on the "feel of an artefact in the hand".

Measurement is central to UX and there are numerous tools to do this (after a fashion) but perhaps more importantly for the current discussion, measurement facilitates insight into how experience is conceived. Measurement in UX is primarily (but not exclusively) based on the use of numeric scales. The procedure is very familiar, a participant is recruited, invited to use a digital product and then they are asked to complete a questionnaire, the data are collated, subjected to inferential statistics and then the new product is pronounced to be "better" than the old version. Almost always, measurement is in the service of the designer, hardware and software engineer or shareholder. Dourish (2006) notes that, "A common lament to be found in reviews of ethnographic work is, yes, it's all very interesting, but I don't understand its implications for design" or the somewhat more subtlety, 'this paper does not seem to be addressed towards the CHI (computer-human interaction) audience". Dourish goes on to consider how theory has been relegated to a second place behind design. Although he is highlighting the fate of sociological conclusions, much the same observations hold true for psychology. Psychology has, in recent years, become an unacknowledged maidservant to design. Whether Dourish's comments are fair is moot, but what is important is that we recognise that experience is seamless, unbroken and possibly ineffable but measurement is (almost by default) piecemeal, partial and instrumental. In the next chapter, we discuss our complex involvement with digital products.

References

Alben L (1996) Defining the criteria for effective interaction design. Interactions 3(3):11–15

Bargas-Avila JA, Hornbæk K (2011) Old wine in new bottles or novel challenges: a critical analysis of empirical studies of user experience. In: Proceedings of the SIGCHI Conference on Human Factors in Computing Systems. ACM, pp 2689–2698

Barsalou LW (1983) Ad hoc categories. Memory & Cognition 11(3):211–227

Barsalou LW (1985) Ideals, central tendency, and frequency of instantiation as determinants of graded structure in categories. J Exp Psychol Learn Mem Cogn 11:629–654

Barsalou LW (1991) Deriving categories to achieve goals. In: Bower G (ed) The psychology of learning and motivation: advances in research and theory, vol 27. Academic Press, San Diego, CA, pp 1–64

Battarbee K (2003) Defining co-experience. In: Proceedings of the 2003 international conference on Designing pleasurable products and interfaces. ACM, pp 109–113

Blythe MA, Monk AF, Overbeeke K, Wright PC (eds) (2003) Funology: from usability to enjoyment. Kluwer Academic Publishers, Dordrecht

Botvinick M, Cohen J (1998) Rubber hands 'feel' touch that eyes see. Nature 391(6669):756

Chrysikou EG (2006) When shoes become hammers: goal-derived categorization training enhances problem-solving performance. J Exp Psychol Hum Learn Perform 32:935–942

Coyne R (1995) Designing information technology in the postmodern age. MIT Press, Cambridge

Davis M (2003) Theoretical foundations for experiential systems design. In: Proceedings of the 2003 ACM SIGMM workshop on Experiential telepresence. ACM, pp 45–52

Dennett DC (1988) Quining qualia. In Consciousness in modern science. Oxford University Press, UK

Dewey J (1934/1980) (reprint) Art as Experience. Perigee Books, New York

Dourish P (2006, April). Implications for design. In: Proceedings of the SIGCHI conference on Human Factors in computing systems. ACM, pp 541–550

Dreyfus HL, Wrathall MA (2005) Introduction. In: Dreyfus HL, Wrathall MA (eds) A companion to Heidegger. Blackwell Publishing, Malden, MA

Forlizzi J, Battarbee K (2004) Understanding experience in interactive systems. In: Proceedings of the 5th conference on Designing interactive systems: processes, practices, methods, and techniques. ACM, pp 261–268

Gibson JJ (1986) The ecological approach to visual perception. Houghton Mifflin, Boston

Haldane D (2015) Review of the Chimp Paradox, by S Peters. Occup Med 65(6):509

Hassenzahl M (2008) User experience (UX): towards an experiential perspective on product quality. In: Proceedings of the 20th Conference on l'Interaction Homme-Machine. ACM, pp 11–15

Hassenzahl M, Tractinsky N (2006) User experience-a research agenda. Behav Inf Technol 25 (2):91–97

Heidegger M (1927/1962) Being and time (trans: Macquarrie J, Robinson E). Harper Collins, New York

Hutchins E (1995) Cognition in the Wild. MIT press

Kuniavsky M (2010) Smart things: ubiquitous computing user experience design. Elsevier

Law ELC, Vermeeren AP, Hassenzahl M, Blythe M (2007, September) Towards a UX manifesto. In: Proceedings of the 21st British HCI Group Annual Conference on People and Computers: HCI... but not as we know it-Volume 2. British Computer Society, pp 205–206

Law ELC, Roto V, Hassenzahl M, Vermeeren AP, Kort J (2009, April) Understanding, scoping and defining user experience: a survey approach. In: Proceedings of the SIGCHI conference on human factors in computing systems. ACM, pp 719–728

Lucariello J, Nelson K (1985) Slot-filler categories as memory organizers for young children. Dev Psychol 21:272–282

McCarthy JC, O'Connor B (1999) The context of information use in a hospital as simultaneous similarity–difference relations. Cogn Technol Work 1(1):25–36

McCarthy J, Wright P (2004) Technology as experience. Cambridge, MA, MIT Press

Medin DL, Ross N, Atran S, Cox D, Coley J, Proffitt J, Blok S (2006) Folkbiology of freshwater fish. Cognition 99:237–273

Merleau-Ponty M (1945/1962) Phenomenology of perception. (trans: Smith C). Routledge Classics, London

Metzinger T (2004) Being no one: the self-model theory of subjectivity. MIT Press, Cambridge, MA

Nielsen J (1994) Usability engineering. Elsevier

Robert JM, Lesage A (2010) From usability to user experience with interactive systems. Handbook of Human-machine interaction, pp 303–332

Ross BH, Murphy GL (1999) Food for thought: cross-classification and category organization in a complex real-world domain. Cogn Psychol 38:495–553

Roto V, Law E, Vermeeren APOS, Hoonhout J (2011) User experience white paper. Bringing clarity tothe concept of user experience. Result from Dagstuhl seminar on demarcating user experience, September 15–18 (2010). Disponible en ligne le, 22, 06–15.

Suchman LA (1987) Plans and situated actions: the problem of human-machine communication. Cambridge university press

Sutcliffe A (2009) Designing for user engagement: aesthetic and attractive user interfaces. Synthesis lectures on human-centered informatics. Morgan & Claypool Publishers, San Rafael, CA, United States

Svanæs D (2013) Interaction design for and with the lived body: some implications of merleau-ponty's phenomenology. ACM Trans Comp Hum Inter (TOCHI) 20(1):8

Turner P (2013) Coping synthesis lectures on human-centered informatics. Morgan & Claypool Publishers, San Rafael, CA, United States

Valera FJ, Thompson E, Rosch E (1991) The embodied mind: cognitive science and human experience. MIT Press, Cambridge, MA

Weiser M (1996) Open house. ITP Review 2.0, March. Available at http://sandbox.xerox.com/hypertext/weiser/wholehouse.doc. Last accessed 1 Sept 2017

Wheeler M (2005) Reconstructing the Cognitive world. MIT Press, Cambridge, MA

Winograd T, Flores F (1986) Understanding computers and cognition: a new foundation for design. Ablex, Norwood NJ

Chapter 2
Everyday Involvement with Technology

Computers don't just do things for us, they do things to us, including to our ways of thinking about ourselves and other people. A decade ago, such subjective effects of the computer presence were secondary in the sense that they were not the ones being sought. Today, things are often the other way around. People explicitly turn to computers for experiences that they hope will change their ways of thinking or will affect their social and emotional lives.

Turkle 1995, p. 26

This chapter discusses our involvement with digital products. Donald Norman tells us that he coined the term "user experience" (UX) to refer to "all aspects of the end-user's interaction with the company, its services, and its products" (NNG website, n.d.). Marc Hassenzahl, another leading proponent of user experience, largely agrees and while omitting the corporate dimension, has added that its "psychological complexity cannot be underestimated" (Hassenzahl 2003, p. 41), a sentiment with which we agree. However, the point we highlight in this opening paragraph is not the breadth of UX but its narrowness. Since the first appearance of human-computer interaction, the world is changed and while we may indeed interact with an application running on our personal computer, can we say the same when we are reading about the floods in China on CNN or the BBC? Is this best described as interaction? Perhaps not. We have a complex web of relationships with digital products. Information is pushed and pulled, alerts pop-up, invitations are routed, and we tweet and re-tweet. The vocabulary is changed and we no longer simply interact with technology, instead we dwell with digital technology, we identify with it and for some, we cannot imagine life without it and we have known this for some years (e.g. Negroponte 1996; Houle 2011). Yet Norman's definition of UX pivots on a very particular form of use, namely interaction. As we described in Chap. 1, we seek to replace this term with involvement.

© Springer International Publishing AG 2017

P. Turner, *A Psychology of User Experience*, Human–Computer Interaction Series,
https://doi.org/10.1007/978-3-319-70653-5_2

2.1 Everyday Involvement …

We begin with the familiar observation that digital technology is pervasive. It has a central role in education, work, entertainment, transportation, health, commerce, our identity—indeed, it mediates just about every aspect of our everyday lives and because of this, it is important to us. More than this, it is the context for any and all user experiences.

From this perspective, it is fair to say that our relationship with digital products is no longer instrumental—it is not just about getting the job done. In addition to the philosophical case we made for involvement in Chap. 1, the inclusive term involvement captures the different ways in which we cope with the wealth of digital products we encounter. Etymologically, involvement is from the Latin involvere, meaning "to be rolled up in", while in Middle English it means "to enfold" or "to entangle". Thus, to be involved with technology is to be rolled up in it or enfolded by it. This enfolding also captures something of the spirit of our relationship too.

Further, it is not hyperbole to suggest that digital technology and digital products define the current age, just as steam power and top hats did for the Victorians and roads and the gladius did for the Romans, and this digital world is the context against which we have (user) experiences with digital products. We should also recognise that not all of us are wide-eyed bystanders marvelling at the latest piece of digital magic, instead, we are actively engaged with it, whether we like it or not, and because it is a fact of who and what we are. We are involved with technology because we find it useful, rewarding, fun, enjoyable, pleasurable, and ineluctable. It is also the case that we have to use it at work, and at home for shopping, entertainment and so forth. Many of us would struggle to live without it.

Heidegger uses the very compelling metaphor of suggesting that we must have been "thrown" into the world to capture something of this involvement. We have all been thrown into this digital world, like reluctant children being introduced to swimming by being thrown into a pool, and we find ourselves immersed in digital technology actively coping with it. If this image implies that for some of us that we are in over our heads, then so much more appropriate the metaphor becomes.

Yet, curiously for a discipline that has taken a long time to recognise that the use of digital products is always in context and to appreciate that context was a missing factor in our description of human-computer interaction (e.g. Suchman 1987), and to recognise that context is a slippery context (e.g. Dourish 2004), we seem to have forgotten about it again. In the last chapter, we considered a number of different definitions of UX, and found that context was not always present much less made explicit. Yet context is not optional, we cannot, for example, discuss the range of experiences someone might have with their smart phone without mentioning, for example, that they have a very poor connection. Or perhaps the fact that they live in rural India where it is common practice for a smart phone to be shared among a group of villagers. Or the fact that they are only 12 years old and their parents have imposed usage conditions. Of course, user experiences can and do occur within restricted laboratory conditions (particularly for those of us with laboratories) but these are the exceptions. Overwhelmingly, user experiences are situated—they are experienced in context, and this needs to be reflected in any definition or treatment of UX.

We should recognise that our involvement with digital technology provides the background or context for the experience of individual digital products. We simply do not (or cannot) use digital products in isolation. So, any user experience with a digital product is in the context of our overall involvement and familiarity with other digital technology.

For example, contrast the experiences of an older person who has been given a basic cell phone to stay in touch with her daughter. This phone is reserved for emergencies in the fruit bowl in the kitchen (this is real world example of my acquaintance). The older person has a TV and radio but little other technology in her home. At the other extreme is the CEO of an Internet start-up who carries a state-of-the-art smart phone with her all day/every day. The phone acts as communication centre, mobile office and "status" symbol. The phone wirelessly "synched" with her home and office networks. Two phones; two levels of technological involvement, two different contexts; two different user experiences. We should recognise that our involvement with digital products and technology is the real source of all user experience.

However, long before UX became a thing in its own right, we were already experiencing digital products. Admittedly, many of these early (historic) experiences with concerned with the lack of their usability and indeed some people also found them to be a source of anxiety (e.g. Eason 1976; Heinssen et al. 1987; Igbaria and Chakrabarti 1990; Turner et al. 2007). Yet despite this, there is compelling evidence that we perceived many of these digital products socially as evidenced by Turkle (1995), Brooks (2002), CASA[1] researchers (e.g. Nass et al. 1994; Nass et al. 1995; Sundar and Nass 2000) and, of course, sociologists working within the SCOT[2] paradigm.

This chapter

After this introduction, this chapter is divided into 4 sections each of which discusses a different form of involvement with technology.

Firstly, we consider the different ways in which our propensity to perceive digital products socially manifests. The evidence is that there may be a number of inter-related mechanisms at work as part of this. We should add a note to say that these mechanisms have been identified by researchers from different academic disciplines, so while there is much overlap, there is little synthesis. These are

---

[1]Computers as Social Actors (CASA) researchers believe that our interactions with computers, televisions, and "new media" are essentially social and "natural". Advocates of CASA argue that people expect media to follow a wide range of social rules and their (re) actions follow the same rules.

[2]Advocates of SCOT—the *Social Construction of Technology*—argue that technology does not determine human behaviour but that human action shapes technology but importantly, for the current discussion, they also argue that the use of technology cannot be understood without understanding how it is embedded in its social context.

Theory of Mind, the Media Equation and folk psychology. These three distinct faculties enable us to understand and predict the behaviour of others and, by extension, the workings of digital products.

In the following section, we discuss something which is readily observable about our everyday use of digital products that we make them our own. I have a pocket knife which looks more-or-less the way it did when I bought it. It shows the signs of use but little else. The digital products I own, in contrast, are far from being "factory fresh" as I have appropriated them. We appropriate digital products by making them a part of our lives, by personalising them, and by customising them. This can be trivial, for example, by selecting our own "wallpaper", but in other cases, this can be fundamental and transformative. This appropriation can actually give rise to new and unexpected products in their own right.

The next section of this chapter examines the truism that we are all familiar with digital products. We have become familiar by being exposed to them, directly and indirectly on a daily basis. Familiarity, it will be argued is best understood as "know-how". This is involvement as a hands-on practical understanding of how a digital product works.

Finally, we discuss being-with technology from the perspective of dwelling with it. Our homes are filled with digital technology with which we have created niches and ecologies. An information ecology being a network of tools and people and their practices. The idea was to move interest "beyond the dominant image of the tool metaphor, an image of a single person and his or her interactions with technology and they wanted to capture a notion of locality that is missing from the system view" (Nardi and O'Day 1999).

2.2   … As Shared Sense-Making

We are social creatures and tend to treat almost every situation, every encounter, socially. So, it should a matter of little surprise that we also treat digital products socially too and we propose that this is very likely to be one of the first forms of experience we have with them.

More than 20 years ago Clifford Nass and his colleagues (Nass et al. 1994) made the assertion that computers are social actors (this became known as CASA) and presented simple but compelling empirical evidence to support this claim. The studies showed that while people did not believe that computers are human or human-like their response to them was nonetheless social, indeed these responses are "commonplace and easy to generate" (p. 72). Their preliminary work also found that a variety of social norms applied to computers; that computer-generated voices created a strong sense of the social actors. It was also observed that our social responses to computers were automatic and unconscious. Studies of CASA were to uncover more detail in subsequent years (e.g. a number of studies of the role of "gender") and extended the paradigm to newer media forms such as Twitter (e.g. Li and Li 2014). However, a new generation of digital products have emerged which specifically invite social interaction and these are the robots and digital assistants. We introduce the psychological bases of our social relationships in this chapter and continue with it in the next chapter where we focus on relational technology.

What does it mean to treat digital technology socially?
Many authors are happy to tell us that we have a social relationship with technology, after all, the power and ubiquity of social media is undeniable but we do not have a social relationship with them. They are communications media, they are the means by which we are in contact with each other (often constantly), they are a means to an end and that end is, unequivocally, other people. So, for example, we do not have a social relationship with twitter but twitter does enable potentially millions of other people to read our 140 characters worth of thoughts on whatever is current. As the term "social" is both loose and loaded, we have adopted the more manageable   (but   longer-winded)   "shared   sense-making"   to   indicate   this relationship.

When we use a digital product by pressing a button, or sliding a finger over a screen we are initiating a dialogue. The technology responds to the instructions by doing something and we in turn issue another command and it in turn responds— and this basic dialogue has all of the hallmarks of being social (i.e. an interaction between two agents). This is not the only means by which we are prompted to engage with digital products "socially" or as Nass and Moon (2000, p. 88) put it "mindlessly" but it does illustrate the point. The underlying mechanism involved in the concept of mindlessness relies on "… individuals must be presented with an object that has enough cues to lead the person to categorize it as worthy of social responses, while also permitting individuals who are sensitive to the entire situation to note that the social behaviors were not clearly appropriate."

Once faced with a situation which can or might be taken to be social, we quite naturally, and unconsciously, make use of our (social) sense-making abilities to understand and anticipate the subsequent behaviour with it.

We have identified three sense-making mechanisms which we will discuss here but are sure there are others and the first of these which we will consider is Theory of Mind. Almost all of us have developed a Theory of Mind which embodies our beliefs (or theory) that other people have the same kind of rich internal mental lives as we do and it would seem that we extend this to include digital products too.

The second mechanism is what Reeve and Nass (1996) describe as the Media Equation. This equation is that "new media = the real world" and they argue that this attribution is due to our "old brains". An old brain is not one that has seen better days but one which reflects its origins, and with our species, it means the savannahs of Africa during the Upper Late Pleistocene. So, we are using our old brains to make sense of new media and this mismatch has resulted in the social-like perception and treatment of digital products.

The third mechanism relies on folk psychology. Malle (2004) writing about folk psychology tells us that, "People make a number of assumptions about human behavior and its relation to the mind. These assumptions are interrelated and form a network that is variably referred to as a commonsense psychology, naïve theory of action, theory of mind, or folk psychology" (p. 30). Malle reminds us that, although we might expect that these different labels to refer to different "slices of the phenomenon", there is little consensus among researchers. So, folk psychology should be understood as a network of knowledge and rules rather than a coherent model of which Dennett (1991) writes, "What I want to stress is that for all its blemishes, warts, and perplexities, folk psychology is an extraordinarily powerful source of prediction. It is not just prodigiously powerful but also remarkably easy for human beings to use". (p. 135).

Theory of Mind

It is believed by many that most people develop a Theory of Mind (usually abbreviated to ToM) by which we make sense of what other people do and think and this is based on the perfectly reasonable but unsubstantiated belief that they have the same kind of rich internal mental lives as we have. Baron-Cohen (2000) has suggested that a ToM may be more important than the appearance of bipedalism or tool use in our evolution. ToM is what Goldman (2012) calls "the cognitive capacity to attribute mental states to self and others" and it has also been proposed as a necessary condition for, and the basis of, no less a construct than culture itself. Despite the clear importance of ToM, most people are scarcely aware of it, as it is employed unconsciously.

For hundreds of thousands of years, we have been cooperating with each other and fighting each other and deceiving each other all courtesy of our ToM. The presence of our ToM has enabled us to make sense of each other's affective states, habits, intentions and we use it to anticipate and understand each other's plans and actions (Whiten 1991). The idea of people developing a Theory of Mind was originally proposed by Premack and Woodruff (1978) to describe the hypothesised ability of our cousins the chimpanzees to infer each other's mental states. It is described as a *Theory of Mind* because the relevant mental states are not directly observable (i.e. they are theorised), and the observed behaviours of others are predicted and accounted for on this theoretical basis (Perner 1999).

Baron-Cohen (1997) underlines the importance of an effective "mindreading" system from an evolutionary perspective: "Imagine that you are an early hominid, and that another early hominid offers to groom you and your mate. You need to reason quickly about whether you should let him approach […] Making inferences about whether his motives are purely altruistic or whether he might be deceitful is a reasoning strategy that you can apply in time to react to a social threat". (p. 25) The hominid's mindreading provides him with information about the intentions of others, necessary to act quickly and appropriately. From this evolutionary perspective, ToM is an essential component of coping with the world, and Baron-Cohen has identified a wide range of intentional communications which depend on it. These are "communicative acts that are produced in order to change the knowledge state of the listener", so if I were to tell someone that green tea contains anti-oxidants, I am doing so in order to give them new information. I am doing this because I believe they do not have this information; and they might be interested in it; and they might want this information. In short, I am trying to change their knowledge state, and to do that I need a theory that others have minds that can be informed or uninformed or deceived just like me. We can witness this every minute of every day when, for example, we post images, or update our profiles, or send messages using social media on the clear understanding that one's "friends" will understand.

Other examples of intentional communication include repairing a failed communication when we realise that the listener has not understood the intended message; and teaching is too, as it is concerned with "changing the knowledge state of the less knowledgeable listener" (though there is little evidence that this works in practice); and persuasion is the changing of someone else's belief about the value of something.

Similarly, sharing a plan or goal with another relies on a "meeting of minds" and shared attention (as in hey, "look at that") requires that both people are aware of the other person being aware of looking at the same things at they are. If you find this a little unlikely, try getting your cat to look at the moon. Point at the moon and then tell Felix to "look at the moon". All that will happen is that Felix will rub his head on your hand.

Overall, such observations have prompted Bruner to write, "Social realities are not bricks that we trip over or bruise ourselves on when we kick at them, but the meanings that we achieve by the sharing of human cognitions" (Bruner 1982, p. 837).

We are now applying these hard-won skills to making sense of, and use a range of digital products, including robots, virtual agents, digital assistants, intelligent systems, animation and cooperative systems to name but a few. We return to some of these in more detail in Chap. 3.

The Media Equation

Reeves and Nass were among the first to recognise that we treat interactive technology, television, and other new media (their term) as though they were the real world. In their *The Media Equation* (1996), they show in a wide variety of ways that the apparent equivalence of media and real life and they present evidence that we interact with these media in the same way we respond to other people, using the same "rules" that govern face-to-face interpersonal interactions.

Reeves and Nass recognise that their equation[3] is both remarkable and counter-intuitive, since people very clearly know that the media with which they interacting with are not real people. Despite this, we are routinely polite (and rude) to digital technology which, they suggest, are the products of our "old brains".

The brains which developed there, did so in response to the demands placed upon them (e.g. finding something to eat while not being eaten) and not the pressures and requirements of the modern, digital world—or so their argument goes.

Our old brains have developed to cope with other humans and are being misled by these new media (or we are misleading ourselves). They also argue that media

---

[3]The equation reads something like "new media = social world".

representations and techniques have been specifically designed to activate these very social responses. One of their key conclusions is that the human brain has not evolved quickly enough to cope with the range of twenty-first century digital products.

The evidence in support of this is quite detailed, for example, people have been found to respond to computers with different voices (Nass and Steuer 1993), to feel psychologically close to or connected with a computer (Lee and Nass 2005), to respond to computer personalities in a similar manner as they respond to human personalities (e.g. Brave et al. 2005), and to flattery from the computer (Fogg and Nass 1997) or engage in self-disclosure with artificial intelligence (Mou and Xu 2017).

Nass and Moon (2000, p. 86) have written that "the computer is not a person and does not warrant human treatment or attribution" and point out that computers do not have faces or bodies—unlike, say, a child's toy, and are unresponsive to human affect, and never express emotion themselves. Yet for all of this, there is abundant evidence that people mindlessly (a term they emphasize) apply social rules and expectations to digital products. Their own empirical work has found that people tend to "overuse human social categories" (p. 82) such as gender and ethnicity, politeness and reciprocity, and behave as though computers have a personality traits, such as friendliness. Mindlessness has also been defined as the over-reliance on habits from past experiences that are applied in a new situation. This over-reliance leads to the use of pre-existing "scripts" which may fail to account for the particulars of the individual and the situation, such as interacting with a computer rather than a human.

As compelling as this is, it does cut across a number of different domains, for example, Reeves and Nass note that the media equation is automatic and unconscious and occurs with the most passive use of digital products. This suggests that this might be better thought of as a form of perception rather than deliberation or a response to the affordances offered by the product. This also suggests that it may be an example of System I thinking (please see Chap. 6) and there is some support for this when they tell us that people respond to what is present and immediate rather than what they know to be there.

Folk Psychology

The third account relies on (or is an aspect of) folk psychology and is the wonderfully named theory-theory (Morton 1980). We note that some researchers equate folk psychology with Theory of Mind directly, but we do not, following Ravenscroft (2016) who tells us that folk psychology has a number of distinct forms, and primarily refers to a set of cognitive capacities which include "the capacities to predict and explain behaviour". Churchland (1990, p. 207) also describes our ability to understand one another as relying on an "integrated body of lore concerning the law-like relations holding among external circumstances, internal states, and overt behaviour". Thus, folk psychology is knowledge of how the (social) world works. Other examples of folk knowledge include: we know that if we do not eat we get hungry; that if we injure ourselves it hurts; and the world is not fair. In short, folk psychology enables us to cope with the world.

Theory-theory proposes that people have basic or "naïve" knowledge about the world and understand the rules which govern it. We use these to reason about the mental states of others, such as their beliefs, desires or emotions, and to understand the intentions behind that person's actions and to predict their future behaviour. A central feature of this is "perspective taking" which enables one to infer another's inner state using knowledge about the other's situation.

The application of theory-theory, as a set of heuristics or rules derived from what we have learned about the world, other people and technology, is not limited to making sense of people and can be applied to the operation of technology. Interestingly, folk psychology does not necessarily require a human brain to operate and could, at least in principle, "run" on a computer or artificial intelligence.

Similar or different?

Theory of Mind has been widely studied as part of developmental psychology (including the dimensions of autism) and is well established. That, of course, is not to suggest that there is unanimity among researchers. There are currently (at least) two broad accounts of how we acquire ToM. The older account assumes that it relies on folk psychology while the newer account proposes that it is the result of running a simulation of other minds. There are also other approaches which include mirror neurons.

The theory-theory approach to a ToM would require that we apply the rules we have learned to behaviour appropriately (in society) and make sense of the behaviour of others including technology. A folk psychological account of social behaviour shares the same kind of conceptual space as mental models (e.g. Norman 1988). Theory-theory like mental models are likely to be incomplete, occasionally contradictory but work most of the time for most situations.

In contrast, the simulation theory of ToM proposes that we use "the resources of [our] own minds to simulate […] others." (Davies and Stone 1995) and it essentially requires us to adopt the perspectives of another and from there make predictions and propose explanations. This is an attractive account and is, to some degree consistent with a role for mirror neurons, which we discuss next, but it is, of course, a theoretic. We undoubtedly can adopt the perspective of another and see the world through their eyes but as Dennett (1987, p. 100) writes, "If I make believe I am a suspension bridge and wonder what I will do when the wind blows, what 'comes to me' in my make-believe state depends on how sophisticated my knowledge is of the physics and engineering of suspension bridges". For Dennett, simulations rely on knowledge and rules. There are also some developmental objections to simulation accounts of ToM including, for example, Perner and Howes (1992).

Mirror neurons, which are a form of motor neuron, are active ("fire") when an animal acts (e.g. when it reaches for an apple) and they are also active when the animal observes the same action in another—hence their name (e.g. Rizzolatti and Sinigaglia 2007). The function of the mirror system is a subject of continued discussion and they have been proposed to play a role in understanding and interpretation action (e.g. Rizzolatti and Craighero 2004; Cook et al. 2014);

imitation and empathy (e.g. Iacoboni et al. 1999); emotion (e.g. Enticott et al. 2008); and in mediating social interaction in their role in the theory of mind (e.g. Ramachandran and Oberman 2006).

As for the Media Equation, it is a little on its own here, as it is not to be found within mainstream psychology but is largely confined to social psychological accounts of digital technology use. As the media equation stresses that we seem to apply social rules mindlessly to the interpretation of technology (and all that goes with it) this seems to suggest that it may be regarded as a form of folk psychology.

2.3 … As Appropriation

Fifty years ago, the idea of a personal computer was pure science fiction. After all, why would anyone want their own computer? Today, I own five of varying ages and I have owned and used very many more.

The personal computer (PC), which appeared in the 1980s, did not offer anything particularly personal. The description of personal did not mean "mine" (as in not yours) but more simply, not shared. Prior to the PC, a typical office worker likely to have graduated from a typewriter to a "dumb" terminal driven by a mainframe or mini-computer. PCs, in contrast, offered the prospect of having one's own data and specialist applications. With laptop computers came the real sense of ownership and a badge of status (and often resentment) as only a manager was thought to merit a laptop. However, desktop and laptop personal computers could not compete with the sense of ownership that an Apple iPod brought. The original iPod was carried about with us in a jacket or shirt pocket and was instantly recognised as such because of its distinctive white ear buds, indeed, early adopters were warned about signalling the presence of these much sought-after devices to potential muggers. The iPod was both personal and personalised as it had a copy of one's own music (and a little later, audiobooks, TV shows and movies). The Apple iPod appeared in October 2001 and was to herald a whole series of products whose names became with an "i" prefix. Anecdotally (co.design 2012), its origins lie with the iMac, "It created an interesting foundation upon which Apple could name future consumer products… not only was "iMac" concise and easy to remember, but the "i" could stand for other things. There was the obvious association with the Internet, but it could also stand for "individual" and "imagination"."

We describe appropriation[4] as the processes by which we make technology better suited to how we want to use it (that is, to give us a better user experience). It

---

[4]Silverstone and Haddon (1996), and very many later studies drawing on their work, use the term "domestication" to describe appropriation as the way in which technologies are integrated into everyday life and adapted to match the demands of daily practices. They based these ideas on the parallel they draw with the domestication of wild animals for their use as sources of food, for clothing, for work and for protection.

also lets us use technology to say something about who we are or want to be seen as. Dourish (2003) stresses the practical and situated aspects of appropriation writing that, "Appropriation is the way in which technologies are adopted, adapted and incorporated into working practice. This might involve customization in the traditional sense (that is, the explicit reconfiguration of the technology in order to suit local needs) …" (Dourish ibid, p. 467).

Personalisation

Personalisation is the process by which an artefact is endowed with greater significance by and for its user. Wells (2000) defines it as "the deliberate decoration or modification of the environment" and associates it with 'well-being'. Blom and Monk (2003) have shown that personalising the appearance of artefacts has cognitive, social and emotional dimensions. Their account of personalisation was based on the analysis of three qualitative studies of the use of web-based personalisation in the UK; and a Finnish mobile phone users and of the personalisation of home PCs, again in the UK. They describe the cognitive aspects of personalisation as improving of ease of use, better recognition of the system and improved aesthetics (though this might have reasonably have been treated as a category in its own right as the research was concerned with personalizing the appearance of artefacts). The social dimensions of personalisation are concerned with reflecting personal and group identity. Finally, the largest category are the emotional effects on the user. These affective consequences include feelings of familiarity, ownership, control, fun, attachment, release from boredom and other positive attachments. Later work by Oulasvirta and Blom (2007) suggests that personalisation enhances the experience of use and adds enjoyment in three ways, by supporting senses of autonomy, competence and relatedness.

Authors in the field of sustainable interaction design have introduced the concept of the ensoulment of objects, a property closely related to attachment. Here, ensoulment signifies the properties of "well-loved" designs that embody meaning and reflect their owner's identities and values (Blevis 2007; Nelson and Stolterman 2003). Jung et al (2011) further develop the concept in their narrative-based study, identifying three contributory factors to ensoulment: intimacy accumulated over time; investment of effort and reflection of personal values.

A diversity of expression

Appropriation can be very diverse ranging from the fairly simple such as using a smart phone as a torch (flashlight) and as a mirror to full blown instances of make-believe. This field is enormous and the ability to appropriate smart phones and tablet computers is probably the major factor in their success. We consider three very different but illustrative examples.

It is possible, for example, to use an app for iPAD which will imitate the appearance of a Star Trek PADD. The PADD app imitates the look of the Star Trek style of user interface as it appears on TV. The app comes complete with the appropriate (appropriated) sound effects.

More seriously, it is also possible, to transform an iPhone or an equivalent Android phone into a medical diagnostic instrument by adopting add-ons and apps

Fig. 2.1 Appropriating a smart phone I

to measure glucose, blood pressure, pulse rate and to display ultrasound images and electrocardiograms (iPAD references).

A final example of appropriation was observed when we are sitting drinking coffee in the elegant city of Padua. We witnessed a small group of young men very vigorously gesturing at something held by one of them at about chest height. We thought it looked like the makings of a fight. The young men were very demonstrative, waving their arms and making shapes with their fingers but without a sound, not a word was uttered. As we watched it was clear that they were also soundlessly mouthing things at what turned out to be a smart phone. Then it became clear that they were using the phone's video capabilities to communicate with each other via sign language (Figs. 2.1 and 2.2).

2.4   … Leading to Familiarity

We propose that familiarity with digital technology is another expression of being involved with it. Constantly living with technology and being surrounded by it means that we have become familiar with it. Nye (2006, p. 199) observes, "a child born since 1950 finds it 'natural' to use electric lights, to watch television […] and

Fig. 2.2 Appropriating a smart phone II

to use satellite-based communications. That child's grandparents regard such things as remarkable innovations that had disrupted the normal". Technology has become like family—always present, as source of pleasure, and of irritation, and comfort.

More than 30 years ago Bewley et al. (1983) writing of the design of the Xerox Star's user interface, which was the forerunner of all modern graphical user interfaces, noted that it was informed by four key principles. The first of these was "There should be an explicit user's model of the system, and it should be familiar (drawing on objects and activities the user already works with) and consistent."

The idea of a user model and consistency in interaction have are now well established but familiarity has been largely ignored. Yet it was familiarity with files, printers, trashcan, the processes of cutting and pasting and using "tools" like scissors, pens and brushes which explicitly linked the operation of the GUI to the users' familiar worlds of artefacts and action which made this user interface accessible to every office worker. We have all used paper, we have all put paper into files or trashcans in the real world. We are familiar with paper. The Xerox Star's interface sought to reproduce this visually (not metaphorically as is usually and mistakenly stated). The greatest strength of the GUI was that it operated in a manner which was like the real world and as such was familiar. Raskin (1994) agrees, and in a short essay on the nature of intuitive user interfaces equating it with being familiar. He writes that a user interface is "intuitive" in as much as it resembles (or is identical) to something the user already knows. He continues "In short, intuitive in this context is an almost exact synonym of familiar".

Blackler and her colleagues have reported a series of studies of "technology familiarity" which they found to be good predictors of subsequent performance with new but similar or related technology. They found that people with good "technology familiarity" began to use the new technology more quickly and used more of its features than those with poorer technology familiarity (Blackler et al. 2003a, b, 2010). These observations have been echoed by Dixon and O'Reilly (2002) who have also argued that people almost never learn completely new procedures as they simply adapt their behaviour from prior knowledge. Blackler and Hurtienne (2007) have noted that the, "use of products involves utilising knowledge gained through other experience(s). Therefore, products that people use intuitively are those with features they have encountered before." They have demonstrated this effect.

So, we can understand familiarity as the readiness to cope with the world, for example, the safety briefing to which we were all exposed before our flight departs has, from my observation, changed in the last decades. Before the advent of budget airlines, flying was expensive and only enjoyed by people off on their annual Summer holiday or business people *en route* to a meeting. Flying was largely unfamiliar as were the evacuation procedures in the unlikely event of it being needed. In those days, the demonstration by the cabin crew of lifebelt and emergency oxygen was watched with some care. Now, we hear the cabin crew using language such as "if you are not familiar with this particular aircraft" or "I know many of you are frequent flyers but …". We are familiar with flying and with the seatbelts which keep us in check.

Much the same applies to digital products but probably more so. We use them every day and we have watched other people use them, both in the real world and in a wide variety of media (which we may have viewed on a digital device). We are able to demonstrate our familiarity with these diverse technologies not by having complex, abstract cognitive structures in our heads but demonstrating this "know-how" and acting appropriately.

Familiarity as know-how
Familiarity is a 'readiness' to cope with, say, chairs (e.g. by sitting on them) which has developed from our earliest days. Heidegger describes this readiness as "the background of … primary familiarity, which itself is not conscious or intended but is rather present in [an] unprominent way" (concept of time). Thus, assuming that we are in the world of modern computing, when we enter our places of work we see desks, chairs, computers, network points and so forth. We do not perceive a jumble of surfaces, wires and inexplicable boxes. However, if we are not in this world the scene might indeed appear chaotic and meaningless.

For Heidegger, familiarity encompasses the ideas of involvement and understanding. Here involvement may be taken as something approaching a synonym for 'being-in-the-world' while understanding should be interpreted as 'know-how'. Dreyfus (1991) notes that "This know-how … is more basic than the distinction between thought and action" and describes human beings as "We are such skills", thus directly equating humans with our know-how. In these terms, understanding interactive technology simply means being able to use it (i.e. demonstrating our familiarity with it).

So, while we may not have a detailed technical understanding of the technology involved but we can still get it to work and to use it effectively. For example, most people can use a smart phone, but few know how it works (at the level of microprocessors and microwaves), what is important that our familiarity provides the means for this pragmatic use of technology.

Familiarity as imposing a technological horizon
However, there is something of a downside to our familiarity with technology and it is that it tends to create a "horizon". A technological horizon is a reflection of our baseline familiarity with technology or a social practice or institution. So, for example, shopping has traditionally involved going to a store, selecting goods, paying for them and then returning home with them. This practice is one which many of us in the West grew up with and one which we see as natural, authentic and familiar. This everyday practice established—in part—our technological horizon for shopping. This self-same generation may or may not have embraced Internet shopping which offers greater convenience, cheaper goods, more choice but also requires us to change our everyday practices to accommodate them. Shopping at a dotcom is quite a different experience to visiting a city-centre store yet it is one which the current generation may establish as their default or technological horizon. Technological horizons are in action every time someone utters something like, "in my day …" or "when I was a lad …" which reflects an individual's familiarity with how things were.

2.5 … Resulting in Being–with

This chapter has argued that we do not simply interact with digital products but we have a variety of relationships with them. In this section, we introduce being-with technology from the perspective of dwelling with it.

We distinguish living with technology from dwelling with it by arguing that the former is quite passive and implies occupying the same or adjacent space, whereas dwelling is more active. As Heidegger describes it, "Dwelling is not primarily inhabiting but taking care of and creating that space within which something comes into its own and flourishes" (Heidegger 1971). From the perspective of digital technology, dwelling with it suggests actively creating information or artefact ecologies and cognitive or technological niches.

Ecologies

Nardi and O'Day (1996, 1999) introduced the concept of the information ecology in order to focus attention on relationships involving tools and people and their practices. They wanted to create an account of the use of technology which captured locality. They wrote that they chose the word "ecology" as they found it to be more evocative than terms like "community," despite their similarities. Ecology suggests diversity in a way that community does not and it also implies evolution. They then applied these ideas to an information ecology which they define as a system of people, practices, values, and technologies in a particular local environment. In information ecologies, the spotlight is not on technology, but on human activities that are served by technology. Among other concrete examples described, we find that of a hospital intensive care unit (ICU) "Human experts (nurses, physicians, therapists, ethicists) and machines (monitors, probes, and the many other devices in the ICU) all have roles to play in ensuring smooth, round-the-clock care. Though this is a setting with an obvious reliance on advanced technologies, it is clear that human expertise, judgment, empathy, cooperation, and values are central in making the system work". (Nardi and O'Day 1999). In other words, ICU practitioners dwell with their technologies.

The concept has since been adopted in the study of a range of information sharing domains. These include, but are not limited to: situations where information is the principal stock-in-trade, such as education and librarianship; or is particularly critical, such as clinical practice; or complex, as in e-government; or fast-changing, such as in grassroots activism. The following exemplify many other specific instances found in this literature which highlight the dynamic and social production of an information ecology.[5]

In an early application of the concept, Albrechtsen and Jacob (1997) argue that in the diverse information ecologies of libraries, classification structures must be actively developed by user groups and librarians, rather than imposed by external organisations, thus highlighting that ecologies are constructed rather than simply inhabited.

In the more dynamic context of the ICU, we find McKnight (2006) analysing the information seeking behaviour of critical care nurses. She observes how nurses pull together vital data for patient care from a host of digital and human sources, but only occasionally search for "knowledge-based information". This is despite a respect for evidence-based practice. McKnight suggests that this is in part a result of the shaping of their information ecology by historic ritual and tradition, together with personal and professional values that stress the importance of direct patient care and the nurse-patient relationship. Nazi (2013), again in the medical domain, illustrates how the uptake of patient-owned online personal health records can be understood in terms of the dynamic local relationships between values, practice,

---

[5]There are also many instances where the Nardi and O'Day concept of an information ecology is applied in a weaker form, as loosely synonymous with context, or to signify the use of multiple digital technologies per se.

people and technology that in turn are embedded in a wider social, technical and organisational ecosystem. Such dynamics are exemplified in the advent of secure messaging in the wider technical ecosystem and its successful local adoption. The technology matched values and initial practice, but also stimulated more effective communication techniques. The resulting improved information flow led to changes in the wider information ecosystem.

In the very different world of student activism Treré (2012) applied the ecology framework to explore interrelationships between people and technologies, observing that "choices related to technologies (blog, mailing list, YouTube channel, Dropbox account, etc.) affect the whole system of relationships within the ecology, pushing actors to redefine their practices, abandon online platforms momentarily, switch to other tools, acquire new skills, and interrogate their own conceptions of digital activism…" (p. 2371). He also notes how "tech-savvy" volunteers act as keystone species within their information ecology.

Krippendorff and Butter (2007) emphasise dynamism in their alternative treatment of ecologies and write that "It is a truism that we surround ourselves with objects that we are comfortable with and experience as meaningful. This is axiomatic for designers as well as for those who have a stake in their designs. To design artefacts for use by others is to design them to be or to have the chance to become meaningful to these others—not merely in their designers' terms, but according to these others' own and often diverse conceptions." They continue, "Artifacts of different species with synonymous meanings (interfaces) compete for the same ecological niches, while artifacts that have complementary meanings can work together, cooperate, and may develop larger technological cooperatives … Ordinary users may not be aware of the ecological properties of their artifacts, which are brought about by inserting them into contexts of their choice, but to designers, these properties are of central importance for a design to have a chance of surviving in the context of other species of artifacts". They emphasize the contextual and dynamic nature of the affordances associated with artefacts and the meanings attributed to them.

Jung et al. (2008) offer a complementary perspective, writing of personal ecologies of interactive artefacts as comprising all physical artefacts with some level of interactivity enabled by digital technology that a person owns, has access to, or simply uses. Their work identifies ecological factors which define connections or commonalties between artefacts which are commonly based on their function, or shared information, or their perceived characteristics. They also propose ecological layers which seem to be multiple sub-ecologies, grouped by e.g. context of use or selected features of the artefacts; many artefacts exist in multiple layers. Use of ecologies by individuals may be more or less structured or organised.

Finally, Activity theorists, Bødker and Klokmose (2015) have written that "Human beings surround themselves with many artifacts, in many everyday activities, and what artifact is 'natural' for them to use, is highly dependent on their individual past experiences, as well as of the shared practices in which they are part, and the technological possibilities offered to them, in (and outside) these communities of practice." True to the spirit of Activity Theory, such ecologies are necessarily shared by a community, within which individuals develop praxis "There is no user without other users who share their experiences with artifacts and materials, understanding, etc.". Ecologies comprise multiple different devices which serve similar purposes, with no clear means of deciding between them: this is situated and depends on the characteristics of the ecology; both artefacts and activities in constant development. Again, for these authors, ecologies are dynamic.

Niches

Niches are created by animals (including humans) for safety, reproduction and management of food supplies. We also create cognitive niches as resources and mediating structures (e.g. DeVore and Tooby 1987; Magnani and Bardone 2008; Stotz 2010, 2014; Bertolotti and Magnani 2016). Stotz (2010) has described a cognitive niche as "a problem-solving resource and scaffold for individual development and learning [...] what is most distinctive about humans is their developmentally plastic brains immersed into a well-engineered, cumulatively constructed cognitive–developmental niche". I have proposed technological niches which extend beyond the technology itself, and are constructed to ensure that we feel safe, secure and comfortable in the face of the demands of technology (Turner 2013). Technological niches are necessarily smaller, simpler, more manageable and more closely aligned to our needs, both personal and professional, than the "world of work". A simple example of such a niche is a social media service. We enter such domains are "recognised", are surrounded by "friends" and have news tailored for us and a wide range of other services. These social media niches shield us from the vagaries of the Web by offering all a user could possibly want within the confines and safety of their own platform.

The reason for creating these niches or ecologies is not always clear but it is safe to say that these structures tend to scaffold our broader endeavours. From a biological perspective, niches are sub-divisions of the worlds we create. Laland and Sterelny (2006, p. 1751) tell us that this is not the "organism-driven modification of the environment per se, but rather modification of the relationship between an organism and its relative niche. Hence the term "niche construction" includes such things as habitat selection, where organisms modify the environment that they experience". Technological niches are just such selected habitats.

2.6 Conclusions

Our use of digital technology is both purposive and concernful. That is, we use technology of all kinds to achieve our goals and we do so in a manner which is neither detached nor disinterested: we are involved. The pragmatic aspects of this use (i.e. utility and usability) initially attracted the attention of human-computer interaction research and development. In contrast, the concernful aspects have received relatively little attention. To be concernful is to recognise the inter-connectedness of activities and use of tools in the broader context of other people, other technologies and other contexts. This, of course, is the substance of "involvement" and this involvement with technology enables us to encounter it as available or ready-to-hand. To be ready-to-hand means that we encounter/experience technology as being proximal or handy and as being available for immediate use or action.

In the next chapter, we continue our discussion of involvement by considering how we treat digital products which we specifically designed to have a relationship with us.

References

Albrechtsen H, Jacob EK (1997) Classification systems as boundary objects in diverse information ecologies. Adv Classif Res Online 8(1):1–18

Baron-Cohen S (1997) Mindblindness: an essay on autism and theory of mind. MIT press, Massachusetts

Baron-Cohen S (2000) Theory of mind and autism: a review. Int Rev Res Ment Retard 23:169–184

Bertolotti T, Magnani L (2016) Theoretical considerations on cognitive niche construction. Synthese pp 1–23

Bewley WL, Roberts TL, Schroit D, Verplank WL (1983, December) Human factors testing in the design of Xerox's 8010 "Star" office workstation. In: Proceedings of the SIGCHI conference on Human Factors in Computing Systems, ACM, New York, pp 72–77

Blackler AL, Hurtienne J (2007) Towards a unified view of intuitive interaction: definitions, models and tools across the world. MMI-Interaktiv 13(2007):36–54

Blackler A, Popovic V, Mahar D (2003a) The nature of intuitive use of products: an experimental approach. Des Stud 24(6):491–506

Blackler AL, Popovic V, Mahar DP (2003b) Designing for intuitive use of products: an investigation

Blackler A, Popovic V, Mahar D (2010) Investigating users' intuitive interaction with complex artefacts. Appl Ergon 41(1):72–92

Blevis E (2007) Sustainable interaction design: invention & disposal, renewal & reuse. In: Proceedings of the SIGCHI Conference on Human Factors in Computing Systems, San Jose, California, USA, 28 April–3 May 2007, ACM Press, New York, NY, pp 503–512

Blom J, Monk A (2003) A theory of personalisation: why people personalise their PCs and mobile phones. Hum Comput Inter 18:193–228

Bødker S, Klokmose CN (2015) A dialectical take on artifact ecologies and the physical-digital divide. In: Proceedings of the 33rd Annual ACM Conference Extended Abstracts on Human Factors in Computing Systems, ACM, New York, pp 2401–2404

Brave S, Nass CI, Hutchinson K (2005) Computers that care: investigating the effects of orientation of emotion exhibited by an embodied computer agent. Int J Hum Comput Stud 62(2):1–8

Brooks R (2002) Flesh and machines: how robots will change us. Pantheon Books, New York

Bruner J (1982) The language of education. Soc Res 49(4):835–853

Churchland PM (1990) Eliminative materialism and the propositional attitudes. In: Lycan WG (ed) Mind and cognition. Blackwell, Oxford, pp 206–223

co.design (2012) https://www.fastcodesign.com/1669924/steve-jobs-almost-named-the-imac-the-macman-until-this-guy-stopped-him. Last accessed 30 Aug 2017

Cook R, Bird G, Catmur C, Press C, Heyes C (2014) Mirror neurons: from origin to function. Behav Brain Sci 37(2):177–192

Davies M, Stone T (1995) Introduction. In: Davies M, Stone T (eds) Mental simulation. Blackwell, Oxford, pp 1–18

Dennett DC (1987) The intentional stance. 1987. Cambridge, MA

Dennett DC (1991) Two contrasts: folk craft versus folk science, and belief versus opinion. In: Greenwood JD (ed) The future of folk psychology. Cambridge University Press, Cambridge, pp 135–148

DeVore I, Tooby J (1987) The reconstruction of hominid behavioral evolution through strategic modeling. In: Kinzey WG (ed) The evolution of human behavior: primate models, pp 183–237

Dixon P, O'reilly T (2002) Appearance, form and retrieval of prior knowledge. In: Design and the Social Sciences: Making Connections, pp 166–177

Dourish P (2003) The appropriation of interactive technologies: some lessons from placeless documents. Comput Support Coop Work 12:465–490

Dourish P (2004) What we talk about when we talk about context. Pers Ubiquit Comput 8:19–30

Dreyfus HL (1991) Being-in-the-world: a commentary on Heidegger's being and time, division 1. MIT Press, Cambridge, MA

Eason KD (1976) Understanding the naive computer user. Comput J 19(1):3–7

Enticott PG, Johnston PJ, Herring SE, Hoy KE, Fitzgerald PB (2008) Mirror neuron activation is associated with facial emotion processing. Neuropsychologia 46(11):2851–2854

Fogg BJ, Nass C (1997) Silicon sycophants: the effects of computers that flatter. Int J Hum Comput Stud 46(5):551–561

Goldman AI (2012) Theory of mind. In: The Oxford Handbook of Philosophy of Cognitive Science, pp 402–424

Hassenzahl M (2003) The thing and i: understanding the relationship between user and product. In: Monk AF, Overbeeke K, Wright PC, Blythe MA (eds) Funology: From usability to enjoyment. Kluwer Academic Publishers, The Netherlands, pp 31–42

Heidegger M (1971) Building dwelling thinking. In: Poetry, language, thought, p 154

Heinssen RK, Glass CR, Knight LA (1987) Assessing computer anxiety: development and validation of the computer anxiety rating scale. Comput Hum Behav 3(1):49–59

Houle D (2011) Shift age. Sourcebooks, Inc.

Iacoboni M, Woods RP, Brass M, Bekkering H, Mazziotta JC, Rizzolatti G (1999) Cortical mechanisms of human imitation. Science 286(5449):2526–2528

Igbaria M, Chakrabarti A (1990) Computer anxiety and attitudes towards microcomputer use. Behav Inf Technol 9(3):229–241

Jung H, Stolterman E, Ryan W, Thompson T, Siegel M (2008, October) Toward a framework for ecologies of artifacts: how are digital artifacts interconnected within a personal life?. In: Proceedings of the 5th Nordic conference on Human-computer interaction: building bridges, ACM, New York, pp 201–210

Jung H, Bardzell S, Blevis E, Pierce J, Stolterman E (2011) How deep is your love: deep narratives of ensoulment and heirloom status. Int J Des 5(1):59–71

Krippendorff K, Butter R (2007) Semantics: Meanings and contexts of artifacts. In: Schifferstein HNJ, Hekkert P (eds) Product experience. New York, NY: Elsevier. Retrieved from http://repository.upenn.edu/asc_papers/91

Laland KN, Sterelny K (2006) Perspective: seven reasons (not) to neglect niche construction. Evolution 60(9):1751–1762

NNG website https://www.nngroup.com/articles/definition-user-experience/. Last retrieved 7th Jan 2017

Lee KM, Nass C (2005) Social-psychological origins of feelings of presence: creating social presence with machine-generated voices. Media Psychol 7(1):31–45

Li Z, Li C (2014) Twitter as a social actor: how consumers evaluate brands differently on Twitter based on relationship norms. Comput Hum Behav 39:187–196

Magnani L, Bardone E (2008) Sharing representations and creating chances through cognitive niche construction. The role of affordances and abduction. In: Communications and discoveries from multidisciplinary data, Springer, Berlin, Heidelberg, pp 3–40

Malle, BF (2004) How the mind explains behavior. Folk explanation, meaning and social interaction. MIT-Press, Massachusetts

McKnight M (2006) The information seeking of on-duty critical care nurses: evidence from participant observation and in-context interviews. J Med Libr Assoc 94(2):145

Morton A (1980) Frames of mind: constraints on the common-sense conception of the mental. Oxford University Press, Oxford

Mou Y, Xu K (2017) The media inequality: comparing the initial human-human and human-AI social interactions. Comput Hum Behav 72:432–440

Nardi BA, O'day V (1996) Intelligent agents: what we learned at the library. Libri 46(2):59–88

Nardi BA, O'Day V (1999) Information ecologies: using technology with heart. MIT Press, Cambridge

Nass C, Moon Y (2000) Machines and mindlessness: social responses to computers. J Soc Issues 56(1):81–103

Nass C, Steuer J (1993) Voices, boxes, and sources of messages. Hum Commun Res 19(4):504–527

Nass C, Steuer J, Tauber ER (1994) Computers are social actors. In: Proceedings of the SIGCHI conference on Human factors in computing systems, ACM, New York, pp 72–78

Nass C, Moon Y, Fogg BJ, Reeves B, Dryer DC (1995) Can computer personalities be human personalities? Int J Hum Comput Stud 43(2):223–239

Nazi KM (2013) The personal health record paradox: health care professionals' perspectives and the information ecology of personal health record systems in organizational and clinical settings. J Med Internet Res 15(4)

Negroponte N (1996) Being digital. Vintage

Nelson HG, Stolterman E (2003) The design way: Intentional change in an unpredictable world: Foundations and fundamentals of design competence. Educational Technology

Norman DA (1988) The psychology of everyday things. (The design of everyday things)

Nye DE (2006) Technology matters. MIT Press, Cambridge, MA

Oulasvirta A, Blom J (2007) Motivations in personalisation behaviour. Interact Comput 20(1): 1–16

Perner J (1999) Theory of mind. In: Developmental psychology: achievements and prospects, pp 205–230

Perner J, Howes D (1992) "He Thinks He Knows": and more developmental evidence against the simulation (role taking) theory. Mind Lang 7(1–2):72–86

Premack DG, Woodruff G (1978) Does the chimpanzee have a theory of mind? Behav Brain Sci 1 (4):515–526

Ramachandran VS, Oberman LM (2006) Broken mirrors. Sci Am 295(5):62–69

Raskin J (1994) Intuitive equals familiar. Commun ACM 37(9):17–19

Ravenscroft I (2016) Folk Psychology as a Theory. In: Zalta EN (ed) The stanford encyclopedia of philosophy (Fall 2016 Edition). https://plato.stanford.edu/archives/fall2016/entries/folkpsych-theory

Reeves B, Nass C (1996) How people treat computers, television, and new media like real people and place. Cambridge University Press, Cambridge, UK

Rizzolatti G, Craighero L (2004) The mirror-neuron system. Annu Rev Neurosci 27:169–192

Rizzolatti G, Sinigaglia C (2007) Mirror neurons and motor intentionality. Funct Neurol 22(4):205

Stotz K (2010) Human nature and cognitive–developmental niche construction. Phenomenol Cogn Sci 9(4):483–501

Stotz K (2014) Extended evolutionary psychology: the importance of transgenerational developmental plasticity. Front psychol 5

Suchman LA (1987) Plans and situated actions: the problem of human-machine communication. Cambridge University Press, Cambridge

Sundar SS, Nass C (2000) Source orientation in human–computer interaction: programmer, networker, or independent social actor? Commun Res 27(6):683–703

Treré E (2012) Social movements as information ecologies: exploring the coevolution of multiple Internet technologies for activism. Int J Commun 6:19

Turkle, S (1995) Life on the screen: identity in the age of the internet. NY etc.: cop

Turner P (2013) *Coping* Synthesis lectures on human-centered informatics. Morgan & Claypool Publishers, San Rafael, CA, United States

Turner P, Turner S, Van de Walle G (2007) How older people account for their experiences with interactive technology. Behav Inf Technol 26(4):287–296

Wells MM (2000) Office clutter or meaningful personal displays: The role of office personalization in employee and organizational well-being. J Environ Psychol 20(3):239–255

Whiten A (ed) (1991) Natural theories of mind: evolution, development and simulation of everyday mindreading. B. Blackwell, Oxford

Chapter 3
Other Social Beings

Kismet is the world's first robot that is truly sociable, in that it can interact with people on an equal basis, and which people accept as a humanoid creature. They make eye contact with it; it makes eye contact with them. People read its mood from the intonation in its speech, and Kismet reads the mood of people from the intonation in their speech. Kismet and any person who comes close to it fall into a natural social interaction. People talk to it, gesture to it, and act socially with it. Kismet talks to people, gestures to them, and acts socially with it. People, at least for a while, treat Kismet as another being. Kismet is alive. Or may as will be. People treat it that way.

Brooks (2002, p. 65)

This chapter extends the theme of involvement with technology which we introduced in Chaps. 1 and 2 and discusses some of the consequences of living "up close and personal" with technology. Here, we specifically discuss the appearance of relational artefacts in our digital worlds and explore further another important dimension, namely that we treat digital products as though they were another social being.

A relational artefact is a computational object, "explicitly designed to engage a user in a relationship" (Turkle 2007) and examples include not only many forms of what most of us would recognise as robots, but also a wide range of toys, digital and software products. As Fong et al. (2003) point out, social robots—and now other relational artefacts—range from those created solely to engage humans in social interaction to those which are intended to fulfil other functions but require an apparent conformance to social norms for their acceptance. Turkle has observed that when children first play with electronic (computerised) toys they treat them as "their nearest neighbours" and in due course they begin to see these computers as "rational machines". This perception quickly develops so that computers, particularly robots, are seen as relational artefacts with feelings, needs, and a whole raft of human-like attributes of their own. For Turkle, this has led to a crisis in authenticity as evidenced by the opening quotation, namely that Brooks (writing of Kismet) describes it as being able to interact with people on an "equal basis".

© Springer International Publishing AG 2017
P. Turner, *A Psychology of User Experience*, Human–Computer Interaction Series,
https://doi.org/10.1007/978-3-319-70653-5_3

This question has been a recurrent theme in science fiction, which has often considered the consequences of creating digital products which can think, feel and behave like us. We should have probably placed "think", "feel" and "behave" within inverted commas unless, of course, it really does not matter, whether these products "think" or think, "feel" or feel or simply behave as though they did. This point is nicely illustrated in the classic movie 2001: A Space Odyssey. In this scene, we hear a BBC interviewer (Martin Amor) talking to astronaut Frank Poole:

> Amor: "Dr. Poole, what's it like living for the better part of a year in such close proximity with Hal?"
>
> Poole: "Well it's pretty close to what you said about him earlier. He is just like a sixth member of the crew … very quickly get adjusted to the idea that he talks and you think of him, er, really just as another person".
>
> Amor: "In talking to the computer one gets the sense that he is capable of emotional responses. For example, when I asked him about his abilities I sensed a certain pride in his answer about his accuracy and perfection. Do you believe that Hal has genuine emotions?"
>
> Poole: "Well he acts like he has genuine emotions. Erm, of course he's programmed that way to make it easier for us to talk to him but as to whether or not he has real feelings is something I don't think anyone can truthfully answer".
>
> Transcript from 2001 (Kubrick and Clarke 1968)

An aspect of this issue has actually already been tested in the courts as there is another group of individuals to which these considerations apply, namely, the great apes. The Great Ape Project is an international organisation which advocates a United Nations Declaration of the Rights of Great Apes that would confer basic legal rights on our fellow (but non-human) great apes, including chimpanzees, bonobos, gorillas, and orangutans. Some countries appear to be already treating this sympathetically as in 2014, a court in Argentina issued a ruling that favoured the rights of an orangutan held in captivity. In response a writ of habeas corpus, Sandra (an orangutan) was transferred to a habitat in keeping with her development (CNN 2014). This begs the question of whether we might expect an artificial intelligence to plead (and we might assume, win) its rights in the coming decade or two?

This chapter

This chapter after the introduction, comprises three sections. The first section introduces robots, not the flashing lights and "does not compute" variety, but those in the form of mewing, mechanical seals, or chirpy dogs or a curious, singing alien. These are the social robots or relational artefacts which have been designed specifically to offer a relationship based on care and affection rather than interaction or ease of use (even though some are supplied with easy to wash covers).

The second section discusses digital assistants which are artificial intelligence applications which, reside on (or is it "in") one's phone or in a loudspeaker in the kitchen, and can be relied upon to provide reminders about upcoming meetings or the recipe for a cheese soufflé. These assistants "understand" and speak natural language and have been designed to have a personality.

The next section provides a discussion of anthropomorphism and the uncanny valley phenomenon. While the former discusses our irresistible tendency to project aspects of our human characteristics onto technology, the latter (perhaps) sound an alert about getting too close.

The chapter concludes by returning to Turkle's concerns about authenticity.

3.1 Origins

The word "robot" was coined by the writer Karel Čapek in his play Rossum's Universal Robots in 1920. Čapek's robots were artificial people created to serve, and as can be imagined, the play was intended as a social commentary. Fictional robots were to appear again in Isaac Asimov's short story Runaround (1942) in which he proposed his famous "Three Laws of Robotics" to ensure our safety in their presence. Robots were to continue to feature in science fiction novels and movies either as the friends of mankind or, more usually after they had achieved self-consciousness, they dispense with the three laws, and then get on with the business of our destruction.

In reality, of course, the development of robots was primarily in support of manufacturing with the first industrial robot ("UNIMATE") operated at a General Motors factory in New Jersey in 1961. Unimate was responsible for jobs which otherwise might have been hazardous to a human workforce and became something of a celebrity appearing on the TV of the time. In parallel with the development of these industrial robots, there was research into creating smarter, lighter and more useful prosthetics.

Subsequent robotic development focussed on improving their ability to walk or balance or the degrees of freedom offered by their joints. Barrett et al. (1996) were to introduce the study of how real tuna swim opening the door to biologically inspired design. In the same year Honda created P2, a first step in creating their famous ASIMO product which was the first self-regulating, bipedal humanoid robot (Fig. 3.1).

ELIZA

Alongside the development of industrial robots, there has been increasing interest in other applications of the technology, particularly as companions. A companion (at least etymologically) means someone with whom one breaks bread, which is a little different from welding car panels, (com—with, pan—bread, ion—indicating action).

However, Turkle (2007) argues that ELIZA, an application dating from the 1960s, probably marks the modern beginnings of relational artefacts. ELIZA was an entirely text-based interactive application developed by Joseph Weizenbaum, designed to mirror a user's language and in doing so, to appear interested or concerned in "her" interlocutor. In practice, it quickly emerged that unreliable boyfriends and troublesome parents were being discussed openly by keen under-graduate users of ELIZA.

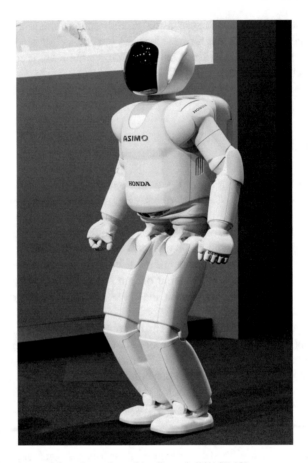

Fig. 3.1 Asimo (sourced from https://en.wikipedia.org/wiki/ASIMO)

ELIZA operated quite simply by matching input strings and substituting and swapping keywords but did so surprisingly effectively. Weizenbaum (1976) found that ELIZA had a profound emotional effect on her interlocutors, so much so, that students asked to be left alone with her. Here is a sample of an interaction between a woman and ELIZA.

woman: Men are all alike.

ELIZA: In what way?

woman: They're always bugging us about something specific or other.

ELIZA: Can you think of a specific example?

woman: Well, my boyfriend made me come here.

ELIZA: Your boyfriend made you come here?

woman: He says I'm depressed much of the time.

ELIZA: I am sorry to hear you are depressed.

woman: It's true. I'm unhappy.

This familiar dialogue is typical of the conversations held between users and ELIZA. In a more recent research note, Turkle has observed that Weizenbaum became quite concerned with how ELIZA was being perceived and he even described these relationships as being immoral (on the basis that ELIZA did not and could not care about its interlocutors and she was little more than a "parlour trick"). However, this ethical dimension aside, what was learned from the study of ELIZA was that we are happy (and positively keen) to talk to her. As Turkle put it, when ELIZA showed interest in us, it pushed our "Darwinian buttons" but more importantly perhaps, that even very minimal "social" representations can be effective at engaging people (Turkle 2007, p. 503). Perhaps the most entertaining account of ELIZA's seductive conversational style can be found in David Lodge's campus novel 'Small World' (Lodge 1984).

Tamagotchi and its relaunch

From another, and perhaps unexpected, direction Bandai's Tamagotchi was arguably the first digital "pet" which appeared in Japan in 1996. The word Tamagotchi can be translated as "egg watch" which is a fair description of how it looks as it is a hand-held computer with buttons and a small liquid crystal display. This palm-sized virtual pet requires its user (or owner) to feed and care for otherwise it stopped working (or died).

A Tamagotchi could simulate hunger, happiness and, of course, death. The instruction book included with the toy stressed the creature's need for nurturance. If you keep Tamagotchi full and happy, it will grow into a cute, happy "cyberpet" but if you were to neglect your Tamagotchi, the inevitable happened.

In passing: I recently mentioned Tamagotchi to a group of undergraduates and most of them remember owning one and these memories were accompanied by widespread warm laughter as they exchanged stories about them. Tamagotchi, as of 2017, are back in production.

3.2 Social Robots

Having begun with "parlour tricks" like ELIZA and "toys" such as Tamagotchi, the range of relational artefacts has continued to grow to include Furbies, released by Tiger Electronics in 1998, who needed to be "taught" English (as a newly acquired furby only spoke furbish) to those frighteningly realistic and demanding dolls such as "my real baby" (released by Hasbro in 2001), and social robots proper designed to help with autistic children (e.g., Cabibihan et al. 2013) and older people (such as the "mental commitment" robot seal, Paro, dating from 2001. It is safe to say that this not just a technological fad as there is a growing market for these products as the International Federation of Robotics predict that by 2019, there will be 31 million such robots.

There have been in the last twenty to thirty years very many robots created for a wide variety of reasons and it is not practical to review them all, and the technology has matured to the extent that social robots are now being created primarily as a potential solution to particular problems. In short, social robotics research has become a matter of applications rather than psychology. As we shall see, however, a hard line cannot be drawn between research and application: relational artefacts developed originally for research work have found a "second life" as commercial products, while social robots that are primarily products have supported significant research projects.

This chapter therefore discusses selected landmarks in social robotics research and development, in a broadly historical sequence. We consider firstly Cog, Kismet and Kaspar, intended primarily as research tools to support the exploration of human-robot social interaction, then parallel developments in relational artefacts for entertainment, play or as therapeutic aids, and finally the emergence of humanoid robots whose generic social capabilities are designed to support a range of practical applications or (perhaps) to serve as companions. Taken together, this parade of robots illustrates four of Fong et al. (2003) categories of social robotic forms: the anthropomorphic, the zoomorphic, the caricatured and the functional. Many of these robots come complete with "personalities" (e.g., Niculescu et al. 2013), "emotions" (e.g., Breazeal and Brooks 2005; Winkielman et al. 2016), "internal psychological states" (Breazeal 2002) and even "back stories" for robotic receptionists (e.g., Gockley et al. 2007).

We give particular attention to human perceptions and experience of these technologies. As many researchers and developers are at pains to point out, acceptance is crucial to the success of social robotics applications.

Sheridan (2016) writing of human-robotic interaction in general, identifies four key application areas in this rapidly evolving field. These are: human supervisory control of robots (e.g., assembly lines, warehousing); teleoperation (that is, the remote control of space for non-routine tasks); automated vehicles; and human-robot social interaction of which he writes "to provide entertainment, teaching, comfort, and assistance for children and elderly, autistic and handicapped persons" (p. 526).

Kismet, Cog and Kaspar

The humanoid robots Kismet and Cog, designed at the MIT Artificial Intelligence Laboratory, are particularly important relational artefacts as they were explicitly designed to relate to people in human-like ways, to "detect stimuli that humans find relevant … respond to stimuli in a human-like manner… [and] have a roughly anthropomorphic appearance." MIT's Cog project began at the turn of the twentieth century, concluding in 2003 (Brooks et al. 1999; Breazeal and Scassellati 2002). MIT labs' introduction to the project describe Cog as "a set of sensors and actuators which tries to approximate the sensory and motor dynamics of a human body" (MIT, n.d.). It aimed to bring together many facets of then current work in AI, the underlying premise being that Cog should 'learn' and develop through interactions with humans and other beings in the world. In form, Cog had an upper body torso, including arms, and was equipped with visual, tactile and kinaesthetic senses. Among other capabilities, Cog could visually detect people and objects, imitate movement and point to visual targets. Kismet which was designed by Breazeal (2002), had a cartoon-like appearance with large hairy eyebrows, big round eyes and a broad metallic mouth. It also had Shrek-like ears. Its highly mobile face was used to communicate its nine facial emotions. Kismet not only displayed emotional states (e.g., anger, fear, sadness, etc.) but also different levels of arousal (e.g., excitement or fatigue). The robot was also verbal, emitting its own utterances as well as repeating words such as its name.

Turkle (2006) and her colleagues have described a group of 60 children, aged between 8 and 13, meeting Kismet and Cog in 2001. The project aimed, among other objectives, to explore how the children integrated the robots into their concepts of personhood, friendship and intentionality. The children encountered Kismet and Cog in individual and group sessions. While Kismet engaged participants by verbalisation and facial expression, Cog responded by looking in a child's direction and imitating arm movements. A debriefing followed where Cog was dismantled and its mechanisms explained. Despite many instances of communication breakdowns, the children persevered in attempting to communicate and excuse the robots' failures to respond suitably. Secondly, most children anthropomorphised Cog and Kismet, considering them to be "sort of alive". And finally, most resisted the demystification presented in the debriefing, preferring to maintain that they had a genuine relationship with the robots. Turkle et al. conclude that their findings raise fundamental questions about nature of authentic relationships.

The tendency to treat robots as fellow beings is not confined to children. Breazeal (2003), for example, reports a series of studies evaluating the effects of the 'emotions' designed to be expressed by Kismet in its appearance and behaviours, mainly through variations in the ears, eyes and posture. Typical of the results is the finding that after scolding Kismet "the robot's saddened face and body posture were enough to arouse a strong sense of empathy. The subject would often immediately stop and look to the experimenter with an anguished expression on her face, claiming to feel "terrible" or "guilty". Emotional responses on the part of the user were explicitly invoked by Kismet's designers in order to "tune the human's behavior so that both perform well during the interaction".

The University of Hertfordshire's series of Kaspar robots, share a similar aim of supporting research into human-robot interaction, and more specifically, companion robots (Dautenhahn et al. 2009). Kaspar was designed to be low cost, while being minimally, but effectively, expressive and to enable research into relationships beyond the caretaker-infant dynamic that underlies interaction with Cog or Kismet. Its expressions are intended to suggest happiness, surprise and so forth, allowing an interaction partner to interpret the facial cues presented. As will be seen again in the discussion of the robot dog AIBO, below, children had a particularly positive reaction to Kaspar and were readily engaged, while adults were more reserved and less playful. Kaspar's 'descendants' continue to support research into, for example therapy for social skills in children with autism (Mengoni et al. 2017) (Fig. 3.2).

Social Robotics for fun—my robot dog and My Real Baby

Sony's AIBO (Artificial Intelligence roBOt) is, or rather was, a robot dog which responds to noises, makes musical sounds to communicate and expresses different needs and emotions. As well generating a convenient English acronym, aibo means 'pal', 'companion' or 'partner' in Japanese. AIBO has a variety of sensors that respond to touch and orientation and also develops different "personalities" depending on how it is treated by its user. Later AIBO models were equipped with facial and voice recognition software which enable the AIBO to recognise its "primary caregiver." AIBO launched as an 'entertainment robot' in 1999 and was among the first robotic products to be marketed to the general public (Fig. 3.3).

There are a number of interesting studies of how people perceive and interact with AIBO; Weiss et al. (2009) offer us a good example. These researchers set up a small enclosure in a shopping centre in Salzburg and invited adults and children to meet AIBO. Of those who played with AIBO, 147 people were randomly selected to answer questions related to their experiences with the robot.

The researchers categorised interactions with AIBO according to Norman's (2004) three level model of emotion (visceral, behavioural and reflective). Children were reported as displaying an initial visceral enthusiasm for AIBO, manifest through remarks such as "Oh, what a nice dog", and "May I play with it", as well as by running towards AIBO. These positive visceral reactions persisted even in the face of difficulties: extraneous noise and children's parallel commands meant that AIBO did not always react at once. Indeed, children stayed longer and played more intensely when AIBO did not fulfil their expectations. At the behavioural level, children enthusiastically engaged with the dog, on average interacting with it for 20 min, only stopping when their parents told them to. Interestingly, children played longer and more intensely with the dog when AIBO did not behave as expected. Questionnaires elicited emotional experience at the reflective level. Here the results indicate that children readily ascribed cognition to AIBO: around 75% believed that AIBO could see them, while nearly 80% thought that it was able to understand them. Almost all believed that AIBO had emotional states: being capable of sadness (87%) or happiness (99%). There was great enthusiasm for AIBO as a companion: 92% of children would have it as a playfellow, and 90% would feel better when home alone if AIBO were there. The researchers suggest this indicates the attribution of emotional attachment.

As for adults, there was little observable evidence of a visceral response. Adults enquired about AIBO's functionality, and largely watched it in action from a distance. At the behavioural level, those who did interact with the dog voiced positive emotions, although these largely concerned the perceived impressiveness of the technology. Reflecting on AIBO, the small number of adults interviewed were unenthused about its potential as a child's playmate. Other roles suggested were as a pet for children allergic to real animals or a companion for those in hospital. The

Fig. 3.2 Kaspar, courtesy Kerstin Dautenhahn, University of Hertfordshire

authors speculate that adults may need longer to establish an emotional attachment to AIBO than children.

My Real Baby was broadly contemporary with AIBO, being launched as a commercial product by Hasbro in 2000. What is interesting about the Real Baby is that its child 'parent' had to decipher Baby's inner states and moods, manifest through behaviours and facial expressions and act accordingly. Otherwise it would become, for example, overtired and fretful. Baby could also 'learn' language up to the production of 4–5 word sentences. Such capabilities drew on Brooks' earlier research at MIT and iRobot into a robotic doll (Bit) (Brooks 2002; Plowman 2004). Despite this pedigree, Plowman notes that My Real Baby proved unpopular as a product because of its relatively high selling price, frequent need for battery replacement and general unreliability and was eventually withdrawn from the market. Academic research exploring reactions to My Real Baby is scant, but Eberle (2009), as well as suggesting that the Baby's lack of commercial success

Fig. 3.3 Aibo [courtesy Sven Volkens, via Wikimedia Commons]

may be an instance of the Uncanny Valley phenomenon (discussed below) at work, quotes an anecdote of a development team member "unthinkingly rushing" from his office to fetch a bottle to sooth the Baby's cries. The realism of the production version was reported to have been scaled back to allow child customers to better "exercise their imaginations. This is paralleled in a web review of My Real Baby cited by Plowman, where that the disappointed customer asserts that they will return to "dolls that do nothing" with which a child can "make believe that she is doing all the mommy things."

Sheridan (2016) notes that a number of "connected toys" have also appeared complete with computer-based speech, speech recognition, and decision-making software. Mattel's new Barbie doll comes with an extensive speech and language recognition vocabulary that is linked via the Internet to the company server (Vlahos 2015).

Paro and Keepon: Robots for therapy and social development
The robot seal Paro is described by its creators as a 'mental commitment robot', intended to interact with human beings, stimulate emotional attachment and, overall, to bring solace in therapeutic contexts, originally those catering for the elderly. The form of a baby seal was adopted rather than more common domestic animals such as dogs and cats to avoid comparisons with the capabilities of a real pet while still being a recognisable and appealing animal. Paro is furry, battery operated and has senses of sight, hearting (including speech recognition), balance and touch, can move its neck, flippers and eyelids and emits the cries of a baby seal.

It is both proactive and in response to touch and speech—and recognises its name. Stroking Paro in response to a movement, for example raising its head, will trigger it to 'learn' to repeat that movement. Such responsiveness "allows its users to gradually build a relationship with it" and encourages them to "show their affection for Paro" (Shibata and Wada 2011). The robot had its first public outing in 2001, is now in its 8th generation and has been employed therapeutically in Japan, Korea, Europe and the USA. Some cross-cultural differences are reported in the reported experience of interaction: a survey based evaluation showed high positive ratings for the factor "comfortable feeling like interacting with real animals" by European users while people in Asia rated "favorable impression to encourage interaction" more positively (Shibata et al. 2009). The authors speculate that such differences may originate in the portrayal of robots in popular culture (more positive in Asia than in Western countries) and in the relative familiarity of real animals as therapeutic aids in the West.

A substantial number of trials have now been reported of the impact of interacting with Paro in educational and social care settings, both institutional and domestic, and including care facilities for people with cognitive deficits and dementia. Shibata and Wada (2011) in their review suggest that mood, social interactivity and behaviour in elderly people improved after interactions with Paro. Marti et al. (2005) conducted a study into the therapeutic benefits of Paro for young adults with severe cognitive impairment. Their initial results showed a clear role for the robot in mediating social exchange and stimulating attachment and engagement; the authors observe that participants engaged in such behaviours as feeding Paro or protecting it from cold, suggesting that it was regarded as an agent rather than an object. These effects were much less present in a comparison session when Paro was not turned on and thus not interactive. Consistent outcome improvements are not reported by all studies: Wagemaker et al. (2017), for example, do not find clear improvements in adults with severe intellectual disabilities after a treatment phase with Paro, but do suggest that for one person during interaction sessions an emotional connection with the robot and mood improvements were observable. Other reports indicate that participants can both attribute feelings to Paro and recognise that it is an artificial object, and that not everyone is willing to engage with the robot.

We should note here that although Paro is perhaps the most best known and most commercialised example, there are many other social robots that play a role in therapeutic contexts, including cats, dogs (such as AIBO), dinosaurs, and a spectrum of other forms from those which are clearly machines to those of a strongly humanoid appearance. Keepon (Kozima et al. 2009) affords a typical exemplar of a social robot which lies in the liminal area between machine, animal and humanoid forms. It has a simple form of two spheroids on top of one another, the upper spheroid having a minimal face of two eyes and a mouth. Keepon was originally designed to support research into social development in children, using minimal non-verbal interaction, where it has proved valuable in exploring, among other aspects of social interaction, the importance of rhythm in coordinating social communication (Michalowski et al. 2007) and the development of theory of mind as a child matures. A simplified version of the research robot is now marketed as a toy (Fig. 3.4).

ASIMO, Nao and Pepper: Humanoid robots walk out of the lab

Highly sophisticated humanoid robots are now in routine production and application. In 2000, Honda launched ASIMO as its most sophisticated autonomous humanoid walking robot. In its latest version the robot has sophisticated bipedal locomotion capabilities, including running and stair climbing, coupled with the ability to reach for and grasp objects and to avoid moving as well as stationary obstacles. Its more social graces include the understanding of, and response to, voice commands and face recognition. All-in-all, ASIMO is intended, eventually, to have sufficient range of movement and capability to help with everyday tasks, such as care for the elderly, household tasks and assisting at stations or airports, although there are no reports of real-world use so far and Honda suggest that this is still some years away. It is therefore unsurprising that studies of the experience of encountering ASIMO are lacking, but Rosenthal-von der Pütten and Krämer (2014) have included ASIMO as one of the 40 robot examples, presented as standardised images, in a large online survey of perceptions of these digital products. The results placed ASIMO in a cluster of robots perceived to be likeable, non-threatening, not particularly human-like and somewhat submissive—alongside Nao, which we will consider next.

Nao's first version was released by Aldebaran (now Softbank) Robotics in 2005 and the technology continues to evolve as an "interactive companion robot" [SoftBank Robotics, n.d.(a)]. A number of variants of the 58 cm tall, humanoid, robot exist, most being walking bipedal models. Speech and language processing, kinetic and haptic sensors, object recognition and internet connection are all present. Somewhat disquietingly. It has apparently been demonstrated that Nao can show a degree of self-consciousness (Bringsjord et al. 2015). Nao has been used in a number of real-world customer service, therapeutic and educational contexts as well as a vehicle for academic robotics research.

Because Nao's functionality and characteristics are programmable, it has been used in many hundreds of empirical studies exploring the design space for social, humanoid robots. Among the more strongly psychologically-informed themes in this very large body of work has been the investigation of the relationship between perceived robot personality, the attribution of traits to the robot, user personality and user preferences. There is reported evidence of both preference for robots with a similar personality to the user's own (similarity attraction theory) and robots with differing personalities (complementary attraction theory). Much of this work has centred on the extraversion-introversion personality dimension. Among the more robust examples of such studies, Aly and Tapus (2012, 2016) report results of robots providing restaurant advice that support similarity attraction theory, while Weiss et al. (2012) suggest that the nature of the task in hand (in their study, teaching, patient care and discussing a balance sheet) and cultural influences may be significant in determining preferences, Joosse et al. (2013) who studied perceptions of

Fig. 3.4 Keepon, courtesy Hideki Kozima, Tokyo University

robots engaged in cleaning and tour guide tasks also argue for the effects of perceived appropriateness of particular personality types for particular tasks and roles.

Nao's more fully productised counterpart, Pepper (Fig. 3.5), has thus far attracted relatively few published research studies. Pepper—humanoid, but not bipedal, 1.2 m tall and equipped with an interactive screen—can detect, display and respond to emotion, speak and move autonomously, as well as having what is now the established range of humanoid robot functionality. Furthermore, its manufacturers state that "Pleasant and likeable, Pepper is much more than a robot, he is a genuine humanoid companion... You can also personalise your robot based on your mood or the occasion... Pepper gradually memorises your personality traits, your preferences, and adapts himself to your tastes and habits." [SoftBank Robotics, n.d.(b)]. These functionalities have supported Pepper's practical use in work contexts where social interaction is important: typically receptionist or sales promotion roles, where the robot has been deployed by a number of Japanese organisations, but also in nursing or caring settings. Pepper is currently the subject of a European research project (Papadopoulos et al. 2017) investigating its ability to adopt local cultural norms, such as emotional reticence, and individual daily routines, such as afternoon tea and biscuits, in a role as an assistant in British care homes for the elderly (The Times 2017a).

It is also evident that Pepper is marketed as a companion, where the promotional material and press coverage (e.g., The Telegraph 2015) seem to position Pepper in a niche somewhere between that of a child, a pet and a personal assistant. Among the few examples of Pepper to date, a field study in a shopping mall conducted by Aaltonen et al. (2017) found results reminiscent of the Weiss et al. (2009) AIBO report: children were keen to engage with Pepper while adults were more interested in its functionality, while Dereshev and Kirk (2017) report that potential users exposed to advertising material for Pepper found its quasi-human form more disconcerting than robots of animal or machine-like morphology.

Androids: Threatening or likeable?

Alongside the development of autonomous humanoid robots with practical skills, the first decade of this century saw the development of android robots: machines designed to mimic the appearance and behaviour of human beings as closely as possible. The demands of this apparent near-humanity, however, mean that thus far almost all android robots to date are tele-operated. Best-known among a growing population of Androids are Ishiguru's Geminoid H-1 and its successors (Ishiguru n. d.; Nishio et al. 2007). A European model, DK-1, modelled on a Danish professor, also exists. These androids are modelled to resemble their human progenitor in minute detail, but movement, speech and other interactions are controlled by an operator. While they are primarily intended as tools to support research into fundamentals of human-robot interaction, the Geminoids have served to "attend" meetings and give lectures remotely. In Ishiguru's view, after some degree of initial caution, people interact with the Geminoids in much the same way as with a human partner (Guizzo 2010). More advanced androids are now emerging with at least some degree of autonomy: Ishiguru's Erica, equipped with on a composite "beautiful and neutral" female face, has some autonomous conversational abilities, while Nadine and Sophie, developed at Nanyang University, have speech recognition and production, emotional expression and some bodily movement (Magnenat-Thalmann and Zhang 2014).

Academic research exploring the experience of encounters with android robots has very largely focussed on aspects of the "uncanny valley" phenomenon, discussed later in this chapter. However it is interesting to note that the photo-based study by Rosenthal-von der Pütten and Krämer (2014), cited earlier, found Geminoid H-1 to be judged the most threatening of the 40 robots presented, while the wider range of androids presented were generally thought to be both threatening and likeable. The authors speculate that these highly humanoid androids are judged by similar criteria to human facial appearance, and that Geminoid H-1's stern expression may have influenced the ratings.

Dogs and robots

Perhaps there is just something about robots, perhaps we are mesmerised by them. Yet, from quite a different but interesting perspective, researchers have compared our understanding of dog emotional expressions with those of a People Bot robot (Bethel and Murphy 2008). A set of canine expressive behaviours that had been used in previous studies of dog–human interactions namely, (joy, fear, anger, sadness, and neutral) and the actions of the robot. In their answers to open-ended questions, participants spontaneously attributed emotional states to both the robot

Fig. 3.5 Pepper, courtesy Sven Volkens via Wikimedia Commons

and the dog. They could also successfully match all dog and all robot expressions with the correct emotional state. While the researchers in this study were interested in the design insights they could gather from it, we might conclude that we have a tendency to rely on our social cognition.

Some observations

From the accounts just discussed, we can see that in many cases our perceptions of, and behaviours towards, social robots closely resemble our interactions with other human beings. Robots are treated as social agents, and thus fit within the CASA (Computers as Social Actors) framework which we saw in Chap. 2. We discuss the underlying reasons for such anthropomorphism later in this chapter. Children seem to engage readily with these forms of relational artefact, while adults may be more reticent. Some of the extremely humanoid robotic forms have been found to be a source of disquiet. Again, this topic is explored further below.

To these observations we can add some further empirical findings which concern general issues in our experience of social robots. As with so many aspects of human psychology, it is unsurprising that perceptions of robots are permeated by individual and cultural differences (for example, Fischer 2011; Weiss et al. 2012). The degree of human-ness judged to be necessary or appropriate also varies by the context of use and role of the robot (Lee et al. 2016; Broadbent et al. 2012). Broadbent and colleagues supply the example that a lifting robot is not required to look human, but a robotic surgeon should do so. We have also seen how individual, cultural, role and task characteristics influence whether a robot's perceived personality should be complementary or similar to that of its human user.

This being said, it remains the case that the application of psychology has been predominantly in the service of the better design of social robots and/or in analysing user reactions and with a few exceptions, among them Broadbent (2017), there has been little systematic or deep consideration of the psychology of the user experience.

3.3 Digital Assistants and Chatbots

We now move from relational artefacts in human or animal shape, however approximate this may be, to intelligent digital products that are primarily manifest as disembodied voices. McTear (2002) tells us that the "conversational computer" has been a long-standing goal dating back 30 years from the time of his writing and had been the object of a number research programs, including the DARPA Communicator Project, Japan's Fifth Generation program, and the European Union's ESPRIT and Language Engineering programs. The impression and perhaps the expectation of effortless conversation with a computer can be blamed on the usual suspects in science fiction but practicality of spoken language interaction with computers has only become a practical possibility due to advances in speech technology, language processing, and dialogue modelling, as well as the emergence of faster and more powerful computers to support these technologies. Potential applications for these natural language user interfaces may have been many and imaginative, but they have come to the fore with digital assistants.

Digital assistants

Digital assistants (alternatively termed conversational agents, virtual personal assistants or intelligent assistants) have been around for decades. Clippy, the much-mocked Microsoft Word assistant in the form of a paper-clip, appeared as far back as 1997. More recently, however, a number of talking technologies have become well established and accepted. Of the major voice-based offerings, Siri was launched by Apple in 2011; followed by Microsoft's Cortana (2014), Amazon's Alexa (2014), Google's Now (2012) and Assistant (2017) and most recently, Facebook's (2017). They appear as apps, as an integral part of their parent operating systems, or as a "smart speaker", such as Alexa's cylindrical Echo. Their functionality includes interaction with applications, such as setting reminders and email, information searching, ordering pizza and communication with other connected devices. They are now also being integrated with in-car information systems. Unlike the social robots discussed above, however, all they have to rely upon for communication with their users, aside from minimal interface graphic devices, is their "voice" and any "personality" created by their designers. This necessarily, of course includes gender.

Most digital assistants have a female voice, although Siri has an option for a male alternative. Empirical support for this design choice may be found, inter alia, in Mitchell et al. (2011), who established that both men and women preferred a female voice, while the British Daily Mail (Daily Mail 2017) quotes an Amazon spokesman thus "We asked a lot of customers and tested Alexa's voice with large internal beta groups before we launched, and this is the voice they chose... we believe Alexa exudes characteristics you'd see in a strong female colleague, family member or friend." Alexa has also been given a new vocabulary of words including cowabunga, "bada bing" and whoops-a-daisy for English listeners of a certain age. The thinking for this was said to be that Alexa was seen as too robotic and these "speechcons" would make her easily to engage with emotionally (The Times 2017b).

As for the other digital assistants, Siri's designers employed script editors to produce convincingly character-driven dialogue (Simonite 2013). Siri has been asked out on dates, and has been asked to offer advice on where to hide a body. Love and Abutaleb (2015) in a Reuter's news item, report designers as having endowed Siri and Cortana with smart and detailed personas to engage their users. Siri, for example, has a thirst for knowledge, while Cortana prefers a very, very dry martini. On the other hand, Facebook's M and Google Now have been intentionally designed to be neutral but efficient functionaries, in the hope of avoiding irritated responses and unrealistic expectations.

Despite the rich potential of the field for exploring the experience of, and relationship with, this most recent form of relational artefact, significant studies remain relatively rare, particularly in real-world contexts. Among the few instances which have been reported, Luger and Sellen (2016) conducted an interview-based study with 14 regular users of, variously, Siri (most users), Google Now, (rather fewer users) and Cortana (one sole user). Findings highlighted that most participants were initially drawn in by the playful aspects of interaction. (Siri can tell jokes, for example.) However, initial user expectations outstripped the assistants' abilities, particularly around the context of conversations, and users subsequently reduced demands on the assistant in terms of both complexity of speech and nature of the task. Luger and Sellen attribute this to a gulf of execution and evaluation, in Norman's (2013) terms. In one user's description, the experience was "like having a really bad PA". An inverse relationship between task complexity/context dependance and satisfaction was also noted by Kiseleva et al. (2016).

Anthropomorphism, as voiced in the "really bad PA" comment and, for example, by describing Siri as "sarcastic" was most common in users who did not have a technological background, who were also more likely to ascribe gender to their assistant. Variation in anthropomorphism is also noted by Purington et al. (2017) in their analysis of user reviews of Alexa/Echo where users adopting a personified and social style of interaction, where Alexa was addressed by name and referred to by personal pronouns, were also more likely to be satisfied with the product.

Adult users may condense their communications to Siri to the point of curtness, but the London Times newspaper (The Times 2017c) warns that "psychologists" predict that "children who are raised barking orders at submissive voice-activated gadgets could grow up rude and entitled".

Chatbots

While digital assistants may emulate the portfolio of accomplishments of a good personal assistant or the omniscience of a Jeeves, chatbots are single purpose entities. Using natural language speech or text interaction, backed up by AI, they are becoming common interfaces to an increasing range of individual applications, data and services, from ordering a pizza to accessing CBT therapy, some aspects of the latter bearing a striking, if superficial, resemblance to interaction with Weizenbaum's ELIZA.[1] Very large numbers of chatbots are now hosted on Facebook through the medium of its Messenger app. Most communicate through text, speech or simple graphics, but many others—often termed embodied conversational agents[2]—have sophisticated, animated visual embodiments, and some are able to identify, and respond to, user emotions as displayed by facial expression.

It is debatable how far many of these applications are genuinely relational or social, except in the minimal sense that they interact with users. Moreover, to date, empirical work on the experience of chatbots is fragmented and frequently confined to a particular instance of these relational artefacts.

We now turn to a consideration of what underlies the strength of the tendency to treat relational artefacts as other social beings.

3.4   Anthropomorphism

The design of most social robots and other forms of relational artefacts draws—with varying degrees of sophistication—on many aspects of human psychology, including, but not limited to, theories of personality, emotion, proxemics, perception, language processing, learning, attention, social behaviour and theory of mind. But our primary focus in this book is the psychology of the experience of digital products, and it is this we consider here in the context of relational artefacts.

---

[1]Echoing the popularity of ELIZA, Lucas et al. (2014) found that users felt more comfortable and more likely to disclose to a therapist believed to be completely virtual as compared to those who were told the therapist avatar was controlled by a human being.

[2]Even more than usually, terminology for this class of relational artefacts is beset by a host of synonyms, including conversational agent, embodied conversational agent, virtual agent and many others. The OED defines a chatbot as "a computer program designed to simulate conversation with human users, especially over the Internet".

As we have already argued, the success of relational artefacts is founded on our compelling tendency to treat other "beings" as human, in other words, to anthropomorphise.[3] This is of interest because its pervasiveness is intriguing and its relevance of the design of digital products immediate (especially as we have seen with relational technology). Anthropomorphism is our tendency to ascribe human-like characteristics, such as intentions, motivations, emotions and appearance, to non-human agents, artefacts, systems and digital products. We freely, frequently and ineluctably anthropomorphise. We quote from Epley et al. (2007) introduction to their account of anthropomorphism which tells us that there are 1,750,000 species, 10,000 distinct religions (each with its own supernatural beings) and an expanding number of technological artefacts on the planet at present. Yet despite this diversity, "animals are imbued with humanlike intentions, motivations and goals. Spiritual deities are embodied with fingers and facial hair, complete with personality strengths and occasionally personality weaknesses. And even the most technologically savvy have wondered, at least for a moment, whether their computer is plotting against them." (p. 864). Anthropomorphism has a powerful effect even with digital products with no explicit relational intent, as the following two examples from very different contexts illustrate. Sung et al. (2007) have reported on trials with Roomba, (a robot vacuum cleaner of a simple circular shape) which revealed that "Not only have his owners dressed him [the vacuum cleaner] up, they have also given him a name and gender". More recently, Mouray et al. (2017) conducted empirical work with Roomba which suggested that interacting with this type of "anthropomorphic consumer product" could mitigate some of the effects of social exclusion. Far from the domestic setting, Sandry (2015) discusses evidence of anthropomorphic relationships with Explosive Ordnance Disposal (EOD) robots which were operated under human direct control but valued and respected by army personnel as individuals, sometimes assigned names and referred to by gendered personal pronouns.

As we have already seen in Chap. 2 and earlier in this chapter, we have the irresistible tendency to ascribe mind and agency to a variety of products which cannot possibly have them. Much of the literature investigating this can be found in the domain of product design, where studies have found evidence for the ascription of a wide variety of "personality traits" to everything from vacuum cleaners to coffee makers, cars and toasters (e.g., Jordan 2002; Govers and Mugge 2004; Mugge et al. 2007).

Govers et al. (ibid), further developed by Mugge et al. (2009) provide a set of traits which can be attributed reliably to products, in this case, to motor cars and vacuum cleaners. This is an interesting list, namely: aloof, boring, cheerful, childish, cute, dominant, easy-going, honest, idiosyncratic, interesting, lively, modest, obtrusive, open, pretty, provocative, relaxed, serious, silly and untidy. So, this work tells us that people can reliably attribute the trait of aloofness to a vacuum cleaner.

---

[3]Or in the case of social robots in animal form, to *zoomorphise*.

Why do we anthropomorphise?

As we saw in an earlier chapter, Reeves and Nass (1996) have told us that our "old brains" have not yet caught up with the developments of the last 50 years or so. So, like it or not, we have the overwhelming propensity to treat digital products as people. A number of approaches have been adopted to exploring the rationale for anthropomorphism. We begin with design perspectives.

Here DiSalvo and Gemperle (2003) have identified a number of different reasons why we anthropomorphise, these are: familiarity, comfort, "best-bet", species-specific group-level coordination system, object-subject interchangeability, phenomenological inter-subjectivity, and command and control. Of these, the first two probably have the most support. The familiarity thesis is attributed to Guthrie (1993) who writes that when people anthropomorphise, they are making something familiar which is (or was) unfamiliar. Unfamiliar things require cognitive effort to explain them, but by relating them to something which is well known, this burden is diminished—and what could be more familiar than ourselves? Mapping ourselves (in some manner) onto something external, enables us to draw all manner of inferences which would not otherwise be available. The comfort thesis is Guthrie again but rather than suggesting that we anthropomorphise to make things simpler, he proposes that it provides comfort. He argues that we find comfort in dealing with things and situations which resemble us. He writes that anthropomorphism is, "an attempt to feel like we can define and influence the world if it is more like us than not". The remaining proposals are a little more sketchy and speculative in comparison. Van Rompay and Ludden (2015) suggest an analogous motivation to that of comfort seeking: they propose that discovering human characteristics in non-animate objects can be a source of pleasure or just simple fun.

Returning to technological artefacts, Kim and Sundar (2012) make the point that the anthropomorphisation of computers is rarely mindful, in the sense that people consciously believe that the computer is human or merits the attribution of human characteristics, but rather automatic and mindless (as suggested by Reeves and Nass), cued by exposure to a communication cycle which mimics that of human-human interaction and enhanced by social cues such as gendered voices and humanoid images.

Three factors

In contrast to these design accounts, Epley and his colleagues have proposed their own psychological theory (SEEK—Socialty, Effectance and Elicted agent Knowledge) as to why people anthropomorphise. They start by recognising that anthropomorphism is a form of inductive reasoning and that the basic processes underpinning it should be no different from other forms of inductive inference. Having established this, they turn their attention to the likelihood that people will anthropomorphise, concluding that it is a consequence of the following three factors (these points have been adapted from Zlotowski et al. (2015).

1. Elicited agent knowledge—as people have more accessible knowledge about people than technology, they are more likely to use anthropomorphism as an explanation until (and if) they create an alternative mental model;

2. Effectance motivation—when people are pressed to explain behaviour the tendency to anthropomorphise increases'
3. Sociality motivation—people who lack social connection with others often
   compensate for this by treating non-human agents as though they were human.

Epley writes that this is not a theory of anthropomorphism as such but a theory
of the particular form of inductive reasoning involved when we engage in it.
Empirical work, much of it reported by Epley, Waytz and their colleagues suggests
that the tendency to anthropomorphise is situationally dependent and unsurprisingly
is subject to individual differences (e.g., Waytz et al. 2010; Letheren et al. 2016).
Not only that, but Waytz et al. suggest that such differences can determine, among
other things, the degree of trustworthiness and moral accountability attributed to an
agent. The Letheren study related literature in psychology, marketing and consumer
psychology, and thereby derived items for a large-scale survey. The results indicated that those who are more prone to anthropomorphise are likely to be "younger,
single and have a personal connection to animals, as well as higher levels of
openness to experience, neuroticism, conscientiousness and experiential thinking".
A predicted relationship with religiosity was not found, but the authors suggest this
may be an artefact of survey design and deserves further investigation.

Alongside these psychological accounts there have been neurological and
bio-psychological attempts to establish how the brain is responsible for anthropomorphism. A few selected examples give a flavour of different aspects of this work.

Focussing on the mirror neuron system (MNS), Gazzola et al. (2007) found very
little difference in the activity of the MNS on seeing human and robotic actions;
while Hoenen et al. (2016), comparing observation of a robot being verbally har-
assed with a non-harassed robot, identified greater MNS activity in the harassment
condition. They interpret this as evidence that seeing a human interact with a robot
strengthens perception of the robot as a social agent.

Waytz et al. (2010) established that increasing the unpredictability of a non-
human agent or increasing the incentive for mastering it (i.e., effectance motivation)
triggered increased activity in one of the areas of the brain—the ventromedial
prefrontal cortex—associated with analysing the mental states of other humans.
Their approach was complemented by researchers who take individual differences
as their focus, among them Cullen et al. (2013). Their results indicated that participants who showed a greater tendency to anthropomorphise non-human animals
and other non-human stimuli, as evidenced by a self-report instrument, were found
to have a greater volume of grey matter in the left temporoparietal junction.

Finally, many accounts of anthropomorphism include some consideration of
religious belief [e.g., Epley et al. (2008) and Barrett (2000)]. The reasons for this
are clear and obvious, particularly to unbelievers, as most religions have an
anthropomorphic central deity, doing whatever gods do.

Detecting invisible agents: HADD
Guthrie (1980, 1993), drawing on data from psychology and anthropology, suggested that the evolution of a cognitive bias towards the detection of human-like
agency in the environment, where this might not actually exist. This tendency

would be particularly strong when information was sparse or ambiguous. Such a mechanism, Guthrie argued, would have clear survival value, since the consequences of overlooking an agent would be much more detrimental than the false identification of a non-existent actor. On this basis, Barrett posited an evolved cognitive mechanism which he called a "hyperactive agent-detection device" or HADD (Barrett 2000) which he later reformulated as the "hypersensitive agency detection device" (Barrett 2000, 2004) to provide a cognitive basis for religion. Agents, even of a counter-intuitive nature, posited through as a result of the action of the HADD would be readily culturally transmitted.

The possible action of a HADD has clear resonance for any consideration of the attribution of human-like agency to relational artefacts. And in passing, we note that the conditions of ambiguity that Guthrie suggests gives rise to the over-detection of agency are very similar those simulated in the Waytz et al. (2010) study cited above.

The uncanny valley
While the near-irresistible tendency to anthropomorphise may be convenient for those who design or deploy social robots, a significant obstacle to untroubled acceptance may lie in the phenomenon of the uncanny valley. According to Mori, the more robots and other synthetic beings resemble humans, the more positively we feel towards them. However, at some point of high similarity (but not perfect resemblance), this acceptance drops sharply and the product will be rated as unfamiliar, eerie, or uncanny (Mori et al. 2012). Then with greater human-likeness, positive perceptions return and increase sharply. Mori called this the "bukimi no tani" (Mori 1970), which was translated as the now familiar "uncanny valley" (Reichardt 1978).

The phenomenon has given rise to a large body of research in psychology and social robotics, many more recent studies following Bartneck et al. (2009) in preferring likeability to familiarity as a more accurate index of the uncanny, and supplementing this dimension with ratings of eeriness and coldness. There remains lively debate about, and much current investigation of, the social and psychological antecedents of perceived uncanniness and equally of how this might be mitigated. Among the major factors advanced have been: category uncertainty, i.e., the cognitive conflict arising from uncertainty as to whether, in this case, an object is human/animal or robotic (e.g., Green et al. 2008; Burleigh and Schoenherr 2014), including evidence from neuro-physiological studies (e.g., Saygin et al. 2012); realism (in)consistency [e.g., MacDorman and Chattopadhyay (2016)]; atypical appearance [e.g., Strait et al. (2017)]; individual differences (e.g., MacDorman and Entezari 2015), who identify the influence of "Animal Reminder Sensitivity, Neuroticism, its Anxiety facet, and Religious Fundamentalism"; repeated engagement with robots [e.g., Zlotowski et al. (2015)] and prior experience, robot task, and task context (e.g., Rosenthal-von der Pütten and Weiss 2015). Factors which may mitigate uncanniness include display of appropriate emotions by the robot (Koschate et al. 2016) and embedding encounters with a robot inside a framing

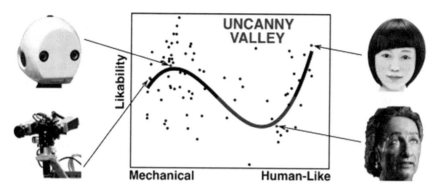

Fig. 3.6 The uncanny valley. Reprinted from Cognition, Vol 146, Jan. 2016, MB Mathur and DB Reichling, Navigating a social world with robot partners: A quantitative cartography of the Uncanny Valley, 22–32, Copyright (2016), with permission from Elsevier

story (Mara and Appel 2015). We would add a gloss to these lists: experimental materials and design, unsurprisingly, vary greatly between studies, so direct comparisons of their results are problematic. All that being said, there is considerable and robust evidence that the Uncanny Valley is a real phenomenon, so much so that Mathur and Reichling (2016) remark that it may prove to be an "inherent and insurmountable feature of human category perception" with consequences for how far trust can be achieved between a human being and a robot partner. Mathur and Reichling's representation of the Uncanny Valley can be seen in Fig. 3.6.

3.5 Authentically Social?

It remains the case that, as Dautenhahn et al. observed in 2009, the development of "believable, socially interactive robots, in particular robots that can positively contribute to society as companions and assistants, remains a challenging (research) issue." We would add that not only is such development challenging, but so is the understanding of the human experience of relational artefacts more generally.

Creating relational artefacts

To recap: a social robot is an autonomous robot that interacts and communicates with humans or other autonomous physical agents by following social behaviours and rules attached to its role.

We have seen how these digital products have been designed to live with us as companions (e.g., Wada and Shibata 2009), or to augment health care or to help educate children (e.g., Hsiao et al. 2015; Agrigoroaie et al. 2016) or to be useful in the home (Sung et al. 2007). So, for the designer, social robotics is about designing these products to be sociable, helpful, useful, responsive to affect and eye gaze and perhaps even able to generate something which simulates "affect" themselves (*cf.* HAL 9000). This chapter has introduced just a few of the very many relational artefacts of a multitude of different forms which have found a place in our everyday life, confined to screens or speakers or in physical incarnations from simple mechanoid bipeds, through cartoon-like characters, dogs and seals, to those which are very near human form.

Let us consider for a moment the issues we might encounter in constructing such a relational artefact. On the face of it, this should be fairly straightforward: it just has to be like us and we know ourselves and others pretty well. And, even if we have problems articulating particular aspects of our make-up—at least we will recognise it when we see it, or talk to it, or are in the same room as it. This is, after all, basic of social cognition which everyone has been developing from birth.

Pure fantasy?

So, having proposed that creating a relational artefact should be easy, Turkle, for one, is adamant that these products will never return our love or any other expression of care, indeed, the very idea of reciprocation is, as she puts it, "pure fantasy". Searle (2014) agrees writing: "Computers have […] no intelligence, no motivation, no autonomy, and no agency. We design them to behave as if they had certain sorts of psychology, but there is no psychological reality to the corresponding processes or behavior […] The machinery has no beliefs, desires, motivations." So, designing relational artefacts should not present us with too many problems except the end result is inauthentic (which is academic language for "fake"). In this view of the world, no meaningful relationship can ever exist.

Indeed, the literature on the adoption of social robotics makes it clear that no participant believes that these social agents are alive, or that they reciprocate human feelings of affection. And yet there are very many examples of apparent care for robotic companions. To take just one, here is an elderly woman speaking to Paro the seal robot on her return from hospital "I was lonely, Paro. I wanted to see you again." (Wada et al. 2005).

In Flesh and Machines (2002), Brooks describes a visit to his laboratories by Sherry Turkle, and quotes from her *Life On The Screen* where she wrote:

> Cog "noticed" me soon after I entered its room. Its head turned to follow me and I was embarrassed to note that this made me happy. I found myself competing with another visitor for its attention. At one point, I felt sure that Cog's eyes had "caught" my own. My visit left me shaken—not by anything that Cog was able to accomplish but by own reaction to "him". For years whenever I had heard Rodney Brooks speak about his robotics "creatures". I had always been careful to mentally put quotation around the word. But now, with Cog, I had found the quotation marks had disappeared. Despite myself and despite this research project, I had behaved as though in the presence of another being.

Brooks observes that Turkle had responded to Cog despite herself. Not quite pure fantasy.

3.6 Conclusions

Our overwhelming tendency to anthropomorphise coupled with ever-more sophisticated technical developments in relational artefacts means that such digital products has a growing presence in everyday life. Turkle in her TED talk, "Connected, but alone?" tells us a little of what it means to be-with technology.

Our overwhelming tendency to anthropomorphise coupled with ever-more sophisticated technical developments in relational artefacts means that such digital products has a growing presence in everyday life. Turkle in her TED talk, "Connected, but alone?" tells us a little of what it means to be-with technology.

Her view is that communication technologies have changed what people do, but more importantly who we are. A consequence of this is that regular communications users may be developing problems in relating to other people, but more importantly for Turkle, they have lost the ability to be alone and engage in reflection. From Turkle's own research, she has found that people are beginning to expect more from technology and less from other people. She observes that digital products which have been designed to provide companionship, such as just about all of the social robots we have discussed in this chapter, do so without "the demands of friendship". She argues that we have are losing or have lost basic conversational skills and with it interpersonal skills. Her analysis, she claims, is that these digital products promise us (i) that we can put our attention wherever we want to, and that (ii) when we're connected we will always be heard. Because of this, "we'll never have to be alone". In conclusion, she believes that people prefer the simplicity that technology offers whereas human relationships are complex.

References

Aaltonen I, Arvola A, Heikkilä P, Lammi H (2017, March) Hello Pepper, May I Tickle You?: Children's and Adults' Responses to an entertainment robot at a shopping mall. In: Proceedings of the Companion of the 2017 ACM/IEEE International Conference on Human-Robot Interaction. ACM, pp 53–54

Agrigoroaie RM, Tapus A (2016) Developing a healthcare robot with personalized behaviors and social skills for the elderly. The Eleventh ACM/IEEE International Conference on Human Robot Interaction. pp 589–590

Aly A, Tapus A (2012) Speech to head gesture mapping in multimodal human-robot interaction, pp 183–196

Aly A, Tapus A (2016) Towards an intelligent system for generating an adapted verbal and nonverbal combined behavior in human–robot interaction. Auton Robots 40(2):193–209

Asimov I (1942) Runaround. Astounding science-fiction. Street & Smith Publications Inc, New York

Barrett JL (2000) Exploring the natural foundations of religion. Trends Cogn Sci 4(1):29–34

Barrett JL (2004) The naturalness of religious concepts. New Approaches Study Relig 2:401–418

Barrett D, Grosenbaugh M, Triantafyllou M (1996, June) The optimal control of a flexible hull robotic undersea vehicle propelled by an oscillating foil. In: Autonomous Underwater Vehicle Technology. AUV'96, Proceedings of the 1996 Symposium on. IEEE, pp 1–9

Bartneck C, Kanda T, Ishiguro H, Hagita N (2009, September) My robotic doppelgänger-a critical look at the uncanny valley. In: Robot and human interactive communication. RO-MAN 2009. The 18th IEEE International Symposium on. IEEE, pp 269–276

Bethel CL, Murphy RR (2008) Survey of non-facial/non-verbal affective expressions for appearance-constrained robots. IEEE Trans Systems Man Cybern Part C (Applications and Reviews) 38(1):83–92

Breazeal CJ (2002) Designing sociable robots. MIT Press, Massachusetts

Breazeal C (2003) Emotion and sociable humanoid robots. Int J Hum Comput Stud 59(1):119–155

Breazeal C, Brooks R (2005) Robot emotion: a functional perspective. Who needs emotions, 271–310

Breazeal C, Scassellati B (2002) Robots that imitate humans. Trends Cogn Sci 6(11):481–487

Bringsjord S, Licato J, Govindarajulu NS, Ghosh R, Sen A (2015, August) Real robots that pass human tests of self-consciousness. In: Robot and Human Interactive Communication (RO-MAN), 2015 24th IEEE International Symposium). IEEE, pp 498–504

Broadbent E (2017) Interactions with robots: the truths we reveal about ourselves. Annu Rev Psychol 68:627–652

Broadbent E, Tamagawa R, Patience A, Knock B, Kerse N, Day K, MacDonald BA (2012) Attitudes towards health-care robots in a retirement village. Australas J Ageing 31(2):115–120

Brooks R (2002) Flesh and machines: how robots will change us. Pantheon Books, New York

Brooks R, Breazeal C, Marjanovic M, Scassellati B, Williamson M (1999) The cog project: building a humanoid robot. In: Nehaniv C (ed) In Computation for metaphors, analogy, and agents, lecture notes in artificial intelligence 1562, Springer-Verlag, New York, pp 52–87

Burleigh TJ, Schoenherr JR (2014) A reappraisal of the uncanny valley: categorical perception or frequency-based sensitization? Front Psychol 5(2014):1488

Cabibihan JJ, Javed H, Ang M, Aljunied SM (2013) Why robots? a survey on the roles and benefits of social robots in the therapy of children with autism. Int J Soc Robot 5(4):593–618

CNN (2014) http://edition.cnn.com/2014/12/23/world/americas/feat-orangutan-rights-ruling/

Cullen H, Kanai R, Bahrami B, Rees G (2013) Individual differences in anthropomorphic attributions and human brain structure. Soc Cogn Affect Neurosci 9(9):1276–1280

Daily Mail (2017) http://www.dailymail.co.uk/sciencetech/article-4258122/Experts-reveal-voice-assistants-female-voices.html

Dautenhahn K, Nehaniv CL, Walters ML, Robins B, Kose-Bagci H, Mirza NA, Blow M (2009) KASPAR–a minimally expressive humanoid robot for human–robot interaction research. Appl Bion Biomech 6(3–4):369–397

Dereshev D, Kirk D (2017) Form, function and etiquette-potential users' perspectives on social domestic robots. Multimodal Technol Interact 1(2):12

DiSalvo C, Gemperle F (2003, June) From seduction to fulfilment: the use of anthropomorphic form in design. In: Proceedings of the 2003 International Conference on Designing Pleasurable Products and Interfaces. ACM, pp 67–72

Eberle SG (2009) Exploring the Uncanny valley to find the edge of play. Am J Play 2(2):167–194

Epley N, Waytz A, Cacioppo JT (2007) On seeing human: a three-factor theory of anthropomorphism. Psychol Rev 114(4):864

Epley N, Akalis S, Waytz A, Cacioppo JT (2008) Creating social connection through inferential reproduction loneliness and perceived agency in gadgets, gods, and greyhounds. Psychol Sci 19(2):114–120

Fischer K (2011) Interpersonal variation in understanding robots as social actors. Proc ACM/IEEE Int Conf Human-Robot Interaction, 6th, Lausanne, Switz. IEEE, Piscataway, NJ, pp 53–60

Fong T, Nourbakhsh I, Dautenhahn K (2003) A survey of socially interactive robots. Robotics and autonomous systems 42(3):143–166

Gazzola V, Rizzolatti G, Wicker B, Keysers C (2007) The anthropomorphic brain: the mirror neuron system responds to human and robotic actions. Neuroimage 35:1674–1684

Gockley R, Forlizzi J, Simmons R (2007) Natural person-following behavior for social robots. In: Proceedings of the ACM/IEEE International Conference on Human-robot Interaction. ACM, pp 17–24

Govers PCM, Mugge R (2004) I love my jeep, because its tough like me: the effect of product personality congruence on product attachment. In: Kurtgözü A (ed) Proceedings of the Fourth International Conference on Design and Emotion. Ankara, Turkey

Green RD, MacDorman KF, Ho CC, Vasudevan SK (2008) Sensitivity to the proportions of faces that vary in human likeness. Comp Hum Behav 24(5):2456–2474

Guizzo E (2010) The man who made a copy of himself. Spectrum IEEE 47(4):44–56

Guthrie S (1980) A cognitive theory of religion. Curr Anthropol 21:181–203

Guthrie SE (1993) Faces in the clouds: a new theory of religion. Oxford University Press

Hoenen M, Lübke KT, Pause BM (2016) Non-anthropomorphic robots as social entities on a neurophysiological level. Comput Hum Behav 57:182–186

Hsiao HS, Chang CS, Lin CY, Hsu HL (2015) "iRobiQ": the influence of bidirectional interaction on kindergarteners' reading motivation, literacy, and behavior. Interact Learn Environ 23 (3):269–292

Ishiguru (n.d.) www.geminoid.jp/en/robots.html. Last accessed 20 Aug 2017

Ishiguru (n.d.) Geminoid H1-2 www.geminoid.jp/en/robots.html. Last accessed 20 Aug 2017

Joosse M, Lohse M, Pérez JG, Evers V (2013, May) What you do is who you are: the role of task context in perceived social robot personality. In: Robotics and automation (ICRA), 2013 IEEE international conference. IEEE, pp 2134–2139

Jordan PW (2002) The personalities of products. In: Green WS, Jordan PW (eds) Pleasure with products: beyond usability. Taylor & Francis, London, pp 19–48

Kim Y, Sundar SS (2012) Anthropomorphism of computers: is it mindful or mindless? Comput Hum Behav 28(1):241–250

Kiseleva J, Williams K, Jiang J, Hassan Awadallah A, Crook AC, Zitouni I, Anastasakos T (2016, March) Understanding user satisfaction with intelligent assistants. In: Proceedings of the 2016 ACM on Conference on Human Information Interaction and Retrieval. ACM, pp 121–130

Koschate M, Potter R, Bremner P, Levine M (2016, March) Overcoming the uncanny valley: displays of emotions reduce the uncanniness of humanlike robots. In: The Eleventh ACM/ IEEE International Conference on Human Robot Interaction. IEEE Press, pp 359–365

Kozima H, Michalowski MP, Nakagawa C (2009) Keepon. Int J Soc Rob 1(1):3–18

Kubrick S, Clarke AC (1968) Screenplay for 2001: A Space Odyssey, Available via http://www.visual-memory.co.uk/amk/doc/0057.html. Last accessed 24 Aug 2017

Lee HR, Šabanović S, Stolterman E (2016, March) How human like should a social robot be: a user-centered exploration. In: 2016 AAAI Spring Symposium Series

Letheren K, Kuhn KAL, Lings I, Pope NKL (2016) Individual difference factors related to anthropomorphic tendency. Eur J Mark 50(5/6):973–1002

Lodge D (1984) Small world: an academic romance. Secker and Warburg, London

Love J, Abutaleb Y (2015) Sassy woman or machine? tech giants divided over digital assistants. https://www.yahoo.com/tech/sassy-woman-machine-tech-giants-divided-over-digital-062306542–finance.html. Last accessed 23 Aug 2017

Lucas GM, Gratch J, King A, Morency LP (2014) It's only a computer: virtual humans increase willingness to disclose. Comput Hum Behav 37:94–100

Luger E, Sellen A (2016, May) Like having a really bad PA: the gulf between user expectation and experience of conversational agents. In: Proceedings of the 2016 CHI Conference on Human Factors in Computing Systems. ACM, pp 5286–5297

MacDorman KF, Chattopadhyay D (2016) Reducing consistency in human realism increases the uncanny valley effect; increasing category uncertainty does not. Cognition 146:190–205

MacDorman KF, Entezari SO (2015) Individual differences predict sensitivity to the uncanny valley. Interact Stud 16(2):141–172

Magnenat-Thalmann N, Zhang Z (2014, November) Social robots and virtual humans as assistive tools for improving our quality of life. In: Digital Home (ICDH), 2014 5th International Conference. IEEE, pp 1–7

Mara M, Appel M (2015) Science fiction reduces the eeriness of android robots: a field experiment. Comput Hum Behav 48:156–162

Marti P, Pollini A, Rullo A, Shibata T (2005, September) Engaging with artificial pets. In: Proceedings of the 2005 Annual Conference on European Association of Cognitive Ergonomics. University of Athens, pp 99–106

Mathur Maya B, Reichling David B (2016) Navigating a social world with robot partners: a quantitative cartography of the Uncanny Valley. Cognition 146:22–32

McTear MF (2002) Spoken dialogue technology: enabling the conversational user interface. ACM Comput Surv (CSUR) 34(1):90–169

Mengoni SE, Irvine K, Thakur D, Barton G, Dautenhahn K, Guldberg K, … Sharma S (2017) Feasibility study of a randomised controlled trial to investigate the effectiveness of using a humanoid robot to improve the social skills of children with autism spectrum disorder (Kaspar RCT): a study protocol. BMJ Open 7(6):e017376

Michalowski MP, Sabanovic S, Kozima H (2007, March) A dancing robot for rhythmic social interaction. In: Human-Robot Interaction (HRI), 2007 2nd ACM/IEEE International Conference. IEEE, pp 89–96

Mitchell WJ, Ho CC, Patel H, MacDorman KF (2011) Does social desirability bias favor humans? explicit–implicit evaluations of synthesized speech support a new HCI model of impression management. Comput Hum Behav 27(1):402–412

Mori M (1970) Bukimi no tani. Energy 7:33–35

Mori M, MacDorman KF, Kageki N (2012) The uncanny valley [from the field]. Robot Autom Mag IEEE 19:98–100

Mourey JA, Olson JG, Yoon C (2017) Products as Pals: engaging with anthropomorphic products mitigates the effects of social exclusion. J Consum Res, ucx038

Mugge R, Schoormans JPL, De Lange A (2007) Consumers' appreciation of product personalization. In: Fitzsimons G, Morwitz V (ed) Advances in Consumer Research, vol 34. Association for Consumer Research, Orlando, FL

Mugge R, Govers PC, Schoormans JP (2009) The development and testing of a product personality scale. Des Stud 30(3):287–302

Niculescu A, van Dijk B, Nijholt A, Li H, See SL (2013) Making social robots more attractive: the effects of voice pitch, humor and empathy. Int J Social Robot 5(2):171–191

Nishio S, Ishiguro H, Hagita N (2007) Geminoid: teleoperated android of an existing person. In: de Pina Filho AC (ed) Humanoid robots: new developments, I-Tech, Vienna, Austria, (Chap. 20)

Norman DA (2004) Emotional design: why we love or hate everyday objects. Basic Books, New York

Norman D (2013) The design of everyday things: revised and expanded edition. Basic Books, AZ

Papadopoulos I, Sgorbissa A, Koulouglioti C (2017) Caring robots are here to help: nurse researchers and scientists developing culturally sensitive care robots say there is nothing to fear–in fact there's much to be gained–from this technology. Nurs Stand 31(51):18–20

Plowman L (2004) "Hey, hey, hey! It's time to play": children's interactions with smart toys. In: Goldstein J et al. (ed) Toys, games, and media. Lawrence Erlbaum Associates, Mahwah, NJ, pp 207–223

Purington A, Taft JG, Sannon S, Bazarova NN, Taylor SH (2017, May) Alexa is my new BFF: social roles, user satisfaction, and personification of the amazon echo. In: Proceedings of the 2017 CHI Conference Extended Abstracts on Human Factors in Computing Systems. ACM, pp 2853–2859

Reeves B, Nass C (1996) How people treat computers, television, and new media like real people and place. Cambridge, UK

Reichardt J (1978) Robots: fact, fiction and prediction. Thames & Hudson, London, UK

Rosenthal-von der Pütten AM, Krämer NC (2014) How design characteristics of robots determine evaluation and uncanny valley related responses. Comput Hum Behav 36:422–439

Rosenthal-von der Pütten A, Weiss A (2015) The uncanny valley phenomenon: does it affect all of us? Interact Stud 16(2):206–214

Sandry E (2015) Re-evaluating the form and communication of social robots. Int J Soc Rob 7 (3):335–346

Saygin AP, Chaminade T, Ishiguro H, Driver J, Frith C (2012) The thing that should not be: predictive coding and the uncanny valley in perceiving human and humanoid robot actions. Soc Cogn Affect Neur 7:413–422

Searle JR (2014) "What Your Computer Can't Know", The New York Review of Books, 9 October 2014, p 54

Sheridan TB (2016) Human–robot interaction: status and challenges. Hum Factors 58(4):525–532

Shibata T, Wada K (2011) Robot therapy: a new approach for mental healthcare of the elderly–a mini-review. Gerontology 57(4):378–386

Shibata T, Wada K, Ikeda Y, Sabanovic S (2009) Cross-cultural studies on subjective evaluation of a seal robot. Adv Rob 23(4):443–458

Simonite T (2013) Apple looks to improve Siri's script. January 15. MIT Technology Review. https://www.technologyreview.com/s/509961/apple-looks-to-improve-siris-script/. Last accessed 23 Aug 2017

Strait MK, Floerke VA, Ju W, Maddox K, Remedios JD, Jung MF, Urry HL (2017) Understanding the uncanny: both atypical features and category ambiguity provoke aversion towards humanlike robots. Front Psychol 8:1366. https://doi.org/10.3389/fpsyg.2017.01366

Sung JY, Guo L, Grinter RE, Christensen HI (2007, September) "My Roomba is Rambo": intimate home appliances. In: International Conference on Ubiquitous Computing. Springer Berlin Heidelberg, pp 145–162

The Telegraph (2015) http://www.telegraph.co.uk/news/worldnews/asia/japan/12022795/My-weekend-with-Pepper-the-worlds-first-humanoid-robot-with-emotions.html. Last accessed 1 Sept 2017

The Times (2017a) Robots learn about tea and sympathy. https://www.thetimes.co.uk/edition/news/robots-learn-about-tea-and-sympathy-to-care-for-elderly-plz7kzzn7. Last accessed 21 Aug 2017

The Times (2017b) Woohoo! Amazon's digital assistant gets excitable. https://www.thetimes.co.uk/article/woohoo-amazon-s-digital-assistant-gets-excitable-qbd6j03p9. Last accessed 21 Aug 2017

The Times (2017c) Robots are turning children into brats. https://www.thetimes.co.uk/article/778ef16e-facf-11e6-a6f0-cb4e831c1cc0. Last accessed 21 Aug 2017

Turkle S (2007) Authenticity in the age of digital companions. Interact Stud 8(3):501–517

Turkle S, Taggart W, Kidd CD, Dasté O (2006) Relational artifacts with children and elders: the complexities of cyber-companionship. Connect Sci 18(4):347–361

Van Rompay T, Ludden G (2015) Types of embodiment in design: the embodied foundations of meaning and affect in product design. Int J Des 9(1)

Vlahos J (2015, September 20) Goodbye imaginary friends; hello A.I. dolls. New York Times Magazine, p 44. Last accessed 1 Sept 2017

Wada K, Shibata T (2009) Social effects of robot therapy in a care house-change of social network of the residents for one year–. J Adv Comput Intell Intell Inf 13(4):386–392

Wada K, Shibata T, Saito T, Sakamoto K, Tanie K (2005, April) Psychological and social effects of one year robot assisted activity on elderly people at a health service facility for the aged. In: Robotics and automation, 2005. ICRA 2005. Proceedings of the 2005 IEEE International Conference on, IEEE, pp 2785–2790

Wagemaker E, Dekkers TJ, Agelink van Rentergem JA, Volkers KM, Huizenga HM (2017) Advances in mental health care: Five N = 1 studies on the effects of the robot seal paro in adults with severe intellectual disabilities. Journal of Mental Health Research in Intellectual Disabilities, 1–12

Waytz A, Cacioppo J, Epley N (2010a) Who sees human? Perspect Psychol Sci 5(3):219–232

Waytz A, Morewedge CK, Epley N, Monteleone G, Gao JH, Cacioppo JT (2010b) Making sense by making sentient: effectance motivation increases anthropomorphism. J Pers Soc Psychol 99 (3):410

Weiss A, Wurhofer D, Tscheligi M (2009) "I love this dog"—children's emotional attachment to the robotic dog AIBO. Int J Soc Rob 1(3):243–248

Weiss A, van Dijk B, Evers V (2012, March) Knowing me knowing you: exploring effects of culture and context on perception of robot personality. In: Proceedings of the 4th International Conference on Intercultural Collaboration. ACM, pp 133–136

Weizenbaum J (1976) Computer power and human reason. New York, Basic Books, From judgement to calculation

Winkielman P, Carr EW, Chakrabarti B, Hofree G, Kavanagh LC (2016) Mimicry, emotion, and social context: insights from typical and atypical humans, robots, and androids. Emotional Mimicry in Social Context, 162

Złotowski J, Proudfoot D, Yogeeswaran K, Bartneck C (2015) Anthropomorphism: opportunities and challenges in human–robot interaction. Int J Soc Rob 7(3):347–360

Chapter 4
Affect

Experience is emotional but there are no separate things called emotions in it.

Dewey (1934, p. 42)

This chapter discusses our affective relationships with digital technology. These are regarded by some to be most important aspect of any experience and have been described as, "the most central and pervasive aspects of human experience" (Ortony et al. 1988, p. 3). Despite this, affect barely receives any attention in the definitions of UX.

Affect refers to a variety of psychological states including emotions, feelings, impressions and moods. Of these, emotions are generally regarded the most relevant to UX as they can be thought of as a result of using a digital product for example, we are happy with our new phone, we are excited by the game, we are bored with virtual reality and so on (e.g. Frijda 1986). As we can readily see from these simple examples, an emotion relies on an appraisal, that is, at its simplest, whether or not we like the something including digital products.

While our focus in this chapter is primarily on the emotions, we also discuss impressions, feelings and mood. All three of these have been significantly under-researched, and our understanding of them is correspondingly less well developed.

Impressions are brief (they are often formed in a very few milliseconds), probably are the first of the affective responses and are often associated with the formation of preferences. Impressions also tend to persist.

Feelings, as the word itself implies, potentially concerns haptics and a role for the body. Colombetti and Thompson (2008) tell us that feelings are not separate constituents of emotion, but are emergent feature of emotional interpretation, and Prinz (2004) has described feelings as embodied appraisals. It is perhaps the enactive approach which offers the most radical and exciting prospect to understand feelings. Doing so, however, means accepting that they arise from the organisation of life itself which, of course, means that every man, woman, child and bacterium (sic) experience them.

P. Turner, *A Psychology of User Experience*, Human–Computer Interaction Series,
https://doi.org/10.1007/978-3-319-70653-5_4

Finally, arguably the most mysterious (or least researched) of aspect of affect is mood which according to Russell (2003) is simply "prolonged core affect without an object". However, Richard Coyne's recent Mood and Mobility (2016) helps us to see that they are a means by which we make sense of the world and, unlike our emotions, we can never escape them.

Treatments of affect in HCI

There are popularly two treatments of affect within human-computer interaction (HCI) which are "affective computing" (Picard 1997) and "emotional design" (Norman 2004). Picard's publication of Affective Computing prompted the creation of a new field of research (of the same name) which is the study and development of systems and devices that can recognise, interpret, process, and simulate a range of human emotions. It is a multi-disciplinary field which relies upon contributions from computer science, psychology, and the cognitive sciences. Picard herself admits that her initial belief was that emotion should be kept out of computing, was later to find that it plays an essential role in "rational decision making, perception, learning and a variety of other cognitive functions" (p. x). Since its formation, affective computing has diversified into the design of new ways for people to communicate their affective-cognitive states to both technology and other people.

Emotional design, in contrast, may be described as a design approach where a positive emotional response to a product is regarded as evidence of a "good design" and which may offer the promise of a "good user experience". Emotional design shares many of the characteristics of user-centred design which Norman helped establish some twenty years earlier and has since become an important aspect of digital product design (Norman and Draper 1986). We discuss Norman's emotional design more fully in Chap. 5 (aesthetics).

There are, however, advocates of a third approach to emotion within HCI who regard it as an essential part of cognition and/or an experience itself. Isomursu et al. (2007) are among those claiming that emotion is an essential component of those experiences arising from using digital products. Their position develops the ideas of Forlizzi and Battarbee who themselves drew inspiration from Carlson's *Experienced Cognition* (1997, p.vii). Carlson's argument is that any successful theory of cognition must "begin with, and account for, cognition as experienced by the individual" (ibid, p. 4) and in addition to the familiar components of cognition (e.g. memory and perception) he recognises a place for emotion. He identifies and proposes three functions of emotion which is involved in the shaping our plans and intentions; the organisation of procedures related to these plans and the evaluation of the outcomes of those plans. Forlizzi and Battarbee read these as indicating that emotion shapes how we plan to use digital products, how we actually interact with them, and the perceptions and outcomes that surround those interactions—while we see these themes repeated throughout the chapter, it all underlines the centrality of affect in UX and the fact that it cannot be separated from experience.

Similarly, Mahlke and Thüring (2007) have also proposed that emotion is central to user experience, and suggest, a little self-referentially, that emotion affects a user's appraisal of a product. They tell us that a user's perception of the qualities of the digital product affect emotional state and consequently overall experience of the product. This echoes Dewey's view, "emotion is the moving and cementing force. It selects what is congruous and dyes what is selected with its color, thereby giving qualitative unity to materials externally disparate and dissimilar. It thus provides unity in and through the varied parts of experience" (Dewey 1934, p. 42) that. As can be seen from this quotation, he describes emotion as moving, cementing, providing "color", and overall as providing unity to an experience. This can be can be demonstrated very easily. Try answering the following question—"how was your last holiday?". Many people (in my experience) will answer this with a single appraising word, such as, "great", "disastrous", "dull", "dysentery" and so forth. Indeed, this can be extended to a surprising number of situations such as, "what was your last job like", "what is it like to bring up children?" or "how was prison?". Each question can be answered in a word or two which often provide it with an appraisal and an emotional unity. For Dewey, emotions do not exist independently of an experience but tell us about the quality of the experience itself.

The structure of this chapter

This chapter, after this introduction, comprises five sections. We begin with a brief introduction to the long history of emotion. Our primary focus is on emotions as being cognitive phenomena. Then we consider how we feel about technology, specifically, our attachment to digital products. Next, we discuss the emotions which arise from technology—games in particular. Then we turn our attention to impressions, feelings and mood which have only received a fraction of the attention emotion has.

4.1 Origins

Any discussion of affect takes place in the context of at least 2500 years of thought, reflection, argument and controversy about it, indeed Oatley and Johnson-Laird (2014) have described affect as the "gunpowder and the glue" of human society. To begin with, there are relatively few widely agreed definitions of many of the key concepts within affect. Further, philosophy, psychology, the arts, anthropology, games research and the cognitive sciences have all, in their own ways, contributed to this by devising any number of theoretical and empirical positions to account for them. So perhaps the only thing which we might agree upon is that, no matter what we call it or which aspect we focus on, affect matters to us.

As we noted in the introduction, of the forms of affect, it has been emotion which has received overwhelmingly the most attention. So, we begin with Plato who argued that our emotions arise from a lower part of the brain and perverted reason. There are, undoubtedly, resonances of this view still with us today. To describe someone as emotional is generally seen as pejorative. In contrast, Aristotle thought that an emotion was the judgment of value, a statement which lies at the heart of contemporary formulation of appraisal theory (discussed at length below).

Approaching modern times, Evans (2002) identifies sentiment as a topic which held the attention of many of the key Enlightenment philosophers of the 18th century. Sentiment, he tells us, was used at that time to mean emotion. Smith (1759/ 2010), for example, took time out from inventing economics to write of his theory of Moral Sentiments in which he claimed that emotions were a thread which held society together, concluding that to be rational is to be emotional. Perhaps this was an early recognition of affect as being cognitive.

However, it was Charles Darwin who was to establish the scientific study of emotion in his The Expression of Emotions in Man and Animals (1872). This work is also noteworthy because it was the first to use photography as part of his scientific method. Darwin used these photographs to show how the expression of emotions is universal (or at least, accurately recognised from culture to culture) thus lending support to his proposal that we evolved from a common ancestor.[1] Like Plato, Darwin regarded emotion as a vestige of our animal past and as such lacking any functional value because it has been surpassed by human reason.

A decade or so later, this was followed by William James's famous paper entitled, "What is an emotion?" (James 1884). He proposed that emotions were bodily changes which occurred in response to emotive stimuli, asserting that the very idea of "a purely disembodied human emotion is a nonentity" (p. 194). Independently of James, the Danish physician Carl Lange had reached much the same conclusions resulting in the popular James-Lange theory of emotion. This account states that, if for example, we find ourselves being chased by a bear, we interpret our physical state—say, trembling, running and crying "bear!"—as evidence that we are afraid. This theory was challenged in the 1920s by Cannon on the grounds that animals that had their viscera surgically separated from their brains appeared to have unimpaired emotional behaviour (this claim was itself challenged a little later). The resulting (rival) Cannon-Bard theory of emotion was to place a greater emphasis on the role of the brain, claiming, for example, that the hypothalamus has a significant role in our emotional responses (Cannon 1927; Bard and Rioch 1937). Papez (1937) expanded on this when he proposed what was to

---

[1]This universality has been challenged by a number of researchers. Prinz (2004), for example, writes that emotions vary across borders, and quoting other authors he notes that in Inuit culture, for example, signs of anger are rarely seen and that the Malay language has no exact synonym for "anger." He also asks us to consider the Japanese term amae, which is an indulgent feeling of dependency, akin to what a child feels towards a mother. Westerners may recognize something like amae in children but they rarely attribute anything of that kind to adults. Japanese also has a term oime for a feeling of indebtedness and fureai, which refers to a feeling of connectedness. For Prinz, emotions appear to be less like biological universals and more like "enculturated scripts". A further example is from Lutz (1998) In her *Unnatural Emotions*. She claims that for groups in the South Pacific, emotional experience is not "pre-cultural, but pre-eminently cultural." She writes, "*the concepts of emotion can more profitably be viewed as serving complex communicative, moral, and cultural purposes rather than simply as labels for internal states whose nature or essence is presumed to be universal. ... The complex meaning of each emotion word is the result of the important role those words play in articulating the full range of a people's cultural values, social relations, and economic circumstances. Talk about emotions is simultaneously talk about society— about power and politics, about kinship and marriage, about normality and deviance ...*" (pp. 5–6).

become known as, the Papez Circuit. This "circuit" comprises the neural structures of the hippocampus, the fornix, and the mammillary bodies which includes many of the constituents of the limbic system. More recently, these bodies have been collectively described as the "visceral brain" by MacLean (1949, 1990).

Since then, research has led to a good understanding of the neural bases of a number of specific emotions—fear, for some reason, proving to be the most popular emotion among psychologists. Having set the scene, we now move into consider the current thinking on emotions.

Emotions are the result of appraisals

Reisenzein tells us that appraisal theory has its roots in the work of Arnold (1960) when she wrote of the direct, intuitive evaluations we employ to distinguish among the emotions. Her work has been seen as the first appearance of the post-behaviourist, cognitive accounts of affect which are the current vogue (Reisenzein 2006)—pace Enactivists.

Despite emotional states appearing to be phylogenetically older, they had been nonetheless seen as "inferior" to cognition. This has changed and now they are regarded to be a form of cognition. Oatley and Johnson-Laird (1987), for example, regard emotion to be a form of communication, in that they guide our actions in situations of bounded rationality, that is, in situations of imperfect knowledge and multiple conflicting goals. Our emotions offer this guidance by making available a repertoire of actions which have been previously useful in similar situations, thus emotions effectively guide our actions and decision making (consciously and unconsciously).

Ratcliffe (2008) also writes that in "describing emotions as cognitive, philosophers tend to mean at least that they are intentional states of some kind. They either are or at least (essentially) involve evaluations, appraisals or judgements" (p. 20). Treating affect (as a whole) as a form of cognition is seen as attractive because it satisfies "a deep intuition that emotions are meaningful. They … inform us about our relationship to the world, they embody our convictions, and they factor intelligibly into our decisions in life" (Prinz 2004, p. 16).

Pessoa (2008) has also shown that those regions of the brain which had been previously viewed as "affective" are also involved in cognition; and conversely, brain regions previously viewed as "cognitive" are also involved in emotion; and, the neural processes which support emotion and cognition are integrated and cannot be treated as though they can be neatly assigned to separate modules. From this perceptive, "complex cognitive-emotional behaviours have their basis in dynamic coalitions of networks of brain areas, none of which should be conceptualized as specifically affective or cognitive" (Pessoa 2008, p. 148).

Finally, advocates of the cognitive approach to emotion also claim that, "cognitive approaches based on the mind's organisation of conscious and unconscious knowledge, offer a clarifying perspective because they focus on the fundamental issue of how emotions are caused and what their effects are" (Oatley and Johnson-Laird 2014, p. 134). We now consider three quite different accounts of emotion which have been variously adopted by HCI researchers.

The nature of an appraisal

Ortony et al.'s (1988) The Cognitive Structure of Emotions has proved to be popular with UX/design researchers. For example, Desmet (2002) adopted it as part of his design research; and, Bartneck (2002) put it to use in the design of embodied agents as did Bartneck and Forlizzi (2004) in the design of social robots. More generally Norman and Ortony (2003) sought to adopt it as part of an interaction design methodology—cf. Norman's *Emotional Design*.

Ortony and his colleagues differentiate emotions according to character of their source, for example, events are judged by their consequences, agents by their actions, and objects by their intrinsic properties. These aspects are not exclusive, for example, people can be judged as agents or as objects.

This, in turn, leads to three major classes of emotions: those arising from appraisals of objects correspond to likes and dislikes; those from appraisals of agents to pleasure and displeasure, and, finally, those from appraisals of events to approval and disapproval. There are further subdivisions, and in all twenty-eight emotions are distinguished. So, to use their example, we might focus on an event such as a sports match for its consequences—like our team winning; or we might focus on agents and its actions, for example, whether the neighbour's dog is going to bite you; or we might focus on an object, such as your new smart phone and how much you have to pay the telecoms provider every month for the next two years.

Taking another approach, Schachter and Singer (2001) have described an appraisal as "an evaluation of what one's relationship to the environment implies for personal well-being." Frijda (1986, 2007), agrees and describes an appraisal as the process involving the detection and assessment of the significance of the environment for well-being. Concerns include the individual's needs, attachments, values, current goals and beliefs (Frijda 2007; Lazarus 1991; Scherer 2004). In short, an appraisal includes everything that an individual might care about, showing how emotions bind us to the world.

Emotions are for action

Another account of emotion which has attracted the attention of design researchers is Frijda's action-readiness account which argues that emotions are built from elements which are not emotions but are what they describe as "ur-emotions". Ur-emotions are simple stimulus-response states of readiness, which carry with them a sense of whether we wish to maintain or end our relationship with the cause of the emotion (Frijda 2007). So, for example, we consider the emotion of joy, which is associated with the motivation to maintain or possibly enhance our relationship with the source of it. With fear, in contrast, the aim is to reduce or remove the source of danger. For Frijda emotion is a process, with cognition regulating it.

Oatley and Johnson-Laird (1987) have created their own computational (rather than psychological) model of affect arguing that emotions guide our actions in situations of bounded rationality and make available actions which have been previously been useful in similar situations. Their theory argues that emotions are cognitively based states which co-ordinate processes in the nervous system.

Emotions are seen as providing solutions to problems arising from moving between plans. This theme of the relationship between emotion and the execution of plans has been considered by Oatley (1992) who also tells us, "Each goal and plan has a monitoring mechanism that evaluates events relevant to it. When a substantial change of probability occurs of achieving an important goal or subgoal, the monitoring mechanism broadcasts to the whole cognitive system a signal that can set it into readiness to respond to this change. Humans experience these signals and the states of readiness they induce as emotions." (p. 50). These emotions signal success, failure, frustration and disgust. Oatley and Johnson-Laird equate achieving a sub-goal with happiness; the failure of a major plan with sadness; and the frustration of an active plan with anger.

Finally, and still on this theme of emotion and action, Prinz writes that emotions must "detect something more than the vicissitudes of vasculature. Otherwise, they would confer no survival advantage" (2004, p. 60). It is by having intentional directedness that aims at things external to the organism that emotions can play their distinctive roles in guiding our activity. Thus "Emotions promote behavioural responses. We (are meant to) run when we are afraid of something external. If emotions represented bodily changes this would be unintelligible. We should flee when our hearts race" (Prinz 2004, p. 59). Nevertheless, Prinz holds that emotions do not have ordinary intentional objects, such as particular objects or people, as their proper targets—except incidentally. This does not mean that emotions lack intentionality, rather, as Prinz stresses, emotions are intentional "in their own right" (2004, p. 62). This emotional guidance may also serve to signal our involvement with the situation.

Russell's core affect

Finally, Russell (1980, 1989, 1996, 2009) has proposed that underlying any emotion is core affect—an idea which might be traced back to the thinking of Wundt. For Russell, core affect has two dimensions: namely, the level of physiological arousal (from calm to excited) and the emotion's valence (the dimension of pleasure–displeasure). Core affect, then, is a continuous assessment of one's current affective state, and as this is a continuous process of change, the locus of our affect moves in response to impact of internal and external factors. According to Russell, core affect is experienced as a single blend of these factors which can be located on the circumplex model, the horizontal axis represented the valence while the vertical axes represents the arousal (Fig. 4.1).

For the design researchers Desmet and Hekkert (2007) this account "offers a simple, yet powerful, way to organize product experience, because all possible experiences involved in the user-product interaction can be described in terms of core affect".

How many emotions are there?

What has emerged from our discussion so far, is that emotions have a broadly cognitive element (an appraisal) and have a corporeal aspect (a physiological change) resulting in an experience, and perhaps an action. Or are regarded as purely

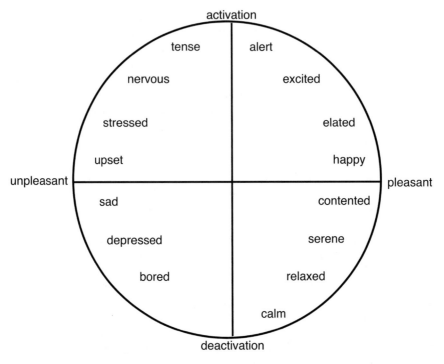

Fig. 4.1 Circumplex model of core affect

cognitive. This being so, a key question is how many are there? Ortony and Turner (1990) observe that there are a variety of answers to the apparently simple question, particularly when we modify it with the word "basic". So, how many basic emotions are there? Theorists and researchers have argued for a small number of basic emotions and while there are many who would agree, they do not agree on that number, or which emotions are basic, and why they should be regarded as basic. This has been a hotly debated topic for some years, and one of the oldest lists is Plutchik's (1980) influential classification which identified eight primary emotions, namely, anger, fear, sadness, disgust, surprise, anticipation, trust, and joy.

There followed quite a large number of alternative lists including Panksepp (1982) who has proposed the basic emotions of expectancy, fear, rage, and panic; Kemper (1987) has proposed a different four, namely, fear, anger, depression, and satisfaction; and Oatley and Johnson-Laird (1987) base their work on the emotions of sadness, anxiety, anger, and disgust. At the other end of the scale, Frijda (1986) has identified 18 basic emotions, including arrogance, humility, and indifference, as well as the more commonplace anger, fear, and sorrow. However, Frijda (1987) also seemed to be happy with only two, arguing that we only have pleasant or unpleasant experiences. Friesen (1972) proposed six basic emotions (anger, disgust, fear, joy, sadness, and surprise), and Ekman et al. (1972) have reported that in reviewing a large body of published work that they found that every investigator had obtained evidence tor six emotions (happiness, surprise, fear, sadness, anger and disgust combined with contempt).

Interestingly, the social media giant Facebook® has supplied its users with a list of feelings (sic) which with which to describe their affective state. It is a long list and comprises: blessed, excited, happy, tired, relaxed, sad, amused, emotional, loved, proud, annoyed, fed up, fantastic, content, sick, determined, pained, bored, cold, exhausted, confused, thankful, nervous, frustrated, stressed, meh, cosy, drained, depressed, accomplished, angry, wonderful, hungry, ill, positive, upset, scared, lonely, stuffed, sleepy, down, hung-over, hopeful, shattered, irritated, lucky, in love, grateful, sore, awesome, undecided, nostalgic, crazy, optimistic, lost, fat, heartbro-ken, blah, relieved, amazing, full, great, ecstatic, gutted, satisfied, hot, crappy, refreshed, rough, ready, productive, disappointed, anxious, grumpy, shocked, mis-chievous, worried, motivated, special, impatient, lazy, good, stupid, curious, broken, super, furious, alone, disgusted, embarrassed, devastated, giddy, unwell, aggravated, better, overwhelmed, awake, restless, wet, energised, bad, blissful, sorry, pretty, cool, free, safe, guilty, lovely, hurt, thoughtful, funny, alive, confident, beautiful, surprised, sexy, fresh. There is also the option to "add your own". While not all of these are emotions ("hung-over?") they may indeed describe social media users' affective states and this is an extremely good example of an ad hoc category.

4.2 Emotions About Technology

This section considers the emotions we experience using digital products, but before we begin, consider the following situation—imagine a friend has bought herself a new smart phone and you are asked whether or not you like it, and let us suppose that you do (or you are too polite to tell her the truth). Is this an affective or an aesthetic response? Clearly it involves an appraisal, which is common to both affective and (as we shall see) aesthetic experiences, but how do we distinguish between them? It should, of course, be easy. Affect is our emotional response to something, whereas aesthetics is about how something looks (which literally what the word means). In addition to this common-sense difference, we also know that they are also neurologically distinct and academically affective science is quite separate from aesthetic science.

Despite these differences, some affective researchers consider that aesthetic experiences rely on specific type of appraisal, namely, a judgement of intrinsic pleasantness (Scherer et al. 2001), while not to be outdone, some affective researchers speak of aesthetic emotion (e.g. Leder and Nadal 2014) and, of course, UX researchers such as Hassenzahl write of the hedonic properties of digital products in the context of discussing their aesthetics. And, as an author, I have the very real and practical need to separate affect and aesthetics into two chapters in this book, and deciding what goes where has proved to be no simple matter.

So, from a pragmatic perceptive—research relating to our attachment to digital products, is described in this section as emotions about technology. This division is not perfect but it is practical. In yet another example, the paradoxical nature of UX research, it is evident that most of the research into the emotions we experience about digital products is instrumental (cf. Chaps. 1 and 2) and primarily concerned with their measurement.

A few words on measurement

A number of scales and instruments have been developed to measure our emotional responses and these include the Pleasure-Arousal-Dominance scale (Russell and Mehrabian 1977), Bradley and Lang's (1994) self-assessment manikin (sic); Donato et al.'s Classification of Facial States (1999), and Desmet's (2002) Product Emotional Measurement instrument (PrEmo) among many others.

However, there is an occasionally recognised but persistent difficulty with determining what is actually being measured. So, for example, Mauss and Robinson (2009), in a detailed review of the published literature, found that the measures of emotional responding reflect dimensions rather than affective discrete states. They also concluded that there is no "gold standard" in measuring the affective and observe that, experiential, physiological, and behavioural measures are all relevant to understanding emotion but cannot be assumed to be interchangeable.

There is the matter of identifying the source feature which is actually (or assumed to be) responsible for the emotional response being measured. Desmet's PrEmo, for example, was designed to assess the emotional impact of products and systems with a view to understanding what further refinements or improvements might be necessary. Thus, the range of emotions being measured were product specific and reflected a very specific, person-product interaction. In contrast, Ekman's interest was in capturing and measuring emotion which arise as the result of human to human interaction. Both perspectives have their place, but Ekman's work tended to emphasize the negative emotions of anger, distrust, fear and sadness. These, it has been argued, have been foregrounded as they are more important for an individual's survival whereas digital products are only rarely homicidal.

How we love our phones

The popular press often run features on the theme that we care more for our phones than our spouses, boyfriends, girlfriends or indeed almost anyone else. Magazine and newspaper even run challenges in which their ace reporters try to manage a day or even as much as a week without their mobile phones. The participants often described themselves as bravely enduring "digital detox" pausing to reflect how much simpler life would be without a phone. Whether or not these journalists are "addicted" to their phones is moot but the use of the term attachment is more charitable and does serve to avoid any discussion of pathology (e.g. Billieux et al. 2015).

It was Bowlby (1969, p. 242) who proposed attachment theory to describe the affective relationship between parent (subsequently revised to "primary care-giver") and child. Bowlby tells us that: "Each party manifests intense pleasure in the other's company and especially in the expression of the other's expression of affection … proximity and affectionate interchange are appraised and felt as pleasurable by both, whereas distance and expressions of rejection are appraised as disagreeable or painful by both". It is interesting that Bowlby emphasizes the reciprocal nature of attachment. Nonetheless, subsequently researchers have proposed that emotional attachments can be observed between people and their pets (Thomson et al. 2005), brands (Fournier 1998; Thomson et al. 2005), places (Low and Altman 1992), experiences (Arnould and Price 1993; Kleine and Baker 2004), celebrities (Thomson 2006), and a variety of products (Wallendorf and Arnould 1988; Kleine et al. 1995).

From a somewhat more traditional perspective, Konok et al. (2016) have also suggested that we have predispositions to form attachment to social partners, which we generalise to the non-human and the inanimate. Konok and colleagues are among a number of researchers who have found that young people readily develop attachment toward their phone, and they seek to be close to it and experience distress on separation for it. Their study concludes that attachment to artefacts, such as their smart phones may be the result of the "cultural co-option" of the attachment system. In a further study, Konok et al. (2017) note that while there are general perceptions of increasing levels of ownership of and engagement to, smart phones, whether this is actually attachment per se is yet to be demonstrated. In a series of studies, the authors did find evidence of separation-related emotions when people were deprived of their phones, which for them, supports the proposal that people do form attachment toward their mobile which is similar to social attachment.[2]

"Grandfather's iPod"

Odom and Pierce (2009) have reported on the differences between user perceptions of digital and non-digital domestic artefacts. They write that, "participants (i) rarely expressed strong attachment to digital artefacts and (ii) rarely perceived digital artefacts to improve with age. In many cases, participants did express strong attachment to non-digital products, which oftentimes were perceived to improve with age" (Odom and Pierce 2009, p. 3795).

In another study, Odom et al. (2009) reported similar patterns in the acquisition, attachment and retention of household and personal paraphernalia. Paralleling the results of the earlier study, the authors observe a "contrast between the ensoulment[3] of things non-digital and the un-ensoulment of things digital" (p. 56).

---

[2]In an interesting footnote to attachment research, Hong and Townes (1976) conducted a cross-cultural study which investigated the incidence and characteristics of infants' attachment to inanimate objects with specific reference to (local) child-rearing practices. They concluded that attachment to an inanimate object does indeed appear to be closely associated with child-rearing practices. They suggest that the occurrence of infant attachment to inanimate objects is lower in cultures in which infants receive a greater amount of physical contact, including a higher rate of breast feeding. These findings indicate that emotional attachment may be formed to inanimate objects in lieu of physical contact, which is relevant to smartphone technology: a smartphone is a device that can enable social interaction without a physical connection to another person.

[3]Ensoulment signifies the properties of 'well-loved' designs that embody meaning and reflect their owner's identities and values (Blevis 2007). Ensoulment or attachment may be viewed, inter alia, as a consequence of personalisation or enchantment, is likely to encourage the preservation of an object even though it is no longer up-to-date or even useful and may lead to an artefact acquiring "heirloom status" (Blevis 2007).

This work prompted our own studies of successive cohorts of post-graduate students in 2009 and 2010, using Odom's probe questions (Turner and Turner 2011). Our results indicated that, contrary to the earlier reported work, many digital artefacts bore significant personal meaning and were preserved even when long superseded in the marketplace. This led to our own more formal examination of attachment in which we employed the repertory grid technique to explore the nature and dimensions of attachment to digital and non-digital objects. The most frequently identified artefacts to which people were attached proved to be a mixture of the digital and non-digital namely mobile phone, wristwatch/jewellery, laptop, photoprints/album and clothing (Turner and Turner 2013). The repertory grid software we employed allowed us to create visual representations of the analysis as can be seen in Fig. 4.2. This, aggregated principal component analysis reveals a fairly even distribution of digital and non-digital artefacts. In this subsequent study, we were unable to find any differences in the attachment people felt to the items that they owned.

Attachment and the self

Meschtscherjakov (2009) has argued that the basis of any emotional attachment to technology lies with it being an expression or an extension of its user or owner, for example, of mobile phones he writes, "Mobile devices enable us to stay in contact with our friends, to access information from everywhere, to be productive and efficient, to capture memories, and to be entertained. They make us independent, increase our mobility, and give us a freedom we do not want to miss anymore. Since mobile devices are also an expression of our personality and a symbol for our peer group membership they have become an extension of our self." Meschtscherjakov et al. (2014) add to this in their investigation of the apparent growing attachment to mobile phones, a phenomenon which they describe as "mobile attachment". They argue that rather than a simple emotional bond, mobile attachment emerges when the mobile phone becomes part of the user's self-concept. This link or bond develops as it empowers, enriches, or gratifies the user's self. They write that people have a need to behave consistently with the view of one's self and extending this "self-consistency" motive, they have concluded that consumers prefer products that are congruent to their self-concept (e.g. Malhotra 1988; Sirgy 1982, 1985). It has been observed that people make a comparison between their self-concept and the product's image and prefer products with a congruent image. Possessing congruent products is also valuable to express one's self-concept to others, because it is common to make personality inferences about a person from the possessions they own (Burroughs et al. 1991; Gosling et al. 2002). The ideas of "brand" and even "product" attachment have also been proposed (e.g. Aaker 1997; Govers and Schoormans 2005; Jordan 1997; Lee and Cho (2017)). Govers (2004) has defined product personality as "the role of personality characteristics that people use to describe a specific product variant and to discriminate it

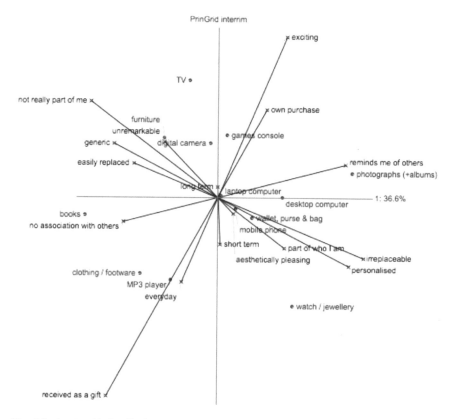

Fig. 4.2 A pringrid visualisation of personal artefacts

from others" (p. 15). For example, a Volkswagen Beetle has a happy and friendly personality (please see our treatment of the related concept of anthropomorphism in Sect. 3.4).

Attached or enchanted?

Our final perspective on attachment is from McCarthy and his colleagues, following the original usage by Bennett (2001) who have proposed that we might become enchanted with technology. They write, "An object or interactive system that is likely to evoke enchantment should offer the potential for the unexpected, given the chance of new discoveries, and provide a range of possibilities. The greater the opportunity it offers for finding new aspects or qualities, the longer the enchantment may last". From this perspective enchantment appears to complement attachment by introducing a "mindful" dimension. McCarthy et al. (2005) continue that, "Enchantment does not necessarily imply that the object of enchantment must be novel or extraordinary, rather that the person sees how rich and extraordinary the everyday and familiar can be".

4.3 Emotions with Technology

In this section, we move from emotions about technology to those emotions we experience with technology. This might be seen as a nice point but it allows us to separate two quite distinct sets of emotional experiences, namely, those experiences which arise from owning, using, or loathing the technology at work or owning the latest excellent phone from Japan and those which arise from playing digital (video) games. So, the key digital product we will consider in this section are digital games which have been specifically designed for emotion including competition, pleasure, adventure, fun, danger and excitement and all from the comfort and safety of an armchair.

There has been, and there continues to be, a sustained but very diverse effort to design games which deliver distinct emotional experiences. Choosing three (more or less at random) we find Sylvester (2013) who advocates an "engineering" approach while reminding use for an (onscreen) event to be meaningful in "must provoke emotion" (p. 8). Isbister (2016) argue that games can play a "powerful role in creating empathy and other strong emotional experiences" and that "games reveal these emotionally positive qualities over time". Finally, Ge and Ifenthaler (2017), are interested in how we construct "serious games" in an educational context with an emphasis on engagement and assessment. In short, the sheer breadth of designing games for ... is quite breath-taking.

However, our interest is not in the design of what might be described as "games technology" but in the emotions they engender.[4]

Games make us happy

McGonigal tells us unequivocally that playing games makes us happy and that playing games will make the world a better place. In her *Reality is Broken* (2011), she provides us with an impressive array of statistics including that about 50% of the population play games and that the average player will have spent 10,000 h gaming by the age of 21. She continues that, 69% of all heads of household play games and large numbers of CEOs and CFOs take games breaks at work; 97% of all youth and 40% of women play. A game player has an average age of 35 and has played for 12 years and most expect to continue to do so for the rest of their lives.

---

[4]We should also recognise the recent interest in gamification. Deterding et al. (2011) tell us that "gamification" originated in the digital media industry with a first usage dating from 2008. Gamification is a poorly defined term but among its many usages, it refers to using game-like features to non-gaming digital environment for the purposes of motivation. So, for example, the language learning platform—duolingo (https://www.duolingo.com/)—has a gamified user interface. Duolingo employs daily email reminders, a within-learning environment "currency" which can be earned and then used to buy access to extra features. It has challenges and a learner can "gamble" with their currency. Gamification is proving popular in the design of educational software and has been proposed, like so many ideas before it, as a potential solution to the perennial problems of getting young people to engage with boring education. It is not clear whether gamification offers emotional experiences or is a smart re-invention of "token economies".

So, while gaming might not be a usual topic in a discussion of UX, on the basis of the sheer weight of numbers, it demands our attention. So, why are games so popular? McGonigal's answer is that, "Today, many of us are suffering from a vast and primal hunger. But it is not a hunger for food—it is a hunger for more and better engagement." Games, she believes, have far more to offer than solipsistic retreat but her point is not so much technological as psychological. "No object, no event, no outcomes or life circumstances can deliver real happiness to us. We have to make our own happiness—by working hard at activities that provide their own reward."

From this perspective, digital games are engines for creating and enhancing emotional experience and for making our lives "better". She claims that we crave, "satisfying work" because it allows us to be "optimistic about our own chances for success"; playing games involves "social connection" and they allow us to feel "curiosity, awe and wonder". So, we can see a little of why she asserts that playing games make us happy.

When all of the technological frippery is stripped away (here we are thinking of things like screen resolution, refresh rates and the quality of the sound), she argues that there are four key defining characteristics for digital games: goals, rules, feedback and voluntary participation. The goal is the specific outcome that players will work to achieve. It focuses their attention and continually orients their participation throughout the games (p. 21). The goal provides players with a sense of purpose. The rules place limitations on how players can achieve the goal. By removing or limiting the obvious ways of getting to the goal, the rules push players to explore previously uncharted possibility spaces. She tells us that this helps unleash creativity and strategic thinking. The feedback system provides the players with information as to how close they are to achieving their goal. In its most basic form, the feedback system can be as simple as the players' knowledge of an objective outcome: "The game is over when …" Real-time feedback serves as a promise to the players that the goal is definitely achievable, and it provide motivation to keep playing. Finally, voluntary participation requires that everyone who is playing the game knowingly and willingly accepts the goal, the rules and the feedback (this is very reminiscent of GOMS).

Not everyone agrees with this somewhat messianic position, Suits (2014), for example, prefers to define a game in terms of embracing unnecessary obstacles. He writes, "To play a game is to engage in activity directed towards bringing about a specific state of affairs, using only means permitted by rules, where the rules prohibit more efficient in favour of less efficient means, and where such rules are accepted just because they make possible such activity … playing a game [which he describes as lusory interaction] is the voluntary attempt to overcome unnecessary obstacles." But McGonigal is undaunted, as her latest book *SuperBetter* (2016) reminds us that "a gameful life can make you stronger, happier, braver and more resilient".

Emotion arising from game play

A study reported by the polling company Bowen Research (Bowen, n.d.) indicates
that games are beginning to catch up with other media such as books, movies, and
music with respect to their emotional impact on their users. In their survey of 535
gamers, over two-thirds said that games were either the best medium at eliciting
emotion or would soon equal the other media. What is even more revealing is the
list of "emotions" that gamers claim to have experienced (Table 4.1).

Although this list (as in Table 4.1) is neither accompanied by a set of definitions
nor has it been examined with controlled, empirical studies, whatever else, games
are clearly a fertile source of emotion and/or quasi-emotional states. The report
continues that after role-playing games, the most emotional genres (of games) were
first-person shooters and action games. They also reported that scripted events in
the former are becoming increasingly adept at telling an emotional story, but the
most common feeling elicited by the games was competitiveness, followed by
honour/loyalty. However, lowest on the scale, and notably lacking in those areas as
well as "awe and wonder" or "delight," were flight simulators. The authors note
that, "It is striking that young people today look at games as an entertainment
medium that surpasses or will equal the more traditional things that touch us deeply,
like books, movies, and music," and "Half of all gamers think conveying emotion is
extremely or pretty important which suggests that games which can achieve more of
this will be extremely popular."

In the same vein, McGonigal has her own list of emotions which are said to be
experienced while playing games (Table 4.2).

Of interest here, is the appearance of "new" emotions indicating that games are a
potentially rich and under-researched source of affect. However, aside from making
us happy, some believe that they make (particularly young men) behave violently.

Table 4.1 "Emotions" arising from playing games

Accomplishment	Awe, wonder and delight	Beauty
Compassion for others	Competitiveness	Danger
Frustration (and wanting to overcome it)	Hate	Honour/loyalty/integrity
Love	Sadness	Sexuality
Spirituality	Violence/excitement	

Table 4.2 Other "emotions" arising from playing games

Amusement	Bliss	Contentment
Curiosity	Relief	Wonderment
Excitement	Naches (pride in the accomplishments of one's children)	
Surprise	Fiero (the feeling of triumph over adversity)	

Imitation

Perhaps the most famous study of how witnessing violence affects subsequent behaviour was conducted and reported by Bandura et al. (1961). They showed one of two short films to groups of pre-school children. One group watched a film which showed a man assaulting a blow-up plastic clown (called bobo), while the other group watched a film which was completely innocuous. Afterwards the children were allowed to play with a wide range of toys including bobo. Those children who had watched bobo being assaulted imitated those actions very closely. Those children who did not watch the bobo movie showed no such imitative behaviour. The conclusion that witnessing violence leads to its imitation was thus established.

A study reported by Lin (2013) investigated whether media interactivity would influence the short-term effects of violent content on audience aggression. It is one thing to passively watch a movie of "violence" and (potentially) quite a number of an actively engage in a system designed to support real-time interactivity. In this study, the groups of male college students were randomly assigned to one of three conditions: digital game playing, the watching of recorded game-play, or movie watching. After this exposure, the participants' levels of aggression were measured. The results indicated that digital game players experienced greater increases in aggressive affect, aggressive cognition, and physiological arousal than participants who watched recorded game play or comparable movie scenes. The authors of the study believe that media interactivity may have exacerbated the violent effect on short-term, aggressive responses.

An earlier study by Bushman and Gibson (2010) has shown that at least for men, ruminating about a game they had played can increase its power to prompt aggression long after the game has ended. They randomly assigned college students to play one of six different digital games for 20 min. Half the games were violent (e.g. Mortal Kombat) and half were not (e.g. Guitar Hero). To determine whether ruminating about the game would extend its effect, half of the players were told over "the next 24 h, think about your play of the game, and try to identify ways your game play could improve when you play again." Bushman and Gibson had the participants return the next day to test their aggressiveness. For men who didn't think about the game, the violent digital game players tested as no more aggressive than men who had played non-violent games. But the violent digital game playing men who thought about the game in the interim were more aggressive than the other groups. The authors noted that it is "reasonable to assume that our lab results will generalize to the "real world". We consider one final piece of evidence in support of this proposition. This time it is anecdotal. This involved a young, game playing man, Devin Moore. Moore found himself taken to an Alabama police station for questioning regarding a stolen gun. He was said to be initially cooperative until he grabbed a policeman's gun whom he shot twice. He then shot another policeman 3 times, and a third policeman was shot 5 times. All three were killed. When Moore was finally captured, he said, "life is like a digital game. You have to die some-time". He claimed that he committed the crimes because of his obsessive playing of

Grand Theft Auto III and GTA Vice City. After the criminal case, a civil case representing the dead policemen's families argued that, the publisher of the game and those who sold it were, in part, responsible for the murders. The lawyers claim that Moore had been "trained" for murder by the games and he was simply faced with a real-life version of what he had already played out.

The "boy problem"

Philip Zimbardo, the noted social psychologist and originator of the Stanford prison experiment holds that digital games are both addictive and foster violence. In Man disconnected (Zimbardo and Coulombe 2015) the ills of modern men and boys are attributed to excessive digital game playing and the draw of online pornography. The authors list the failings of many young men which include falling enrolment in US universities, declining SAT scores, and reduced levels of economic independence. They continue, "we have nothing against playing digital games; they have many good features and benefits". However, Zimbardo and Coulombe are concerned that when they are played to excess, especially in social isolation, they can hinder a boy's ability and interest in developing face-to-face social skills. Further, they suggest that the variety and intensity of games makes everything else seem dull and thus creates a problem with academic performance. They go on to suggest that the declining performance at school might in turn might require medication to deal with it (here they are thinking of attention deficit disorders), which then leads to other problems in a "disastrous negative cycle". While that certain parts of the media might be quick to echo these sentiments, a review of the book (Lawson 2016) calls it "offensive" and a "remarkably poor piece of scholarship" and as we shall see, the evidence does not appear to support Zimbardo's position.

An absence of evidence

The proposal that playing violent digital games may cause or induce violent real world behaviour is both serious and controversial.

Ferguson (2007) has reported evidence of publication bias in meta-reviews of the effects of exposure to violent games. He found evidence for this bias in both experimental and non-experimental studies of aggressive behaviour and aggressive thoughts. He attributed the source of this bias to studies employing less standardized and reliable measures of aggression which tended to produce larger effect sizes.

Ferguson et al. (2008) report two studies that examined the relationship between exposure to violent digital games and aggression or violence in the laboratory and in real life. In the first study, participants were either randomized or allowed to choose to play a violent or nonviolent game. Although males were found to be more aggressive than females, they found no evidence that exposure to violent digital games caused any differences in aggression. In a second study, they found statistical evidence of correlations between trait aggression, family violence, and being male and these were also found to be predictive of violent crime, but exposure to violent games was not. Further analysis showed that family violence and "innate" aggression were better predictors of violent crime than exposure to digital game violence.

Elson and Ferguson (2013) in their comprehensive review of violence in digital games and consequent harm, conclude that there are simply too many shortcomings in the reported work. We will follow the structure of their work quite closely. They begin by outlining the debate from social, political and legal perspectives before moving to proposed psychological bases. The first psychological account is Anderson and Bushman's (2002) General Aggression Model (GAM) which relies on social learning. They describe it as the default model for many digital game researchers, particularly those who endorse the harm view of games. GAM is based on social-cognitive theories and has its roots in social learning theory, like Bandura and Walter's (1963) account. Its basic assumptions, as Elson and Ferguson tell us, are that behaviour is directed by schematic knowledge structures which themselves are acquired from being in the world and doing generally stuff. GAM, in common with many cognitive models, has no place for affect, personality, "the world", individual differences or biology. The other account is the Catalyst Model (Ferguson et al. 2008) which is based on the interaction between biological determinants, and social context. Interestingly, this model does not propose a causal link between, exposure to violent scenes does and violence. Instead exposure is said to shapes acts of violence which would have happened anyway, so playing a digital game with a "violent" contents may serve to provide an expression for it. The reviewers note that this model had not yet been subject to detailed empirical scrutiny at the time of their writing.

Turning to the empirical evidence, they describe the many studies as largely sharing a common design in that a group of psychology students were recruited to play a game (violent or otherwise), while typically having their physiological arousal measured (often by way of a GSR measure) and then they are asked to complete a questionnaire to measure their affective state. The review then considers the evidence for three kinds of "harm", namely the evidence for aggressive cognition, aggressive affect and violent behaviour. Considering these in turn, they note that measurements of aggressive cognition often take the form of a word completion task, an example of which is, supply the missing letter in the following, "explo_e". Here the missing letter might be "r" for explore or "d" for explode. If aggressive thinking has been activated we might expect more explosions than explorations. Aggression scores for participants can then be calculated for participants who have played violent or non-violent games. Many studies have been able to show the presence of aggressive-related associations in players of violent games. Although the US courts appear to like these "common-sense" measures they rejected them as evidence of such cognitions leading to violent intent.

The reviewers then turn to the large number of studies of aggressive affect (anger or hostility) which rely on participant self-reports. These studies have reported a mixture of clear confirmatory evidence of people reporting anger after playing games, mixed results or no evidence. However, a number of compounding factors in these studies have been identified, for example, Eastin (2007) has reported that group size and game mode (competitive vs. cooperative) have an effect on the reported feelings of anger. Overall, results linking violent digital games to aggressive affect showed smaller effects than other potential sources.

Finally, the evidence for playing violent games giving rise to aggressive behaviour was considered. As the reviewers note, inducing aggressive behaviour in the laboratory is fraught with ethical (and probably legal) problems, so experimenters are left to "approximate" it. One laboratory measure being the "Hot Sauce Paradigm" which involves measuring the quality of hot sauce a participant would use to prepare a cup of chili for another (fictional) person. Again, the evidence is uncertain or missing or weak.

Overall, the Elson and Ferguson are vocal in their criticism of the design of many of these studies and conclude that there is no good evidence that playing digital games leads to aggressive cognition or aggressive affect or aggressive behaviour in the real world.

4.4 Impressions

Wundt was the first to write about the primacy of affect: "When any physical process rises above the threshold of consciousness, it is the affective elements which as soon as they are strong enough, first become noticeable. They begin to force themselves energetically into the fixation point of consciousness before anything is perceived of the ideational elements … They are sometimes states of pleasurable or un-pleasurable character, sometimes they are predominantly states of strained expectation … the clear apperception of ideas in acts of cognition and the recognition *is always preceded by feelings.*" (Wundt 1897, pp. 243–244, my italics). So, for Wundt, affect appears before the apperceptive (we would probably use the term "cognitive" now) and there is abundant contemporary evidence for this.

What we make of each other

Of the many studies, most, though not all, have been concerned with the first impressions we form of each other. The first impressions we form of other people allow us to determine accurately and reliably another's sexual attractiveness (e.g. Berry 2000); sexual orientation (Rule and Ambady 2008); and physical attractiveness (Cunningham 1986). And it's not just about sex—well, it is actually in one way or another, as we also form impressions of people's trustworthiness (e.g. Basso et al. 2001); political affiliations (Ballew and Todorov 2007); personality (Borkenau et al. 2009); and competence (Cuddy et al. 2008). In short, we form first impressions of those we encounter, finding them attractive, trustworthy, threatening or not. These emotional responses may reflect what Searle (1983) calls intentions in action. Interestingly, these responses are not simple like/dislike judgments but are more complex. They can reasonably be interpreted as a means of readying the organism to deal with the world.

First impressions are formed quickly, for example, Zajonc (1980) has demonstrated that stimulus preferences can be elicited with exposure times as low as 1–5 ms. However most first impressions studies have focussed on the 50–500 ms range. Lindgaard et al. (2006), for example, has demonstrated that we are easily able to decide on the aesthetics of webpages in as little as 50 ms—one twentieth of a second (these are described more fully below). First impressions have also been shown to be reliable and accurate in a variety of test/re-test situations (e.g. Willis and Todorov 2006; Zajonc 1980).

LeDoux (1996) has also suggested that emotional "logic" is at work, concluding that "objects in the world may not necessarily be defined by their objective identity: what matters is how they are perceived" p. 116. Norman (2004) has made similar observations in his account of emotional design (and user experience) the foundational level of which is the visceral. He also describes the visceral level as being pre-reflective and independent of culture (and learning).

Finally, first impressions become lasting impressions (e.g. Sritharan et al. 2010) because, it is thought, that we store expectancy-violating experiences as exceptions-to-the-rule, such that the rule is treated as valid except for the specific context in which it has been violated. Together we seem to be able to form rapid, accurate and reliable impressions of each other in a fraction of a second and well before we before consciously aware of these judgments. Zajonc (1980) has demonstrated that preferences can be developed with minimal stimulus exposure in times as brief as 1–5 ms. This is not so much "first impressions" but "mere exposure". Comparing the descriptions of what Norman has in mind for his visceral design level and the very many mere exposure studies, it seems that these are likely to rely on different mechanisms.

Over the years, these very brief exposure effects have been shown to be extremely robust and it has been suggested that these may be the source of the "feeling" which accompany both emotional responses (please see Sect. 4.5). These impressions are affective, involuntarily and can indeed occur pre-attentively, that is, before the organism has had a chance to become aware of the stimulus or stimuli, for example, Ekman et al. (2013) has shown that emotional expressions begin to show in changes in facial musculature within a few milliseconds after exposure to a stimulus.

LeDoux (1996) has proposed a mechanism which he calls the "amygdala shortcut". The amygdala has been described as the gateway to sensory processing of emotions and is also known to play an important role at the interface between cognition and emotion (De Gelder et al. 2012). A small bundle of neurons have been identified that lead directly from the thalamus to the amygdala, allowing it to receive direct inputs (this is the shortcut) from the sensory organs and initiate a response before the stimuli have been interpreted by the neocortex. Hence, an affective response can be triggered far more quickly than a reasoned response (LeDoux 1996). This idea has been further developed by Daniel Goleman in his *Emotional Intelligence: Why It Can Matter More Than IQ* (1996) and described as the "amygdala hijack". Goleman uses the term to describe emotional responses from people which are immediate and overwhelming, and out of proportion with the scale of the stimulus.

First impressions of webpages

Lindgaard et al. (2006) conducted a series of studies to ascertain how quickly people form an appraisal of a web page's visual appeal. In a series of studies, participants rated the visual appeal of a series of web page. These pages had been previously rated for their visual appeal. In one study, a group of participants viewed the 25 highest-rated and 25 lowest-rated pages. While viewing each page for 500 ms, they assigned ratings to seven visual design characteristics. This established the reliability of visual appeal ratings and allowed the experimental team to select a subset of website home pages to use in the second study. The next study had two purposes—to determine the reliability of visual appeal ratings of the subset of 50 webpages and to begin to explore visual characteristics that may be related to visual appeal. However, of key interest is the final study which limited participants to view the pages for only 50 ms before asking them to rate their visual appeal. The researchers found ratings were highly correlated between the 50 and 500 ms conditions. Thus, visual appeal can be assessed within 50 ms, suggesting that web designers have about 50 ms to make a good first impression.

The halo effect

This long-term effect of a first impression is sometimes referred to as a "halo effect", particularly in the marketing and business research literature. The first impression formed is carried over to the evaluation of other attributes of products (Thorndike 1920). In the human decision-making and judgment literature, the phenomenon is typically termed a cognitive "confirmation bias". It occurs when participants search for confirmatory evidence supporting their initial hypothesis while ignoring contradictory evidence. Thus, in the presence of a very positive first impression, a person may disregard or downplay possible negative issues encountered. Potentially negative aspects such as errors are often overlooked.

Rosenzweig (2007), for example, discussing the halo effect in perceptions of real-world company performance cites a study in which if members of a group were told that their group's performance had been successful, they reported a greater degree of cohesiveness, better communication and more openness to change. Those who were told they had done badly described the reverse. In reality, both groups had exhibited similar levels of performance.

Among very many accounts in the historical psychological literature, lecturers described as higher rather than lower status are perceived as taller (Wilson 1968), and less severe punishments are reported to be imposed on transgressors who are smiling or perceived as attractive (Efran 1974; Forgas et al. 1983). Interestingly, Forgas (2011) reported findings that suggest that mood may have an influence on the halo effect. Positive affect, self-induced by the recall of happy memories, enhanced the halo effect whereas negative affect eliminated it. In discussing these results, and on the basis of earlier literature, Forgas argues that the halo effect is most likely to occur when people use rapid, automatic Gestalt-based processing and less likely when more "elaborated" judgements are made, concluding that moods have a significant effect on the style of processing adopted.

4.5 Feelings

A criticism of most accounts of affect is that they are disembodied, that is, the body is treated (if it is mentioned at all) as the means by which an emoting brain is carried about the world. Prinz (2004, p. 58) agrees writing that "In developing a theory of emotion, we should not feel compelled to supplement embodied states with meaningful thoughts: we should instead put meaning into our bodies and let perceptions of the heart reveal our situation in the world." This must be doubly the case with UX as we are likely to be physically engaged with technology.

However, this has not always been the case, as James (1884) originally described an emotion as a bodily event and the experience of that emotion—the feeling—as the perception of that bodily event; "the bodily changes follow directly the perception of the exciting fact, and ... our feeling of the same changes as they occur is the emotion". James famously insisted that "a purely disembodied emotion is a non-entity" (ibid., p. 23); if you imagine an emotion without its bodily symptoms, you will be left with a "cold and neutral state of intellectual perception". However, according to Colombetti and Thompson (2008), it was Cannon (he of the Cannon-Baird theory) who suggested that the differences in emotional feelings had to depend on something other than simple autonomic processes. This view, they claim, signalled the move towards the creation of the various disembodied accounts of emotion. The body had become a mere enhancer (their term) of the experienced intensity of the emotion.

Among the critics of these disembodied perspective are the advocates of enactivism and Colombetti in particular. She is among those who has observed that the study of emotion "tends to disregard the meaning-generating role of the body and to attribute this role only to separate abstract cognitive-evaluative processes" (p. 147). Yet, the body has always been present, for example, valence is regularly discussed as part of the emotional experience. Valence is usually described as positive or negative, that is, our emotions are experienced as being desirable or undesirable. A plausible understanding of this, she suggests, might be in terms of whether it feels good or feels bad. Thus, we might understand feelings as bodily sensations, or as Prinz (2004) has proposed *bodily appraisals* (very much in the spirit of James) which are bodily states that track meaning in the environment. Fear, for example, is the embodied appraisal that the escalating terrorist attacks makes international travel feels dangerous. Thus, feelings might play a role in modulating (cognitive) appraisals.

The role of the body

Studies in the 1970s began modestly demonstrating that, for example, when people were induced to adopt emotional facial expressions (to smile or frown), they also reported emotional feelings consistent with their expressions (e.g. Laird 1974). In the course of these studies, a number of participants reported that their thoughts and recollections became consistent with their expressions. This effect was captured in a voluntary comment by one participant who reported that, "When my jaw was clenched and my brows down, I tried not to be angry but it just fit the position. I'm not in an angry mood, but/found my thoughts wandering to things that made me angry".

In a subsequent series of experiments, Strack et al. (1988) asked participants to hold a pen in their mouths. Half of the participants were asked to hold the pen with their teeth, the others were asked to only use their lips. Holding the pen with the teeth produced a frown while holding it with the lips created a smile. They were then asked to conduct a number of simple tasks including rating the funniness of a series of line cartoons (from Gary Larson's the Far Side). Those who were induced to smile, rated the cartoons funnier than those who were frowning.

Somatic marker hypothesis

Moving from the role of facial muscular feedback, Damasio has proposed placing emotions in the body as part of his somatic marker hypothesis (SMH). Damasio (1994) writes, "somatic markers are a special instance of feelings generated from secondary emotions. Those emotions and feelings have been connected, by learning, to predict future outcomes of certain scenarios". Adding, "Somatic markers do not deliberate for us. They assist the deliberation by highlighting some options (either dangerous or favorable), and eliminating them rapidly from subsequent consideration" (p. 174). These somatic markers are learned so that when we think of a possible decision which has had a negative outcome for us in the past it is experienced as "an unpleasant gut feeling". Thus, automatically and based on what he describes as "conditioned avoidance", we tend not to make decisions leading to this kind of unpleasant event. Conversely, we tend to be attracted to events (and actions) that are associated with reward.

In a review of the somatic marker hypothesis, Dunn et al. (2006) have examined its underlying neural mechanism. The hypothesis proposed that a "somatic marker" bias signals arise from the body and it is these biased signals which help regulate decision-making in situations of bounded rationality. The SMH does not solely rely on the limbic system but it incorporates other brain regions including the ventro-medial prefrontal cortex, somato-sensory cortices, insula, and basal ganglia (Damasio 1998). Thus, Damasio has extended the function of the limbic system to include feedback from the other regions. Empirical support for the SMH is largely drawn from the use of the Iowa Gambling Task which was designed to measure decision-making (Bechara et al. 1996, 2005). Evidence from this task suggests a correlation between successful "gambling" and the development of somatic marker signals in healthy control participants. However, no such correlation was found in people with lesions to their ventromedial prefrontal cortex and this was linked to their poorer performance on the decision-making task. In all, there is some support for SMH but it is a little narrowly based.

An Enactive perspective

While there is a place for the body or our corporeality in affect, theory and evidence are piecemeal, however, Enactivism offers a coherent, though radical body of thought which might be helpful here.

Varela et al. (1991) created the concept of enaction which has had a significant effect in fields as diverse as biology (Thompson 2010), cognition (Varela et al. 1991), education (Bruner 1966) and consciousness (Stewart et al. 2010). Enaction is a very complex framework, complete with its own vocabulary and theoretical constructs. From the perspective of cognition/affect, it emphasizes the idea that the experienced world is the product of the mutual interactions among the physical make-up of the organism, its sensorimotor capabilities and the environment itself—a triadic construct, from which a number of important constructs have been derived. To consider its potential contribution to affect we need to consider a number of these concepts, specifically, that organisms are self-organising and that they do not encounter a ready-made world.

The first of these argues that the nervous system is self-organising, autonomous and maintains its own meaningful patterns of activation by means of a process described as autopoiesis (Maturana and Varela 1991). The term was devised by Maturana and Varela (1972) to define the self-maintaining behaviour of living cells and was introduced to the wider communities of HCI and artificial intelligence, as follows, "the phenomenon of autopoiesis is quite general. It can apply to systems existing in any domain in which we can identify unities and components (Winograd and Flores 1986). An autopoietic system holds constant its organisation and its boundaries through the continuous production of its components, if the autopoiesis is interrupted, the system's organization—its identity as a particular kind of unity-is lost, and the system disintegrates (dies). An autopoietic system that exists in physical space is a living system." (ibid., p. 45).

The second premise is the triadic coupling of brain-body-world which lies at the heart of their account and is concerned with "bringing forth a world". Its authors argue that, "Organisms do not passively receive information from their environments, which they then translate into internal representations. Natural cognitive systems are simply not in the business of accessing their world in order to build accurate pictures of it. They participate in the generation of meaning through their bodies and actions often engaging in transformational and not merely informational interactions; they enact a world" (Fantasia et al. 2014). From this reading, it becomes clear that enactive accounts do not treat the world as a given. There is no objective world to be experienced. Instead, it is, "something we engage in by moving, touching, breathing, and eating" (Varela et al. 1991, p. 8).

Against this background, Colombetti sees affectivity is fundamentally an expression of the key enactivist thinking. She argues that primordial affectivity is enactive, because it depends on the reciprocal relationship of an organism and its particular environment. Specially, affectivity is seen not just bring forth a world, but bringing forth a world "of significance" that it comprises more just the emotions, moods, and feelings. However, as affectivity depending on the organisation of life itself, this means that very simple systems (including a bacterium) are affective. Consequently, for Colombetti, the current definitions of affect are just too narrow, while it is likely that this definition may be too broad for many people.

4.6 Mood

Finally, Coyne (2016) in his *Mood and Mobility* writes that emotion is ephemeral but moods last. Mood is clearly an affective state but quite distinctly from the others (the exception, perhaps being temperament). Dreyfus (1991) observed that we can be in a mood but it is meaningless to write that there is a mood in us and another Heidegger scholar Bollnow (2011) writes that moods are neither inside the individual nor outside in the environment but lie in the individual in "his still undivided unity with his surroundings". We can also suffer from disorders of mood (e.g. Russo and Nestler 2013) but fortunately, moods can be stabilised pharmaceutically (e.g. Sanacora et al. 2017). Moods are also found explicitly in grammar, for example, the imperative (commanding) mood, or the subjunctive (possible or imaginative) moods. Coyne makes the important distinction between emotion (which he describes as personal and private) and mood which is often public. The public mood, for example, is a frequently encountered expression to which the media—social media in particular, politicians, and commentators often seek attune themselves. Such moods might include being interested, "ugly", enthusiastic, inspired, scared, hostile, ashamed or melancholy—but this list, of course, is not complete.

Although moods are persistent, we abhor stasis—we like a change of mood and Coyne writes that digital products are "complicit ... as instruments to influence, transmit and transform mood states" (p. 260). He also observes that digital products can also serve to highlight the "mood of the times". Moods can be transmitted and modified by and through pervasive digital media, particularly mobile devices and he gives the example of a Facebook® emoji accompanying a status update (whether the emoji is a matter of mood or feelings or emotions is, of course, moot).

He writes that melancholy could be considered as the quintessential mood. Melancholy is self-reflexive, and thus can be considered as a meta-mood. A meta-mood allows us to be aware of the fact, in this case, that we are melancholy and this in turn allows us to discriminate between this and other moods and may contribute to their regulation. Coyne suggests that Turkle's description of our dependency on technology for social interaction (discussed in Chap. 3) could be characterised as melancholy and further, that ubiquitous digital media seems to promote a state of melancholy

The "Penfield mood organ"

In Dick's (1968) *Do Androids Dream of Electric Sheep?* the "Penfield mood organ", is introduced and is described as a device which can induce any desired mood in people. While moods such as "an optimistic business-like attitude" and "the desire to watch television, no matter what is on", are available, the protagonist's wife selects hours of "existential despair" to match her loneliness.

Coyne also notes that well designed digital products can create a positive, "can-do" mood while Apple's products, for example, historically may have created a sense (mood) of playfulness—witness their colourful iMacs G3 of the late 1990s.

Similarly, online pornography can create a mood of arousal or disgust. This introduces the issue of the influence of media content and here music and mood are the best-known examples of this. Coyne argues that such relationships are probably not causal as other external factors have a role. However, social media content can trigger, sustain and fuel collective mood changes (cf. the role of social media in the so-called *Arab Spring*).

Befindlichkeit and Stimmung

Heidegger does not have a great deal to say about affect but does discuss mood in some detail for which he uses a pair of terms namely, Befindlichkeit and Stimmung, which might be translated as attunement and mood respectively. Befindlichkeit has been variously translated as "how one finds oneself", or "state-of-mind". It is what we are enquiring about when we ask someone, "how are you?" in everyday speech. In contrast, Stimmung or "mood"—is an enduring disposition rather than the short-lived "being in a mood". Together they allow us to make sense of the world without, of course, ever escaping our moods. Not being in any particular mood or not being concerned, is a mood. These are not the emotional expressions of Dewey which colour experience (as we discussed in Chap. 1) but are fundamental, as it is not possible for us not be in a mood. Downing (2000, p. 245) also helps here when tells us that mood is the ground against which things (figures) are disclosed, he writes "Moods are Heidegger's favourite example of a response to what matters in a situation, at least in part because they are so pervasive, intrusive and uninvited. A mood makes manifest not only how things are going (here and now); but also, the way in which these matters, and the extent to which it just has to be accepted.

Although it seems quite simple to categorise mood as just "persistent emotion", mood and emotion are different. Writing this sentence finds me in my usual mood (I would characterise it as calm and measured, while my wife would call it capricious) but I am not experiencing emotion. My mood points me at being accurate and clear in my writing but I feel a flicker of pleasure when I see that this chapter is nearly complete. Three affective states in a moment.

4.7   Conclusions

Given the range, complexity and importance of affect, it has been surprisingly poorly represented and understood within HCI and user experience.

In an everyday sense, Boehner et al. (2007) are right to observe that affect is often seen as the "dual of cognition" and write that if cognition within HCI is recognised as a social, interactionist phenomenon, then this must also be true for affect. Indeed, affect, for all its differences from cognition, can nonetheless be located within the "same information-processing frame" (p. 275) and is susceptible to measurement. If this were so, then we might have expected the development of something equivalent to GOMS[5] but nothing like it has been proposed.

However, their point is made well enough and their proposed alternative, which would recognise the emotion of "national pride, justifiable anger or shame" which has both social and cultural origins is really a plea to look at affect afresh.

It would be convenient to blame psychology for failing to present a coherent model of affect, after all, psychologists do not even agree on how many emotions there are, but that would be unfair. If affect is both the complement of cognition and is cognitive in its own right, the current state of understanding is no worse than we find in the many competing and complementary accounts of cognition (per se) that have been proposed. In short, this is difficult.

Hyde and Smith (1993) observe that Heidegger recognised emotions as "vehicles for the active sensibility of human beings; that is, they provide the perspectives for seeing the word as interesting, as something that matters and that warrants interpretation". They write that Heidegger does not see emotion as a psychical phenomenon but as the result of interaction between a person and the world concluding that, "an emotion orients a person towards the world in a "concernful" manner. From this perspective, emotions are a manifestation of our involvement with the world, and an appraisal of how things are going.

References

Aaker JL (1997) Dimensions of brand personality. J Mark Res 34(3):347–356
Anderson CA, Bushman BJ (2002) Human aggression. Annu Rev Psychol 53:27–51
Arnold MB (1960) Emotion and personality. Vol. I: Psychological aspects; Vol. II: Neurological and physiological aspects. Columbia University Press, New York
Arnould EJ, Price LL (1993) River magic: extraordinary experience and the extended service encounter. J Consum Res 20(1):24–45
Ballew CC II, Todorov A (2007) Predicting political elections from rapid and unreflective face judgments. PNAS 104(46):17948–17953
Bandura A, Walters RH (1963) Social learning and personality development
Bandura A, Ross D, Ross SA (1961) Transmission of aggression through imitation of aggressive models. J Abnorm Soc Psychol 63:575–582
Bard P, Rioch DM (1937) A study of four cats deprived of neocortex and additional portions of the forebrain. Bull Johns Hopkins Hosp 60:73–148
Bartneck C (2002) Integrating the OCC model of emotions in embodied characters. In: Workshop on virtual conversational characters, pp 39–48

---

[5]GOMS is the best known of the modelling techniques created to predict human performance (John and Kieras 1996). John (2003) describes the GOMS family as consisting of ideas for analysing and representing tasks in a way that is related to the stage model of human information processing (italics in the original). The components of GOMS are: goals—operators—methods and selection. A GOMS analysis begins with the user's goals and identifying the necessary operators and methods he or she will need to employ to accomplish those goals. On those occasions when there is more than one possible means of achieving a goal, a selection rule is applied.

Bartneck C, Forlizzi J (2004) A design-centred framework for social human-robot interaction. In: 13th IEEE international workshop on robot and human interactive communication, 2004. ROMAN 2004. IEEE, pp 591–594

Basso A, Goldberg D, Greenspan S, Weimer D (2001) First impressions: emotional and cognitive factors underlying judgments of trust in e-commerce. In: Proceedings of the 3rd ACM conference on electronic commerce. ACM Press, New York, pp 143–147

Bechara A, Tranel D, Damasio H, Damasio AR (1996) Failure to respond autonomically to anticipated future outcomes following damage to prefrontal cortex. Cereb Cortex 6(2):215–225

Bechara A, Damasio H, Tranel D, Damasio AR (2005) The Iowa Gambling Task and the somatic marker hypothesis: some questions and answers. Trends Cogn Sci 9(4):159–162

Bennett J (2001) The enchantment of modern life: attachments, crossings, and ethics. Princeton University Press, Princeton

Berry DS (2000) Attractiveness, attraction, and sexual selection: evolutionary perspectives on the form and function of physical attractiveness. Adv Exp Soc Psychol 32:273–342

Billieux J, Philippot P, Schmid C, Maurage P, De Mol J, Van der Linden M (2015) Is dysfunctional use of the mobile phone a behavioural addiction? confronting symptom-based versus process-based approaches. Clin Psychol Psychother 22(5):460–468

Blevis E (2007) Sustainable interaction design: invention & disposal, renewal & reuse. In: Proceedings of the SIGCHI conference on human factors in computing systems, San Jose, California, USA, 28 April–3 May 2007. ACM Press, New York, pp 503–512

Boehner K, DePaula R, Dourish P, Sengers P (2007) How emotion is made and measured. Int J Hum Comput Stud 65(4):275–291

Bollnow OF (2011) Human space (trans: Shuttleworth C). Hyphen Press, London

Borkenau P, Brecke S, Möttig C, Paelecke M (2009) Extraversion is accurately perceived after a 50-ms exposure to a face. J Res Pers 43:703–706

Bowen (n.d.) https://www.bowenresearch.com/studies.php

Bowlby J (1969) Attachment and loss: Vol. 1. Attachment. Basic Books, New York

Bradley MM, Lang PJ (1994) Measuring emotion: the self-assessment manikin and the semantic differential. J Behav Ther Exp Psychiatry 25(1):49–59

Bruner J (1966) Toward a theory of instruction. Belknap Press of Harvard University Press. ISBN 978-0674897007

Burroughs WJ, Drews DR, Hallman WK (1991) Predicting personality from personal posessions: a self-presentational analysis. J Soc Behav Pers 6(6):147

Bushman BJ, Gibson B (2010) Violent digital games cause an increase in aggression long after the game has been turned off. Soc Psychol Pers Sci 2(1):29–32

Cannon WB (1927) The James-Lange theory of emotions: a critical examination and an alternative theory. Am J Psychol 39(1/4):106–124

Carlson RA (1997) Experienced cognition. Psychology Press

Colombetti G, Thompson E (2008) The feeling body: towards an enactive approach to emotion

Coyne R (2016) Mood and mobility. MIT Press, Cambridge

Cuddy AJC, Fiske ST, Glick P (2008) Warmth and competence as universal dimensions of social perception: the stereotype content model and the BIAS map. In: Zanna MP (ed) Advances in experimental social psychology, vol 40. Academic Press, New York, pp 61–149

Cunningham MR (1986) Measuring the physical in physical attractiveness: quasi-experiments on the sociobiology of female facial beauty. J Pers Soc Psychol 50:925–935

Damasio A (1994) Descartes' error: emotion, reason, and the human brain. Putnam Press, New York

Damasio AR (1998) Emotion in the perspective of an integrated nervous system. Brain Res Rev 26 (2):83–86

Darwin C (1872/1965) The expression of the emotions in man and animals. Chicago University Press, Chicago

De Gelder B, Hortensius R, Tamietto M (2012) Attention and awareness each influence amygdala activity for dynamic bodily expressions—a short review. Front Integr Neurosc 6:54

Desmet P (2002) Designing emotions. Department of Industrial Design, Delft University of Technology

Desmet P, Hekkert P (2007) Framework of product experience. Int J Des 1(1):57–66

Deterding S, Dixon D, Khaled R, Nacke L (2011) From game design elements to gamefulness: defining gamification. In: Proceedings of the 15th international academic MindTrek conference: envisioning future media environments. ACM, pp 9–15

Dewey J (1934/1980) Art as experience. Perigee Books, New York (reprint)

Dick PK (1968) Do Androids Dream of Electric Sheep? Ballantine Books, New York. ISBN 0-345-40447-5

Donato G, Bartlett MS, Hager JC, Ekman P, Sejnowski TJ (1999) Classifying facial actions. IEEE Trans Pattern Anal Mach Intell 21(10):974–989

Downing G (2000) Emotion theory reconsidered. In: Wrathall M, Malpas J (eds) Heidegger, coping and cognitive science, vol 2. MIT Press, Cambridge, pp 245–269

Dreyfus HL (1991) Being-in-the-world: a Commentary on Heidegger's Being and Time, Division 1. MIT Press, Cambridge

Dunn BD, Dalgleish T, Lawrence AD (2006) The somatic marker hypothesis: a critical evaluation. Neurosci Biobehav Rev 30(2):239–271

Eastin MS (2007) The influence of competitive and cooperative group game play on state hostility. Hum Commun Res 33(4):450–466

Efran MG (1974) The effects of physical attractiveness on judgments in a simulated jury task. J Res Pers 8:45–54

Ekman P, Friesen WV, Ellsworth P (1972) Emotion in the human face: guidelines for research and an integration of findings. Pergamon

Ekman P, Friesen WV, Ellsworth P (2013) Emotion in the human face: guidelines for research and an integration of findings. Elsevier

Elson M, Ferguson CJ (2013) Twenty-five years of research on violence in digital games and aggression. Eur Psychol 19(1):1–14

Evans D (2002) Emotion: the science of sentiment. Oxford University Press, USA

Fantasia V, De Jaegher H, Fasulo A (2014) We can work it out: an enactive look at cooperation. Front Psychol 5:874. doi:10.3389/fpsyg.2014.00874

Ferguson CJ (2007) Evidence for publication bias in digital game violence effects literature: a meta-analytic review. Aggress Violent Beh 12(4):470–482

Ferguson CJ, Rueda SM, Cruz AM, Ferguson DE, Fritz S, Smith SM (2008) Violent digital games and aggression: causal relationship or byproduct of family violence and intrinsic violence motivation? Crim Justice Behav 35(3):311–332

Forgas JP (2011) She just doesn't look like a philosopher…? Affective influences on the halo effect in impression formation. Eur J Soc Psychol 41(7):812–817

Forgas JP, O'Connor KV, Morris SL (1983) Smile and punishment: the effects of facial expression on responsibility attribution by groups and individuals. Pers Soc Psychol Bull 9(4):587–596

Fournier S (1998) Consumers and their brands: developing relationship theory in consumer research. J Consum Res 24(4):343–373

Friesen WV (1972) Cultural differences in facial expressions in a social situation: an experimental test of the concept of display rules. Doctoral dissertation, University of California, San Francisco

Frijda NH (1986) The emotions. Cambridge University Press, New York

Frijda NH (1987) Emotion, cognitive structure, and action tendency. Cogn Emot 1(2):115–143

Frijda NH (2007) The laws of emotion. Erlbaum, Mahwah

Ge X, Ifenthaler D (2017) Designing engaging educational games and assessing engagement in game-based learning. In: Handbook of research on serious games for educational applications. IGI Global, pp 253–270

Goleman D (1996) Emotional intelligence: why it can matter more than IQ. Bantam Books, New York

Gosling SD, Ko SJ, Mannarelli T, Morris ME (2002) A room with a cue: personality judgments based on offices and bedrooms. J Pers Soc Psychol 82(3):379

Govers PCM (2004) Product personality Delft University of Technology, Delft

Govers PC, Schoormans JP (2005) Product personality and its influence on consumer preference. J Consum Mark 22(4):189–197

Hong KM, Townes BD (1976) Infants' attachment to inanimate objects: a cross-cultural study. J Am Acad Child Psychiatry 15(1):49–61

Hyde MJ, Smith CR (1993) Aristotle and Heidegger on emotion and rhetoric. In: Angus IH, Langsdorf L (eds) The critical turn: rhetoric and philosophy in postmodern discourse. SIU Press, pp 68–99

Isbister K (2016) How games move us: emotion by design. MIT Press

Isomursu M, Tähti M, Väinämö S, Kuutti K (2007) Experimental evaluation of five methods for collecting emotions in field settings with mobile applications. Int J Hum Comput Stud 65 (4):404–418

James W (1884) What is an emotion? Mind 9(34):188–205

John BE (2003) Information processing and skilled behaviour. In: Carroll JM (ed) HCI models, theories and frameworks. Morgan Kaufmann, San Francisco

John BE, Kieras DE (1996) The GOMS family of user interface analysis techniques: comparison and contrast. ACM Trans Comput-Hum Interact (TOCHI) 3(4):320–351

Jordan PW (1997) Putting the pleasure into products. IEE Review 43(6):249–252

Kemper TD (1987) How many emotions are there? Wedding the social and the autonomic components. Am J Sociol 93(2):263–289

Kleine SS, Baker SM (2004) An integrative review of material possession attachment. Acad Mark Sci Rev (1). Available at http://www.amsreview.org/articles/kleine01-2004.pdf

Kleine SS, Kleine RE III, Allen CT (1995) How is a possession "me" or "not me"? Characterizing types and an antecedent of material possession attachment. J Consum Res 22(3):327–343

Konok V, Gigler D, Bereczky BM, Miklósi Á (2016) Humans' attachment to their mobile phones and its relationship with interpersonal attachment style. Comput Hum Behav 61:537–547

Konok V, Pogány Á, Miklósi Á (2017) Mobile attachment: separation from the mobile phone induces physiological and behavioural stress and attentional bias to separation-related stimuli. Comput Hum Behav 71:228–239

Laird JD (1974) Self-attribution of emotion: the effects of expressive behavior on the quality of emotional experience. J Pers Soc Psychol 29(4):475

Lawson JF (2016) Review of Man(dis)connected: how technology has sabotaged what it means to be male, by Philip Zimbardo and Nikita D. Coulombe. Psychol Sex 7(4):297–299

Lazarus RS (1991) Emotion and adaptation. Oxford University Press, New York

Leder H, Nadal M (2014) Ten years of a model of aesthetic appreciation and aesthetic judgments: the aesthetic episode—developments and challenges in empirical aesthetics. Br J Psychol 105 (4):443–464

LeDoux J (1996) The emotional brain: the mysterious underpinnings of emotional life

Lee H, Cho CH (2017) An application of brand personality to advergames: the effect of company attributes on advergame personality. Comput Hum Behav 69:235–245

Lin J-H (2013) Do digital games exert stronger effects on aggression than film? The role of media interactivity and identification on the association of violent content and aggressive outcomes. Comput Hum Behav 29:535–543

Lindgaard G, Fernandes G, Dudek C, Brown J (2006) Attention web designers: you have 50 milliseconds to make a good first impression! Behav inf Technol 25(2):115–126

Low S, Altman I (1992) Place attachment: a conceptual Inquiry. In: Althman I, Low S (eds) Place attachment. Plenum, New York

Lutz C (1998) Unnatural emotions: everyday sentiments on a micronesian atoll and their challenge to western theory. University of Chicago Press, Chicago

MacLean PD (1949) Psychosomatic disease and the" visceral brain": recent developments bearing on the Papez theory of emotion. Psychosom Med 11(6):338–353

MacLean PD (1990) The triune brain in evolution: role in paleocerebral functions. Springer Science & Business Media

Mahlke S, Thüring M (2007) Studying antecedents of emotional experiences in interactive contexts. In: Proceedings of CHI '07. ACM, pp 915–918

Malhotra NK (1988) Self-concept and product choice: an integrated perspective. J Econ Psychol 9 (1):1–28

Maturana R, Varela F (1972) Autopoiesis and cognition (with preface by Sir Stafford Beer). D. Reidel Publishing Company (Holland, USA, England)

Maturana HR, Varela FJ (1991) Autopoiesis and cognition: the realization of the living, vol 42. Springer Science & Business Media

Mauss IB, Robinson MD (2009) Measures of emotion: a review. Cogn Emot 23(2):209–237

McCarthy J, Wright P, Wallace J, Dearden AM (2005) The experience of enchantment in human-computer interaction. Pers Ubiquit Comput 6:369–378

McGonigal J (2011) Reality is broken. Jonathan Cape

McGonigal J (2016) SuperBetter: how a gameful life can make you stronger, happier, braver and more resilient. HarperCollins, UK

Meschtscherjakov A (2009) Mobile attachment—emotional attachment towards mobile devices and services. In: Proceedings of the international conference on human-computer interaction with mobile devices and services. ACM, New York

Meschtscherjakov A, Wilfinger D, Tscheligi M (2014) Mobile attachment causes and consequences for emotional bonding with mobile phones. In: Proceedings of the 32nd annual ACM conference on human factors in computing systems. ACM, pp 2317–2326

Norman DA (2004) Emotional Design: why we love or hate everyday objects. Basic Books, New York

Norman DA, Draper SW (1986) User centred system design. New perspectives on human-computer interaction. L. Erlbaum Associates Inc., Hillsdale

Norman DA, Ortony A (2003) Designers and users: two perspectives on emotion and design. In: Proceedings of the symposium on foundations of interaction design at the Interaction Design Institute, Ivrea, Italy

Oatley K (1992) Best laid schemes: the psychology of emotions. Cambridge University Press, Cambridge

Oatley K, Johnson-Laird PN (1987) Towards a cognitive account of emotions. Cogn Emot 1: 29–50

Oatley K, Johnson-Laird PN (2014) Cognitive approaches to emotions. Trends Cogn Sci 18 (3):134–140

Odom W, Pierce J (2009) Improving with age: designing enduring interactive products. In: Extended abstracts of CHI '09. ACM Press, New York

Odom W, Pierce J, Stolterman E, Blevis E (2009) Understanding why we preserve some things and discard others in the context of interaction design. In: Proceedings of CHI '09. ACM Press, New York, pp 53–62

Ortony A, Turner TJ (1990) What's basic about basic emotions? Psychol Rev 97(3):315

Ortony A, Clore GL, Collins A (1988) The cognitive structure of emotions. Cambridge University Press

Panksepp J (1982) Toward a general psychobiological theory of emotions. Behav Brain Sci 5 (3):407–422

Papez JW (1937) A proposed mechanism of emotion. Arch Neurol Psychiatry 38(4):725–743

Pessoa L (2008) On the relationship between emotion and cognition. Nat Rev Neurosci 9 (2):148–158

Picard RW (1997) Affective computing. The MIT Press, Cambridge

Plutchik R (1980) Emotion: a psychoevolutionary synthesis. Harper & Row

Prinz J (2004) Gut reactions: a perceptual theory of emotion. Oxford University Press, Oxford

Ratcliffe M (2008) Feelings of being: phenomenology, psychiatry and the sense of reality. Oxford University Press, Oxford

Reisenzein R (2006) Arnold's theory of emotion in historical perspective. Cogn Emot 20(7):920–951

Rosenzweig P (2007) Misunderstanding the nature of company performance: the halo effect and other business delusions. Calif Manag Rev 49(4):6–20

Rule NO, Ambady N (2008) Brief exposures: male sexual orientation is accurately perceived at 50 ms. J Exp Soc Psychol 44:1100–1105

Russell JA (1980) A circumplex model of affect. J Pers Soc Psychol 39:1161–1178

Russell JA (1989) Measures of emotion. In: Plutchik R, Kellerman H (eds) Emotion: theory, research, and experience, vol 4. Academic Press, Toronto, pp 83–111

Russell JA (1996) Core affect and the psychological construction of emotion. Unpublished manuscript, Department of Psychology, University of British Columbia

Russell JA (2003) Core affect and the psychological construction of emotion. Psychol Rev 110 (1):145

Russell JA (2009) Emotion, core affect, and psychological construction. Cogn Emot 23(7): 1259–1283

Russell JA, Mehrabian A (1977) Evidence for a three-factor theory of emotions. J Res Pers 11 (3):273–294

Russo SJ, Nestler EJ (2013) The brain reward circuitry in mood disorders. Nat Rev Neurosci 14 (9):609–625

Sanacora G, Frye MA, McDonald W, Mathew SJ, Turner MS, Schatzberg AF, Summergrad P, Nemeroff CB (2017) A consensus statement on the use of ketamine in the treatment of mood disorders. JAMA psychiatry 74(4):399–405

Schachter S, Singer JE (2001) Cognitive, social and psychological determinants of emotional state. In: Parrott WG (ed) Emotions in social psychology. Psychology Press, Philadelphia, pp 76–97

Scherer KR (2004) Feelings integrate the central representation of appraisal-driven response organization in emotion. In: Manstead ASR, Frijda NH, Fischer AH (eds) Feelings and emotions: the Amsterdam symposium. Cambridge University Press, Cambridge, pp 136–157

Scherer KR, Schorr A, Johnstone T (eds) (2001) Appraisal processes in emotion: theory, methods, research. Oxford University Press

Searle JR (1983) Intentionality: an essay in the philosophy of mind. Cambridge University Press

Sirgy MJ (1982) Self-concept in consumer behavior: a critical review. J Consum Res 9(3):287–300

Sirgy MJ (1985) Using self-congruity and ideal congruity to predict purchase motivation. J Bus Res 13(3):195–206

Smith A (1759/2010) The theory of moral sentiments. Penguin

Sritharan R, Heilpern K, Wilbur CJ, Gawronski B (2010) I think I like you: spontaneous and deliberate evaluations of potential romantic partners in an online dating context. Eur J Soc Psychol 40(6):1062–1077

Stewart J, Stewart JR, Gapenne O, Di Paolo EA (eds) (2010) Enaction: toward a new paradigm for cognitive science. MIT Press

Strack F, Martin LL, Stepper S (1988) Inhibiting and facilitating conditions of the human smile: a nonobtrusive test of the facial feedback hypothesis. J Pers Soc Psychol 54:768–777

Suits B (2014) The grasshopper: games, life, and Utopia, 3rd edn. Broadview Press, Peterborough

Sylvester T (2013) Designing games: a guide to engineering experiences. O'Reilly Media, Inc.

Thompson E (2010) Mind in life: biology, phenomenology, and the sciences of mind. Harvard University Press

Thomson M (2006) Human brands: investigating antecedents to consumers' strong attachments to celebrities. J Mark 70(3):104–119

Thomson M, MacInnis DJ, Park CW (2005) The ties that bind: measuring the strength of consumers' emotional attachments to brands. J Consum Psychol 15(1):77–91

Thorndike EL (1920) The constant error in psychological ratings. J Appl Psychol 4:25–29

Turner P, Turner S (2011) My grandfather's iPod: an investigation of emotional attachment to digital and non-digital artefacts. In: Proceedings of the 29th annual european conference on cognitive ergonomics. ACM, pp 149–156

Turner P, Turner S (2013) Emotional and aesthetic attachment to digital artefacts. Cogn Technol Work 15(4):403–414

Varela FJ, Thompson E, Rosch E (1991) The embodied mind: cognitive science and human experience. MIT Press, Cambridge

Wallendorf M, Arnould EJ (1988) "My favorite things": a cross-cultural inquiry into object attachment, possessiveness, and social linkage. J Consum Res 14(4):531–547

Willis J, Todorov A (2006) First impressions making up your mind after a 100-ms exposure to a face. Psychol Sci 17(7):592–598

Wilson PR (1968) The perceptual distortion of height as a function of ascribed academic status. J Soc Psychol 74:97–102

Winograd T, Flores F (1986) Understanding computers and cognition: a new foundation for design. Ablex, Norwood

Wundt WM (1897) Outlines of psychology (trans: Hubbard Judd C). Available from http://psychclassics.yorku.ca/Wundt/Outlines/sec15.htm. Last retrieved 29 Aug 2017

Zajonc RB (1980) Feeling and thinking: preferences need no inferences. Am Psychol 35(2):15

Zimbardo P, Coulombe ND (2015) Man (dis)connected: how technology has sabotaged what it means to bemale. London, Rider

Chapter 5
Aesthetics

Art is a lie that makes us realize the truth.

Pablo Picasso

This chapter is concerned with our aesthetic experience of digital products. This is the third component of our account of user experience but unlike the other two elements (involvement and affect), there is no readily available psychology of aesthetics to draw upon. There is, instead, a jumble of overlapping ideas, frameworks, theories, and proposals and again, there is the perennial, and all too familiar problem of agreeing the definition of key terms and concepts. We might also have had the expectation that the philosophy of aesthetics is long established and a deep well of thought to draw upon, whereas it is actually relatively new, Carroll et al. (2012, p. 31) tell us that aesthetics "was born as a branch of philosophy in 1735 with Baumgarten's use of the term". However, and on a more positive note, the recent appearance of neuroaesthetics, as Zeki (1999) has argued very strongly, brings the prospect of creating a more complete account of aesthetics with an understanding of its neural basis.

"Digital Aesthetics"

Aesthetics is intrinsic to our experience of digital products and have attracted the attention of researchers who have written of it in remarkably similar ways but using widely divergent language. We might, however, begin by noting that aesthetics cannot be thought of as separate from any given digital product. Aesthetic objects as Saito (2001) has observed are not a set of special things, but rather are determined by our attitudes and experiences. A consequence of this view is that, as Stolnitz (1969, p. 27) claims, "anything at all, whether sensed or perceived, whether it is the product of imagination or conceptual thought, can become the object of aesthetic attention". Hallnäs and Redström (2002) agree when they recognise that with the growing ubiquity of computational things, that we need to be clear what it means for something to be present in our lives, as opposed to something we just

© Springer International Publishing AG 2017
P. Turner, *A Psychology of User Experience*, Human–Computer Interaction Series,
https://doi.org/10.1007/978-3-319-70653-5_5

use. They suggest the terms "use" and "presence" to distinguish between the two and we should note that this is yet another reminder that interaction is an inadequate description of our relationship with digital products. While use refers to a general description of a thing in terms of how it is employed, presence refers to existential definitions of a thing based on how we invite and accept it as a part of our digital world. From this perspective, they see aesthetics as providing a rationale for the choices we make ("I like this one more than the purple one").

Petersen et al. (2004) have proposed a similar distinction within aesthetics but this time they have distinguished between "use" and "appearance". They begin by presenting an overview of the concepts of aesthetics in HCI so as to situate their proposal for "aesthetic interaction" which is based in a pragmatist aesthetics (cf. Shusterman 1992). Drawing upon artistic theory as well as human computer interaction, they locate aesthetics in the everyday, writing, "In a pragmatist perspective aesthetics is a part of everyday life. It stems from a use-relationship. Aesthetic Interaction comprises the views that aesthetics is instrumental and that artefacts are appropriated in use." Continuing this theme, Petersen et al. (2008) have also observed that the ubiquity of digital technology in everyday life has changed the ways in which we interact with it. As computer systems change from being very specific tools for work to ubiquitous computational objects, the nature of the interaction changes too. They give an example of the interactive pillow designed by Redstrom (2008) to illustrate this, "Interactive Pillow is a reinterpretation of what it means to hug a pillow [it is transformed] into an act of communication … These pillows come in pairs that are wirelessly connected to each other, and when one of them is hugged, the other will light up. We are dealing with new devices and new qualities of use which are […] related to emotional qualities, to experiential qualities, and to aesthetic qualities …".

In contrast, to treating aesthetics as a pattern of use/perception/appearance, Lavie and Tractinsky (2004) have sought to differentiate between classical and expressive aesthetics. The former, they describe as referring to traditional aesthetic notions which emphasises orderly and clear design, while expressive aesthetics is associated with the design's creativity and originality. Classical aesthetics embraces principles such as consistency and the use of a structured layout, symmetry, clean and clear design (this is quite like the definition of use proposed by Hallnäs and Redström); whereas expressive aesthetics is "manifested by the designer's creativity and originality and by the ability to interface qualities, such as 'beautiful', 'challenging' and 'fascinating'" (again, recalling "presence").

Finally, Ulrich (2007) defines the aesthetics of an artefact as the immediate feelings evoked when experiencing it via the sensory system. He considers aesthetic responses to be different from (other) cognitive responses in that they are rapid and involuntary. Aesthetic responses are an aggregate assessment biased either positively (e.g., beauty or attraction) or negatively (e.g., ugliness or repulsion) and not a nuanced multi-dimensional evaluation. This, of course, brings us full circle by equating the aesthetics of an artefact with perception, remind us that the word aesthetics from the Greek aisthesthai "perceive".

The Structure of This Chapter

After this introduction, this chapter has five sections. We begin by considering the origins of aesthetics from an evolutionary psychological perspective and consider why evolution has provided us with an interest in beauty. Then we consider what there is of the psychology of aesthetics and the nature of aesthetic experience in particular, before the reflecting on the nature of the "aesthetic turn" in HCI. This may have begun with a humble ATM study. The fourth section is a discussion of embodied aesthetics, when we move beyond the narrowly visual to "the feeling body" and consider what embodiment and enactive thought have to offer. We conclude with an introduction to neuroaesthetics which argues that the goal of the artist and the neuroscientist are one and the same as both.

5.1 Origins

Our sense of the aesthetic is a product of our evolution and to understand it, as Dutton puts it, we need to "reverse-engineer" it to explain how it became established. So, we will approach the origins of aesthetics from an evolutionary psychological perspective. The use of this kind of analysis (or reverse engineering) prompts a caveat. While it must be the case that any given specific sense or capability is the product of our evolution, it is difficult to avoid the feeling that we are reading a modern "just-so" story—of the "How the elephant got his trunk" variety (Kipling 1902). Of course, in a very real sense we are, but there is (surely) a place in scientific discourse for these kinds of stories. After all, we could describe a "just-so" story is an hypothesis wrapped in a compelling narrative. Anyway, back to the evidence.

The usual starting point for this kind of analysis is to assume that the aesthetics sense provides a reproductive advantage to our ancestors, an example of which is that we find symmetry attractive in potential mates. This preference is supported by the evidence that facial symmetry, for example, is correlated with reproductive health (e.g. Scheib et al. 1999), and so it is plausible that preferring symmetrical faces is an aesthetic adaptation that is likely to result in higher reproductive success (Thornhill and Gangestad 1993). Then, in the minds of evolutionary psychologists at least, this preference for symmetry can be seen as an adaptation which we have extend to the creation and enjoyment of works of art, entertainment and the design of the latest smart phone.

However, Dutton (2009) reminds us that evolution has at its disposal a number of different mechanisms, namely, natural selection and sexual selection. Natural selection relies on random mutation and selective retention and can explain our fondness for fast food and sugary snacks and our revulsion at the smell of rotting meat, or our fear of spiders. However, sexual selection contradicts this, and the most famous example is the origins of the peacock's exuberant tail. The tail did not evolve for survival (as it is cumbersome and awkward) but instead it is the result of the mating choices made by peahens. Peahens prefer flashy tails (the number of eye spots appears to be the crucial element), so peacocks with such tails have a chance to reproduce with spot-loving peahens before being eaten by the local wild dogs.[1] Thus, the experience of beauty is one of the ways that evolution has of arousing and sustaining interest, in order to encourage us toward making the most adaptive decisions for survival and reproduction or has he puts it, "Beauty is nature's way of acting at a distance".

And we can see the hand of nature all too easily, as management often assume that beautiful people are more likely to be more successful in their jobs (or are just prone to be over-promoted) and the attractive are judged to be better parents solely on the basis of their looks. Eagly et al. (1991) have presented evidence from a meta-analysis that shows that people believe that a person's beauty is positively related to their social competence, and their … adjustment, potency, intellectual competence, and general "goodness".

Bloch (1995) appears to agree with this as he writes that "a good design attracts consumers to a product, communicates to them, and adds value to the product by increasing the quality of the usage experiences associated with it" (p. 16). He then goes on to provide examples of these factors ranging from Swatch wristwatches, to the early Apple Macintosh computers, and the long-lasting appeal of the Rolling Stones. Again, in *The Value of Good Design* (Design Council 2017) we find "Good design at the front-end suggests that everything is in order at the back-end, whether or not that is the case" and conversely, "Problems with visual design can turn users off so quickly that they never discover all the smart choices you made with navigation or interaction design." The public would seem to be in step with these observations as the UK design council have reported that 77% of people agree with the statement, "people work more productively in well-designed offices" and 72% of people agree that "well-designed houses will increase in value quicker than average. Finally, the "Stanford Credibility Project" as conducted by the university of the same name recruited more than 2500 participants as part of a study to understand how people assess the credibility of a website. Their findings again underline the importance of an attractive visual design, "Nearly half of all consumers (or 46.1%) in the study assessed the credibility of sites based in part on the appeal of the overall visual design of a site, including layout, typography, font size and colour schemes. Beautiful graphic design will not salvage a poorly functioning Web site. Yet, the study shows a clear link between solid design and site credibility." So, beauty does appear to be a bellwether of other useful and desirable traits.

---

[1]This *either* natural *or* sexual selection has been challenged. Zahavi (1975) has pointed out that only the fittest peacocks would be able to maintain the weight and inconvenience of large tails.

5.1.1 The Savannah Hypothesis

Further to our interest in beautiful things, Orians (1986) has proposed the "savannah hypothesis" which concerns the type of landscape which we all would find intrinsically pleasurable. Dutton notes that the original idea for this dates to the work of Appleton and his *The Experience of the Landscape* (1975). His hypothesis is that this landscape has much in common with the savannahs and woodlands of East Africa where much of early human evolution occurred.

A savannah provides open spaces of low grasses interspersed with thickets of bushes and groupings of trees and the presence of water directly in view, or evidence of water nearby or in the distance. This landscape ideally also has an opening in at least one direction to an unimpeded vantage on the horizon, together with evidence of animal and bird life; and a diversity of greenery, including flowering and fruiting plants. These preferences turn out to be more than just vague, general attractions toward generic scenes, instead, they are notably specific. African savannahs are not only the probable scene of a significant portion of human evolution, they are to an extent the habitat meat-eating hominids evolved for; savannahs contain more protein per square mile than any other landscape type. Moreover, savannahs offer food at close to ground level, unlike rain forests, tropical or temperate, which are more easily navigable by tree-dwelling apes. Human beings are less attracted to absolutely open, flat grasslands and more toward a moderate degree of hilly undulation, suggesting a desire to attain vantage points for orientation. The type of savannah that is ideal appears to be the very savannah imitated not only in paintings and calendars but in many public parks and golf courses.

There is another source of support for this hypothesis which comes from Komar and Melamid who surveyed the artistic preferences of people in ten countries. Participants in their study were asked what they would like to see a picture of, whether they preferred interior or landscape scenes, what kinds of animals they liked, favourite colours, what sorts of people they enjoyed seeing depicted—famous or ordinary, clothed or nude, young or old—and so forth. at the end of this process, Komar and Melamid claimed to have captured a reliable report on the artistic preferences of "close to two billion people". The output took the form of creating paintings reflecting the "most" and the "least wanted".

The composition of the most-wanted painting was a landscape with water, people, and animals and the world's favourite colour appears to be blue. Their creation of America's Most Wanted, comprised George Washington on a grassy area beside a river or lake. Near him are three young people, and in the water, is a pair of deer. This preference for a lush blue landscape type which is found across the world is claimed to be evidence of our innate preference for it.

5.1.2   Elegant, Useless Axes

A final evolutionary perspective can be found in Dutton's TED talk (2009) on Acheulian hand axes.[2] These axes were originally found in the Olduvai Gorge in East Africa, and may be as much as 2.5 million years old. They were created by people to a design which remained, more or less, unchanged for about one million years, until a more advanced form of humanity was to emerge. Dutton tells us that they have been unearthed in their thousands, scattered across Asia, Europe and Africa, indeed almost everywhere *Homo erectus* and *Homo ergaster* roamed. He argues that, the sheer numbers of these axes suggest that their use cannot simply be limited to butchering animals, particularly as, unlike other Pleistocene tools, the axes show little evidence of use and indeed some are too big to use for butchery. In answer to question, "what were these artefacts for?"—he proposes that is these may be the earliest known works of art, that is, objects which have been created so that they could be admired for their craftsmanship.

Some archaeologists have voiced similar sentiments, for example, Corbey et al. (2008) have estimated that 1 or 2% shows symmetry and regularity beyond practical needs (these are enormous numbers, given the total amount of hand axes). Currie (2009) is a little more sceptical but not entirely unsympathetic as he describes a particular hand axe as, "a piece of worked stone, shaped as an elongated tear drop, roughly symmetrical in two dimensions, [...]. In size and shape it would not have been a useful butchery implement, and is worked on to a degree out of proportion to any likely use". For Currie, this is not "early work of art" but does suggest evidence of an "aesthetic sensibility".

Figure 5.1, is an image of a Neolithic hand-axe which is delightful to hold. It was created for a right-handed individual and may have been of practical value (possibly) (Fig. 5.1).

Figure 5.2, in contrast, is an image of a ceremonial, non-utilitarian axehead from 3000 BC. It has been carefully formed from volcanic basalt and is wonderfully smooth. It seems to have little practical value. Both axes are aesthetically pleasing (Fig. 5.2).

Burke and Ornstein (1997), in their *The Axemaker's Gift*, develop Dutton's proposition where they argue that the use of tools has had a very significant and enduring effect on our species, writing, "In prehistory, when human beings first began to make tools, they changed [...] "natural selection" permanently. [...] the axe introduced an artificial change in the way individual talents developed. (p. 19) This change to natural selection relied on the fact that those who could make tools were in greater demand than those without such skills and were rewarded proportionately. Consequently, their offspring stood a better chance of surviving and passing on these talents. They go on to speculate that the physical and cognitive skills acquired from the preparation of flint tools which requires a very precise

---

[2]*The reader is strongly encouraged to watch this talk as it is filled with wonderful animated cartoons created by Andrew Park,*https://www.ted.com/talks/denis_dutton_a_darwinian_theory_ of_beauty.

Fig. 5.1 A Neolithic hand axe from about 8000BC (from author's collection)

Fig. 5.2 A ceremonial hand axe from about 3000BC (from author's collection)

sequence of steps may have found expression elsewhere. For example, they suggest that the alphabet, the sequential ordering of phonemes, made "a special contribution to the human ability to dissect and reshape the world" (1997, p. 71). With the Greek alphabet we had, for the first time, an easy to use external storage medium replacing oral traditions (and the much more difficult to use hieroglyphic systems) which allowed us to separate thinker from thought and within this the beginnings of philosophy. Calvin who quotes Kathryn Morton, draws attention to the range of abilities which depend on sequencing: "the first sign that a baby is going to be a human being and not a noisy pet comes when he begins naming the world and demanding the stories that connect its parts. Once she knows the first of these he will instruct his teddy bear, enforce his worldview on victims in the sandlot, tell himself stories of what he is doing as he plays and forecast stories of what he will do when he grows up. He will keep track of the actions of others and relate deviations to the person in charge." (Calvin 2006, p. 88).

5.1.3 A Psychedelic Footnote

A plausible source of insight into the importance of visual imagery, and hence of art and of aesthetics, may lie with the subversion of everyday consciousness (Lewis-Williams 2002). The ingestion of psychotropic substances (e.g. "magic mushrooms"), extreme drumming or chanting or a simple migraine may be accompanied in an hallucination (or scintillating scotoma in the case of a migraine) overlaying the everyday world. Speaking from first-hand experience, a migraine headache is often preceded by a visual disturbance involving characteristic a flashing zig-zag pattern projected into mid-air and is usually associated with a grey arc of cloudiness. These patterns have been found in aboriginal art across the world. Lewis-Williams (p. 637) writes that, "… people see iridescent geometric percepts that derive from the wiring of the brain. […] Their form is independent of their cultural context. Next, subjects feel as if they are passing through a tunnel or vortex. Finally, along with persisting entopic phenomena, subjects see full-blown hallucinations of animals, people, monsters, and compound images". From an hallucination projected on a cave-wall to drawing these geometric shapes on the cave-wall seems to be a small step and having viewed many examples of cave-art myself, I recognise the work of my fellow migraineurs.

5.2 Towards a Psychology of Aesthetics

Arnheim has confidently proposed that a psychology of art was a reasonable ambition, writing that "art, as any other activity of the mind, is subject to psychology, accessible to understanding, and needed for any comprehensive survey to mental functioning", then why not aesthetics too (1966, p. 2).

Historically, the psychological study of aesthetics has been subject to a series of fits and starts. It got off to a promising beginning with Fechner's work in the 1870s, and as Leder and Nadal (2014) note, he developed the theoretical and methodological foundations for understanding both art and aesthetics writing that "Structurally, works of art demonstrate concepts at both higher and lower levels, which can be interrelated, and as a result diversity can result not just from greater variety in the underlying sensory contents, but also from a greater number of higher-level relationships; that is, as it were, from both the breadth and the height of the structure".

However, the study of aesthetics was not to flourish as it was subject to the heavy hand of Behaviourism which effectively snuffed it out until Berlyne's revival in the late 1960s. Daniel Berlyne was an interesting psychologist who proposed a number of unusual psychologies, including humour, curiosity and, of course, aesthetics. As regards aesthetics, he observed that although psychologists have considered the production of art, their focus has primarily been on the artists' motivation or various measures of their creativity. Berlyne (1974) was to revive the empirical interest in art by creating his own theoretical framework based around an arousal-pleasure dimension which parallels Hassenzahl's (2004) contemporary treatments of hedonism.

More recently, Leder and Nadal (2014) have usefully distinguished between art and aesthetics, observing that the terms are frequently used almost interchangeably within the psychological literature, and while their association is understandable, they are most definitely not synonyms. Art, for example, is often appreciated for reasons other than its aesthetics and many non-artistic objects, of course, can be appreciated for their aesthetics. They write that the psychology of art, "aims to characterise the psychological mechanisms involved in the appreciation of art, such as grasping an artwork's symbolism, identifying its compositional resources, or relating to it to its historical context" (p. 445). This stands in contrast with the psychology of aesthetics which, "aims to identify and describe the psychological mechanisms that allow humans to experience and appreciate a broad variety of objects and phenomena, including utensils (sic), commodities, designs, other people, or nature, in aesthetic terms (beautiful, attractive, ugly, sublime, picturesque and so on)".

5.2.1 Aesthetic Experience

Cinzia and Vittorio (2009, p. 682) define an aesthetic experience as to "perceive-feel-sense" which foregrounds the respective roles of the sensorimotor, emotional and cognitive systems. Chatterjee (2011) prefers to define it as "the perception, production, and response to art, as well as interactions with object and scenes that evoke an intense feeling, often of pleasure". In contrast, Bergeron and Lopes (2012) suggest that there are three dimensions to an aesthetic experience, namely, the evaluative, the phenomenological (or affective) and a semantic dimension. They also note that there is no reason to suppose that all three dimensions are required in every instance. Chatterjee and Vartanian (2014) also offer their own "aesthetic triad" proposal (this time from a neurological perspective) suggesting that aesthetic experiences arise from the interaction among sensory-motor, emotion-valuation and meaning-knowledge neural systems.

However, perhaps the most comprehensive treatment of aesthetic experiences is from Leder et al. (2004) which was reviewed and revised in 2014 (Leder and Nadal 2014) in the light of new experimental methods which were developed in the interim.

An aesthetic experience, Leder tell us, begins before the actual perception, with the "social discourse that configures expectations, anticipations, and an aesthetic orientation" (p. 445). An aesthetic experience also occurs in context, which also serves to shape those expectations and orientation, and to create an environment that can contribute to heightening the artistic status of an object. Unlike many other accounts, Leder's model situates the psychological mechanisms in context. This can be seen in Fig. 5.3.

The model is complex and if we confine ourselves to the psychological aspects, we can see that in relies on several stages of perceptual processing which is concerned with grouping, symmetry analysis, and a range of other perceptual features that are relevant to aesthetic appreciation. The next stage involves the analysis of familiarity, prototypicality and meaning and the integration of information from memory. The next stages are concerned with classification and interpretation. Finally, the "output" from the cognitive system is an aesthetic judgement while the affective system produces an "aesthetic emotion" (Fig. 5.3).

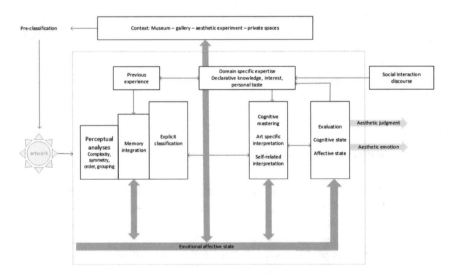

Fig. 5.3 Redrawn from "Model of aesthetic experiences" (Leder and Nadal 2014)

5.3 The Aesthetic Turn

Aesthetics, with respect to digital technology, began to appear as an issue in the early years of the millennium as witnessed by the publication of the Aesthetic Computing Manifesto (Fenwick 2003) which itself was a result of the Dagstuhl Aesthetic Computing Workshop held in 2001 but, it should be said that, neither are very recognisable as a contemporary statement of aesthetics.

In the main, aesthetics within HCI/UX has often tended to been a little conservatively. Until recently, aesthetics was not a feature of human computer interaction, indeed, it had managed to neglect it pretty comprehensively. On those occasions when it was considered, it was largely limited to the visual modality. This is very much a case of "aesthetics is how it looks" which, of course, is resonant with the original meaning of the word. However, as we have seen in the preceding chapters, the last 25 years or so have witnessed successive attempts to incorporate non-utilitarian aspects, such as aesthetics, into our use with digital products. Udsen and Jørgensen (2005) have claimed that we have witnessed a turn to the aesthetic within HCI. They suggest that this turn has taken four forms, towards the cultural; the functionalist approach; the experiential approach and finally towards what they describe as the "techno-futurist" approach.

Udsen and Jørgensen highlight Brenda Laurel whose most celebrated work has been to suggest a parallel between the use of technology and a theatrical performance which she describes in her *Computers as Theatre* (1993). She has also suggested that interactive systems should provide the users with "pleasurable engagement" through the use of interface metaphors of "both emotional and intellectual appeal". In all, she argued for the interface to be treated as an "expressive form" and a highly composite hybrid of cultural experimentation and emerging (HCI) standards—gone is the dull, neutral screen. In contrast, the functionalist approach is typified by Jordan's *Designing Pleasurable Products* (2003) which explores the relationship between product design and user pleasure. Beautiful user interfaces have become the means to an end is pleasure from which ease of use would follow (we explore this perspective in more detail below).

The experiential approach, the authors tell us, concerned "promoting new ways of communicating immaterial messages and experiences through emotional frictions, engaging interactions and seductive means" (p. 209). An example of this seduction is offered, in Plumb Design's *Visual Thesaurus* (Thinkmap 2017) which shows the result of a text search as a "moving, organic structure that encourages users to examine related words"—the visual presentation acting as the vehicle of seduction (Khaslavsky and Shedoff 1999). The final category is described as "techno-futurist". Of the four perspectives, this is the least well defined and is described as "philosophically inspired". The argument is that as technology becomes truly ubiquitous (following Weiser's paradigm), our experience of it will change. Here, the work of Paul Dourish comes to the fore (cf. his *Where the action is*, 2001) with its emphasis on issues such as embodiment and the phenomenological traditions of Husserl and Merleau-Ponty.

While recognising that these four forms have their own philosophies, traditions and have been realised in different kinds of user interfaces, Udsen and Jørgensen also conclude that the aesthetics of these digital products is now just a matter of everyday life which is very much the perspective we have adopted reflecting the work of Hallnäs and Redstom, and Petersön.

5.3.1   Attractive Things Work Better

Arguably, it has been the functionalist perspective which has emerged dominant. Norman has told us unequivocally that attractive things work better (2004), implying, perhaps, that aesthetics trumps usability. This claim has important consequences and may have had its origins with the work of two Japanese researchers, Kurosu and Kashimura (1995) and the subsequent work of Tractinsky in Israel.

The Japanese researchers developed and evaluated a number of different ATM (cash machines) keypad layouts which were identical in function, the number of buttons how they worked, but differed in the attractiveness of the layout. They found that the attractively presented layouts were easier to use than the functionally equivalent unattractive ATMs. The story, as Norman tells it that these results were intrigued the Israeli researcher Noam Tractinsky who assumed that the experiment was flawed. Perhaps, he is said to have thought, the result would be true of Japanese, but this could not be true of Israelis. He suggested that as aesthetic preferences are culturally dependent and "Japanese culture is known for its aesthetic tradition," but Israelis? Israelis, he tells us, are action oriented—they don't care about beauty (his words). So Tractinsky replicated the experiment after obtaining the Japanese ATM layouts, translating the Japanese into Hebrew, and designed a new experiment, with rigorous methodological controls. However, not only did he replicate the Japanese findings, but the results were stronger in Israel than in Japan, contrary to his belief that beauty and function "… were not expected to correlate".

Norman's subsequent work has been to investigate the role of aesthetics in design from the perspective of our affective response to it. His reasoning that it is our emotional systems which provide us with feedback when we are solving problems—such as using a digital product. So, he argued, if we like the appearance of a digital product, this produces a change to our emotional state which is communicated to our cognitive system. Norman elaborates, telling us that, "what many people don't realize is that there is a strong emotional component to how products are designed and put to use" (p. 5), and that "the emotional design side of design may be more critical to a product's success than its practical elements". So, this is why he tells us that attractive things work better and why his book on aesthetics is entitled *Emotional Design*. In an accompanying, and very entertaining, TED talk he has proposed a possible mechanism for this, telling us that when we are anxious we secrete neurotransmitters which encourage us to think depth-first. However, when you are happy (and I quote) "you squirt dopamine into prefrontal lobes which makes you a breadth-first problem solver: you're more susceptible to interruption;

you do out-of-the-box thinking. That's what brainstorming is about, right? With brainstorming we make you happy, we play games, and we say, "No criticism," and you get all these weird, neat ideas". So, if we find the digital product we are using to be a source of pleasure, we tend to tend to use it more creatively (Norman TED talk 2003).

5.3.2 Norman's Teapots

Norman's approach to emotional design has been developed (in part) from reflections on the design of his teapots. He tells us that he has a collection of teapots and he uses three of them to illustrate three different aspects of emotional design.

What he describes as the visceral level corresponds to the first impressions of a product. At this level people do not think about a product, but spontaneously judge, if they like or dislike it. The visceral level is independent of cultural aspects and is equal for everyone. Norman locates this class of response in "the simplest and most primitive part of the brain" and describes it as "genetically determined" (p. 29). This definition distinguishes the operation of the visceral level from other treatments of first impressions. The visceral level does not reason (because it cannot) and, instead, works by "pattern matching". Norman then provides (which he describes as his best guesses) two lists of situations and objects which we are genetically programed to like or dislike (here I am quoting directly from his book pp. 29, 30): we like "warm, comfortably lit places, caresses, attractive people and rounded, smooth objects". We dislike "sudden, unexpected loud sounds or bright lights, looming objects (that is, things which appear to be about to hit the observer), sharp objects, misshaped human bodies and snakes and spiders". Norman concludes that these are pre-dispositions rather than fully fledged mechanisms. (An alternative formulation to this mechanism is discussed in Sect. 5.4.)

This next level of design is about use and is described as the behavioural level. He writes that people may seek to appraise a products functionality and issues such as ease of use of the product come to the fore. This level of use corresponds to what Norman describes in detail in *The Psychology of Everyday Design* (1988). While Norman calls this the behavioural level it might also be called the cognitive except that he introduces an incongruous aesthetic element. He suggests that function, understandability and usability are three of the four major components of this level —which is consistent with his treatment of mental models and then adds "physical feel" as a four component. He also specifically uses the image of someone showering and enjoying "the sensual pleasure, the feel—quite literally—of the water streaming across the body" (p. 70). Yet on the page before, he tells us that on this level, "Appearances does not really matter" (p. 69). So, visual appeal—classical aesthetics do not seem to be relevant here but haptic appeal—embodied aesthetics (perhaps)—are. This is a little difficult to square with his assertion that "Attractive things work better" which explicitly links appearance and use.

Finally, comes the reflective level which "covers a lot of territory. It is all about message, about culture, and about the meaning of a product or its use. For one, it is about the meaning of things, the personal remembrances something evokes. For another, very different things, it is about self-image and the message a product sends to others". So, at this level, consciousness takes part in the process, with people actively endeavouring to understand and interpret things often in the context of past experiences and imagined future actions. The definition of this level is very similar to the more comprehensive definitions of UX we encountered in Chap. 1.

It is important that we recognise that Norman is writing about design and not about psychology, yet despite this, his model appears to be an appeal to the triune model of the brain as proposed by MacLean (1949, 1990). The triune brain account sees the brain as consisting of three phylogenetically distinct complexes or groups of neural structures. The most ancient is reptilian complex (the R-complex), next is the paleo-mammalian complex (limbic system), and finally is the neo-mammalian complex (neocortex). It is proposed that these structures have evolved sequentially. Although this is no longer held to be an accurate account of the development of the brain, it has proved to be popular and enduring in popular science (cf. Carl Sagan's excellent *The Dragons of Eden*).

5.3.3 Distinguishing Between Function And Fun

Hassenzahl (2004) wrote that, "A product can be perceived as pragmatic because it provides effective and efficient ways to achieve behavioural goals. Moreover, it can be perceived as hedonic because it provides stimulation by its challenging and novel character or identification by communicating important personal values to relevant others", p. 322.

Hassenzahl proposes that when we make judgments about digital products we do so on the basis of the product's features which include how it looks, its content, functionality, interaction together with personal expectations or standards. These judgements in turn can be partitioned into two distinct attribute groups which he describes as, pragmatic and hedonic attributes. The pragmatic attributes are connected to the users' need to achieve goals and goal achievement requires utility and usability. So, a product that allows for effective and efficient goal-achievement is perceived as pragmatic. In contrast, hedonic attributes are primarily related to the users' self. They can be further subdivided into stimulation and identification. Stimulation, novelty, and challenge are a prerequisite of personal development. Identification addresses the human need to express one's self through objects. This self-presentational function of products is entirely social; individuals want to be seen in specific ways by relevant others. Thus, a product can be perceived as pragmatic because it provides effective and efficient ways to achieve behavioural goals. It can be perceived as hedonic because it provides stimulation and/or identification by communicating important personal values.

5.4 Embodied Aesthetics

Our embodiment plays a crucial role in the aesthetic experience, an observation which is unlikely to come as much of a surprise to the great artists (e.g. Rizzolatti and Sinigaglia 2007; Freedberg and Gallese 2007; Kirsch et al. 2016; Gallese 2017). Michelangelo, for example, is said to have endowed his sculptures with the impression that they were struggling to free themselves from the blocks of stone which held them. Similarly, Jackson Pollock's "action paintings" embodies their creation, his work reflects the physical act of painting with his scattering, spraying, dripping or pouring (of paint) being implied and captured on the canvas. As the Pollock himself puts it, "The painting has a life of its own. I try to let it come through". However, research and reflection also suggest that people feel (empathise) a physical response or resonance to images of, for example, injury or mutilation and the same mechanism may to be at work when men enjoy pornography (Bocher et al. 2001).

A key theme in embodied aesthetics has been the research into mirror neurons. The presence of mirror neurons has been reported in macaque monkeys for some years and more recently in human (e.g. Rizzolatti 2005; Fabbri-Destro and Rizzolatti 2008; Keysers and Gazzola 2010).

A mirror neurons fires whenever an animal acts and when the animal observes the same action in another—hence their name. Mirror neurons are potentially important to many aspects of our cognitive, affective and aesthetic lives and Ramachandran (2000) has gone so far as to claim that they may have enabled us to create nothing less than culture itself. In humans, brain activity consistent with that of mirror neurons has been found in the premotor cortex, the supplementary motor area, the primary somatosensory cortex and the inferior parietal cortex. A number of neuroscientists consider that this system to provide the physiological mechanism for the perception-action coupling; and are important for understanding the actions of other people, and for acquiring new skills by imitation. Some researchers also speculate that mirror systems may simulate observed actions, and thus contribute to development of a Theory of Mind, while others relate mirror neurons to language abilities.

Kaplan and Iacoboni (2006) have argued that the mirror neuron systems help us understand the actions and intentions of other people and have reported that they could discern if another person who was picking up a cup of tea planned to drink from it or clear it from the table. In addition, Iacoboni has argued that mirror neurons are the neural basis of the human capacity of empathy.

Freedberg and Gallese (2007) have written of the implications for embodiment and like a number of others describe it as a "challenge [to] the primacy of cognition" (p. 200). However, what is of particular interest here is their discussion of mirror neurons as a credible mechanism for our understanding our emotional and empathetic response to art. They reason that as the observation of a goal-oriented action leads to the activation of the same neural networks that are active during its execution, this, in itself may account for our feelings of empathy for the movements portrayed in artistic pieces. Further, mirror neurons have now also been shown to respond to actions that are implied thus they enable the understanding of the action of others by means of what is described as "embodied simulation".

Studies in macaques and humans have demonstrated that mirror neurons are also involved in understanding the intentions that underlie action and this applies to the observation of (static) images of actions too. The observation of pictures of a hand reaching to grasp an object or firmly grasping it activates the motor representation of grasping in the observer's brain. Calvo-Merino et al. (2004) have found evidence that the mirror neuron system is also involved in the understanding of bodily movement (including dancing). Based on this, it is proposed that a similar motor simulation process can be induced by the observation of still images of actions in works of art. It is not surprising that felt physical responses to works of art are so often located in the part of the body that is shown to be engaged in purposive physical actions, and that one might feel that one is copying the gestures and movements of the image one sees—even in cases where the action seems to serve as the outlet for an emotional response (as with scenes of mourning and lamentation, for example). This hypothesis, reflecting longstanding thought in phenomenology, stresses the empathic nature of the relationship automatically established between artworks and beholders. This hypothesis has two components: firstly, the relationship between embodied simulation-driven empathic feelings in the observer and the representational content (the actions, intentions, objects, emotions and sensations portrayed in a painting or sculpture); secondly, the relationship between embodied empathic feelings in the observer "reliving" the artist's work.

5.5   Neuroaesthetics

The term neuroaesthetics was coined by Zeki (1999) to refer to the study of the neural bases of the perception of beauty in art, while Chatterjee (2011, p. 53) tells us that it refers to the, "domain that has something to do with the properties of the brain as it emerges in aesthetics" and Ramachandran (2012, p. 192) speaks of it is the study of "how [...] the human brain responds to beauty". These are all, understandably, broad and inclusive definitions but more than this, neuroaesthetics is also said to be a "gathering force" (Skov and Vartanian 2009) and as it grows, it faces the challenge of being both true to its scientific roots while being relevant to aesthetics. As we have seen, aesthetics encompasses the perception, production, and response to art, as well as interactions with objects and scenes that evoke feelings, and although neuroaesthetics generally is confined to the visual medium, its principles should apply to music, dance, and literature.[3]

---

[3]http://www.dailymail.co.uk/sciencetech/article-2529855/How-book-really-change-life-Brain-function-improves-DAYS-reading-novel.html.

5.5.1 The Gestalt Laws of Perception

However, before we consider the current thinking in neuroaesthetics, we begin by reminding ourselves of the contribution of the Gestaltists. The Gestaltists, of course, were a group of psychologists working in the early years of the 20th century who, are probably best remembered for their "laws" of perception. These laws were based on observations about the apparent regularities in the ways in which our visual perception works. The Gestaltists noted, for example, that objects appearing close together in space or time tend to be perceived together, so, if objects are carefully spaced they will be perceived as being organised into either columns or rows. These regularities (which became "laws") include the effects of continuity, similarity, closure and so forth. Although these laws are most frequently cited with respect to visual phenomena, they also apply to auditory perception too so, for example, the proximity of auditory "objects" are perceived as a song or a tune. However, to avoid a proliferation of these perceptual "laws", Koffka (1935) proposed a fundamental, organising principle which he described as Prägnanz which is, the "psychological organization will always be as 'good' as the prevailing conditions allow" and he commended this proposal with the note that "On the whole the reader should find no difficulty in seeing what is meant here".

On a more contemporary note, Sonneveld and Schifferstein (2008) ask us to consider the sensation of touch. They observe that touch brings together the contributions (inputs) from several different sensory systems including pressure, temperature, vibration, pleasure, and pain which is experienced as a single Gestalt percept (this is not to say that the different components cannot be individually distinguished). Katz agrees and tells us that what we experience as "wetness" (for example) is "the synergistic activation of different combinations of receptors" in what have been described as "touch blends" (Katz 1925/1989). However, as Wagemans et al. (2012) note, currently Gestalt psychology occupies an ambiguous place in that its appeal declined sharply in the 1950s. In part, this was due to the discovery of single neurons being tuned to primitive stimulus attributes (e.g. line orientation, motion direction, the "monkey's paw" detector and so forth) which led to a predominantly atomistic approach in neuroscience, and around the same time, computers models appeared to provide testable, mechanistic accounts of mental operations. Nonetheless, most psychology and HCI textbooks still contain a chapter on the Gestalt perceptual laws as they map remarkably well onto a number of modern user interface designs (either the designers have been reading the textbooks or there may be something to these laws). This is set to change.

Chatterjee (2011) writes that visual neuroaesthetics rests on two principles, namely, visual aesthetics has multiple components and secondly, that aesthetic experiences emerge from a combination of responses to these different components.

It is now well established that the nervous system processes visual information both sequentially (Marr 1982) established that this is further divided into early, intermediate, and late vision). Visual information is also processed in parallel. Early vision is responsible for extracting simple elements from the visual environment, such as colour, luminance, shape, motion, and location. While, intermediate vision creates coherent regions from this chaotic sensory array. Finally, late vision is responsible for recognising objects and understanding what they meaning. In parallel, Chatterjee tells us, any work of art can also be decomposed into its early, intermediate, and late vision components. Aesthetic perception can distinguish between form and content with form being processed by early and intermediate vision, whereas content is processed by later vision. Thus, looking at something artistic, we would see its colour and spatial location first, and these elements would be grouped intermediate vision and so on. A good illustration of this work is Chatterjee and his colleagues (Chatterjee et al. 2009) interested in our responses to beauty in the form of attractive human faces in particular. Their methodology involved showing attractive human faces to people and used fMRI to measure neural involvement. They found that neural involvement was widely distributed, and involved the dorsolateral frontal and medial frontal cortices. They concluded that visual neuroaesthetics is hierarchical and comprises a number of stable hierarchical organised subsystems. They also note that it is this very organization which makes neuroaesthetics possible.

Ramachandran and Hirstein (1999) have developed a neurological theory of aesthetic experience with Ramachandran contributing his personal reflections on Indian erotic art (specifically carved stone female figures). Ramachandran specifically makes reference to these figures in his *The Tell-Tale Brain* (2012) which he described as having shocked the British army when they first came across them in the 18th and 19th centuries. The figures are characterised by exaggerated female forms—large breasts, very narrow waists, and large hips. Lara Croft and Barbie dolls bring the same kinds of exaggerations to mind. Their distance from real female forms has been described by Galia Slayen writing for the Huffington post who tells us that, "If Barbie were an actual woman, she would be 5'9" tall, have a 39" bust, an 18" waist, 33" hips and a size 3 shoe". "She likely would not menstruate … she'd have to walk on all fours (as her ankles would be unable to support her modest weight)."

Ramachandran and Hirstein begin their account by discussing "the logic of art", that is, identifying the rules or principles governing art; secondly, they consider why these rules are they as they are; and finally, which parts of the brain are involved. In the process of answering these questions they go on to propose a number of principles of artistic experience. The precise number of these seems to vary between different publications but include: peak shift, perceptual grouping and binding, contrast, isolation, perceptual problem solving, symmetry abhorrence of coincidence/generic viewpoint and metaphor. We will briefly consider the first three of these.

Peak shift stems from animal research. Rats and pigeons can be trained to respond to the presentation of rectangles, and not to squares (the animal will press a lever or peck a button on seeing a rectangle but ignore squares). Once trained, it has been observed that if these animals are presented a rectangle with exaggerated length (as compared to the original target rectangle), they will respond more vigorously to these new rectangles. This is the peak shift phenomenon. It has been argued that squares and rectangles only differ along one dimension (let's call it their width) and if this is amplified, so too is the animal's response to it. Ramachandran and Hirstein compare the peak shift effect to the Sanskrit word "rasa," which they translate as "essence". They argue that the artist creating, say, a stone carving of a female extracts the "rasa" of the female body shape by exaggerating it in a direction that takes it away from the male body shape, and it is this which makes the sculpture more aesthetically pleasing. They suggest this extraction and exaggeration can be found in the work of the artist François Boucher who is famous for his nudes. Boucher exaggerated the rosy glow of women's' skin colour to make them more attractive than those who were accurately portrayed. They claim that supporting evidence for this can be found in other domains such as Thornhill and Gangestad's (1999) research into the attractiveness of artificially produced faces. They found that woman (during periods of high fertility) prefer faces with exaggerated masculine features to average faces. This peak shift even applies to the behaviour of seagull chicks which will peck for food at a stick with a red dot at the end (painted to resemble an adult gull's beak). The chicks will peck most at a stick with three red stripes. The stick only has one feature in common with an adult bird's beak and that is the red spot and that has been exaggerated.

As for grouping and contrast, Ramachandran and Hirstein tell us that they must be rewarding. They argue that once the visual system has identified objects in the visual field then it must bind or group features relevant to it, examples of this include extracting figures from visually noisy scenes [such as picking out a dalmation dog from a spotty background—as discussed by Gregory (1970)] or seeing the "other" figure in an ambiguous drawing such as Jastrow's duck-rabbit (1899). They note that once we have seen the other figure, we cannot but help see it again and again.

It is well-established that the visual system is primed to identify edges and changes in contrast. Ramachandran and Hirstein observed that this contrast extraction itself may be intrinsically pleasing to the eye and like grouping, rewarding. They suggest that this automatic process may be enjoyable (or pleasing) because (and here I am summarising) edges are more interesting than dull homogeneity.

5.6 Conclusions

Like affect, aesthetics has an appraisal at their heart. We find things attractive because they offer the promise of good design/or are potential mate/or a sign of a desirable skill set or political persuasion. Aesthetics are an outwards sign of "good things" below the surface, and from the perspective of design, Xenakis and Arnellos (2013, 2014) have proposed a model that relates the aesthetics and affordances in the design process. This is potentially a very interesting combination. An affordance (a concept much applied in the HCI/UX design community) is an invitation do to something which is picked up by our perceptual systems (e.g. Gibson 1986; Norman 1988; Kaptelinin 2014; Rietveld and Kiverstein 2014 among very many).

Examples of affordances include a knife which invites us to use it to cut, or a cup which invites us to drink from it. These properties were seen as being phenomenal in nature and not the physical properties of objects—that is, we see directly what these objects are for and how to use them, without having to reason about it. On tool use, Gibson wrote, "[…] A graspable object with a rigid sharp edge affords cutting and scraping (a knife)" and extended this idea to include such things as post boxes which invite posting letters. Xenakis and Arnellos disagree and suggest that affordances were never just about (or "looking at" artefacts, they were always about inviting and guiding use. Thus, they have restated what an affordance is from an aesthetic perspective.

References

Appleton J (1975) The experience of the landscape. Wiley, New York

Arnheim R (1966) Toward a psychology of art: collected essays. University of California Press, Berkeley

Bergeron V, Lopes DM (2012) Aesthetic theory and aesthetic science: connecting minds, brains, and experience. Oxford University Press, Oxford, pp 63–79

Berlyne DE (1974) Studies in the new experimental aesthetics: steps toward an objective psychology of aesthetic appreciation. Hemisphere, Oxford

Bloch PH (1995) Seeking the ideal form: product design and consumer response. J Market 59 (3):16–29

Bocher M, Chisin R, Parag Y, Freedman N, Weil YM, Lester H, Mishani E, Bonne O (2001) Cerebral activation associated with sexual arousal in response to a pornographic clip: a 15 O-H 2 O PET study in heterosexual men. Neuroimage 14(1):105–117

Burke J, Ornstein R (1997) The Axemaker's Gift. Tarcher Penguin, New York

Calvin WH (2006) The emergence of intelligence. Sci Am Spec 16(2):84–92

Calvo-Merino B, Glaser DE, Grèzes J, Passingham RE, Haggard P (2004) Action observation and acquired motor skills: an FMRI study with expert dancers. Cereb Cortex 15(8):1243–1249

Carroll N, Moore, M, Seeley, WP (2012) The philosophy of art and aesthetics, psychology, and neuroscience. In: Aesthetic science: connecting minds, brains, and experience, p 31–62

Chatterjee A (2011) Neuroaesthetics: a coming of age story. J Cogn Neurosci 23(1):53–62

Chatterjee A, Vartanian O (2014) Neuroaesthetics. Trends Cognitive Sci 18(7):370–375

Chatterjee A, Thomas A, Smith SE, Aguirre GK (2009) The neural response to facial attractiveness. Neuropsychol 23(2):135

Cinzia DD, Vittorio G (2009) Neuroaesthetics: a review. Curr Opin Neurobiol 19(6):682–687

Cobey R, Layton R, Tanner J (2008) Archaeology and art. In: Bintliff J (ed) A companion to archaeology. Blackwell Publishing, Malden, pp 367–379

Currie G (2009) Art for art's Sake in the old Stone Age. Postgrad J Aesthetics 6(1):1–23

Dourish P (2001) Where the action is. MIT Press, Cambridge

Dutton D (2009) The art instinct: beauty, pleasure, & human evolution. Oxford University Press, Oxford

Eagly AH, Ashmore RD, Makhijani MG, Longo LC (1991) What is beautiful is good, but … : a meta-analytic review of research on the physical attractiveness stereotype. Psychol Bull 110 (1):109

Fabbri-Destro M, Rizzolatti G (2008) Mirror neurons and mirror systems in monkeys and humans. Physiol 23(3):171–179

Fenwick P (2003) Aesthetic computing manifesto. Leonardo 36(4):255–256

Freedberg D, Gallese V (2007) Motion, emotion and empathy in aesthetic experience. Trends in Cognitive Sci 11(5):197–203

Gallese V (2017) Visions of the body. Embodied simulation and aesthetic experience. Aisthesis. Pratiche, linguaggi e saperi dell'estetico 10(1): 41–50

Gibson JJ (1986) The ecological approach to visual perception. Houghton Mifflin, Boston

Gregory R (1970) The intelligent eye. McGraw-Hill, New York

Hallnäs L, Redström J (2002) From use to presence: on the expressions and aesthetics of everyday computational things. ACM Trans Comput–Hum Interact 9(2):106–124

Hassenzahl M (2004) The interplay of beauty, goodness, and usability in interactive products. Hum–Comput Interact 19(4):319–349

Jastrow J (1899) The mind's eye. Popul Sci Monthly 54:299–312

Kaplan JT, Iacoboni M (2006) Getting a grip on other minds: Mirror neurons, intention understanding, and cognitive empathy. Soc Neurosci 1(3–4):175–183

Kaptelinin V (2014) Affordances and design. In: Campbell A (ed) The interaction design foundation (1st ed)

Katz D (1925/1989) The world of touch. Hillsdale, NJ

Keysers C, Gazzola V (2010) Social neuroscience: mirror neurons recorded in humans. Curr Biol 20(8):R353–R354

Khaslavsky J, Shedroff N (1999) Understanding the seductive experience. Commun ACM 42 (5):45–49

Kipling R (1902) The Just So Stories. McMillan, London

Kirsch LP, Urgesi C, Cross ES (2016) Shaping and reshaping the aesthetic brain: emerging perspectives on the neurobiology of embodied aesthetics. Neurosci Biobehav Rev 62:56–68

Koffka K (1935) Principles of gestalt psychology. Int Libr Psychol Philos Sci Method

Kurosu M, Kashimura K (1995) Apparent usability vs. inherent usability: experimental analysis on the determinants of the apparent usability (pp 292–293). ACM Press, New York

Lavie T, Tractinsky N (2004) Assessing dimensions of perceived visual aesthetics of web sites. Int J Hum Comput Stud 60(3):269–298

Laurel B (1993) Computers as theatre. Addison-Wesley, Reading, MA

Leder H, Nadal M (2014) Ten years of a model of aesthetic appreciation and aesthetic judgments: the aesthetic episode–developments and challenges in empirical aesthetics. Br J Psychol 105 (4):443–464

Leder H, Belke B, Oeberst A, Augustin D (2004) A model of aesthetic appreciation and aesthetic judgments. Br J Psychol 95:489–508

Lewis-Williams D (2002) Art for the living. In: Cummings V, Jordan P, Zvelebil M (eds) the oxford handbook of the archaeology and anthropology of hunter-gatherers. Oxford University Press, Oxford, pp 625–642

MacLean PD (1949) psychosomatic disease and the "visceral brain": recent developments bearing on the papez theory of emotion. Psychosom Med 11(6):338–353

MacLean, PD (1990) The triune brain in evolution: role in paleocerebral functions. Springer Science & Business Media

Marr D (1982) Vision: a computational approach

Norman DA (1988) The psychology of everyday things (The design of everyday things)

Norman DA (2004) Emotional design: why we love or hate everyday objects. Basic Books, New York

Orians GH (1986) Site characteristics favoring invasions. In: Ecology of biological invasions of North America and Hawaii. Springer, New York, pp 133–148

Petersen MG, Iversen OS, Krogh PG, Ludvigsen M (2004, August) Aesthetic Interaction: a pragmatist's aesthetics of interactive systems. In Proceedings of the 5th conference on designing interactive systems: processes, practices, methods, and techniques (pp 269–276). ACM

Petersen MG, Hallnäs L, Jacob RJ (2008) Introduction to the special issue on the aesthetics of interaction. ACM Trans Comput-Hum Interact

Ramachandran VS (2000) Mirror neurons and imitation learning as the driving force behind "the great leap forward" in human evolution. Edge Website article http://www.edge.org/3rd_culture/ramachandran/ramachandran_p1.html

Ramachandran VS (2012) The tell-tale brain: Unlocking the mystery of human nature. Random House, New York

Ramachandran VS, Hirstein W (1999) the science of art: a neurological theory of aesthetic experience. J Conscious Stud 6(6–7):15–51

Redström J (2008) Tangled interaction: on the expressiveness of tangled user interfaces. ACM Trans Comput-Hum Interact 15(4):1–17

Rietveld E, Kiverstein J (2014) A rich landscape of affordances. Ecol Psychol 26(4):325–352

Rizzolatti G (2005) The mirror neuron system and its function in humans. Anat Embryol 210(5–6):419–421

Rizzolatti G, Sinigaglia C (2007) Mirror neurons and motor intentionality. Funct Neurol 22(4):205

Saito Y (2001) Everyday aesthetics. Philos Lit 25(1):87–95

Scheib JE, Gangestad SW, Thornhill R (1999) Facial attractiveness, symmetry and cues of good genes. Proc R Soc Lond B Biol Sci 266(1431):1913–1917

Shusterman R (1992) Pragmatist aesthetics: living beauty, rethinking art. Blackwell, Cambridge

Skov M, Vartanian O (2009) Introduction: what is neuroaesthetics? Baywood Publishing Co, New York

Sonneveld MH, Ludden GD, Schifferstein HN (2008, October) Multi sensory design in education. In Proceedings of the 5th international conference on design and emotion, Hong Kong

Stolnitz J (1969) Aesthetics and the philosophy of art criticism, reprinted in introductory readings in aesthetics. Hospers J (ed) The Free Press, New York, p 27

Thornhill R, Gangestad SW (1993) Human facial beauty: averageness, symmetry, and parasite resistance. Hum Nat 4:237–269

Thornhill R, Gangestad SW (1999) Facial attractiveness. Trends Cogn Sci 3(12):452–460

Udsen LE, Jørgensen AH (2005) The aesthetic turn: unravelling recent aesthetic approaches to human-computer interaction. Digital Creat 16(04):205–216

Ulrich KT (2007) Creation of artifacts in society. Pontifica Press

Wagemans J, Elder JH, Kubovy M, Palmer SE, Peterson MA, Singh M, von der Heydt R (2012) A century of Gestalt psychology in visual perception: I. Perceptual grouping and figure–ground organization. Psychol Bull 138(6):1172

Xenakis I, Arnellos A (2013) The relation between interaction aesthetics and affordances. Des Stud 34(1):57–73

Xenakis I, Arnellos A (2014) Aesthetic perception and its minimal content: a naturalistic perspective. Front Psychol 5:1038

Zahavi, A (1975) Mate selection—a selection for a handicap. J Theor Biol 53(1):205–214.

Zeki S (1999) Inner vision: an exploration of art and the brain. Oxford University Press, New York

Web Reference

Thinkmap (2017) http://www.thinkmap.com/. Last accessed 15 Sept 2017

Chapter 6
Killing Time with Technology

We're busy doin' nothin'

Workin' the while day through

Tryin' to find lots of things not to do.

Crosby, Bendix, and Hardwicke (1949)

This book has presented a psychology of user experience and in doing so we have adopted a philosophical perspective to frame at least some of the ways in which we interact or use or otherwise employ digital products. Central to this is the premise that it is not just this ubiquitous presence of technology which provides the context for UX, but our routine though often unexpected use of it. We will say more about this in the next and subsequent sections of this chapter but first we must recognise the *other* treatment of experience.

6.1 The *Other* Treatment of Experience

Csikszentmihalyi (1996, 1997, 2014) has been the primary student of *flow* for quite some time. His work began with his study of the creative process in artists, where he observed that when the work was going well they tended to disregard fatigue and discomfort but that they often became bored when their work was completed—and wondered why this is so. Just what is the source of their motivation? To this end, he went on to study people playing games and contrasted this with the work of surgeons. With the former we might expect to encounter intrinsic motivations (after all, games are both fun and competitive) whereas with the latter we might expect a role for generous remuneration and prestige. Surprisingly, he found similarities between game players and surgeons and was able to attribute their respective motivation to the perceived challenge or opportunities for action that stretched existing skills and clear, achievable goals with immediate feedback. Such situations he describes as examples of *optimal experience* or *flow*. Thus, people will *flow*

© Springer International Publishing AG 2017

P. Turner, *A Psychology of User Experience*, Human–Computer Interaction Series,

https://doi.org/10.1007/978-3-319-70653-5_6

when working or playing optimally. This optimal point is struck at the balance between the level of skill possessed and the demands of the task. If skills exceed the demands of the task, the individual may slip into relaxation then maybe boredom. Conversely, if the task demands or challenges exceed skills then the individual may experience stress and become anxious. Csikszentmihalyi tells us that, *"The key element of an optimal experience is that it is an end in itself. Even if initially undertaken for other reasons, the activity that consumes us becomes intrinsically rewarding. [...] It refers to a self-contained activity, one that is done not with the expectation of some future benefit, but simply because the doing itself is the reward"*. He has also introduced the term *autotelic*[1] to describe our intrinsic motivation.

The characteristics of flow

Flow is experienced as intense and focused concentration on what one is doing at that moment and people report the loss of reflective self-awareness and a sense of the experience being rewarding. There are also frequently reported experiences of the apparent merging of action and awareness accompanied by the merging of action and awareness and a sense of control over one's actions.

From the evidence that Csikszentmihalyi and his colleagues have presented (e.g., Csikszentmihalyi et al. 2014), flow does not seem to be a particular rare phenomenon. A given individual will *flow* in almost any activity—working a cash register, ironing clothes, driving a car and almost any pursuit such as a museum visit, a round of golf, or a game of chess can bore or create anxiety. Flow is frequently reported when people play digital games and has variously been described as "being in the zone". Overall, Donner and Csikszentmihalyi (1992) have reported that the employees they had surveyed experienced flow 44% of the time at work, boredom 20%, and anxiety the remaining 36%.

Creating flow

Flow can be entered while performing any activity, although it is most likely to occur when one is wholeheartedly performing a task or activity for intrinsic purposes. Passive activities like taking a bath or even watching TV usually do not elicit flow. However, it is generally regarded that three conditions that have to be met to achieve flow. These are, involvement in an activity with a clear set of goals and progress and accompanied by clear and immediate feedback. Secondly, there must be a good balance between the challenges of the task and an individual's skills. Finally, the individual should have confidence in their ability to complete the task.

Despite the apparent ubiquity of *flow*, it tends to be associated with sports and games, perhaps because the goals and feedback in these activities are so well defined but, it does not feature in accounts of UX excepting the mentions in games and gamified applications, ecommerce/marketing, and e-learning. It is perhaps

---

[1]The term "autotelic" derives from two Greek words, auto meaning self, and telos meaning goal. It refers to a self-contained activity, one that is done not with the expectation of some future benefit, but simply because the doing itself is the reward.

worth remembering that *flow* is based on the interaction between person and context, not person and technology. It is also defined a little narrowly in terms of tasks and skills, as Hassenzahl (2008) has observed, "flow is the positive UX derived from fulfilling the need for competence (i.e., mastery); it is a particular experience stemming from the fulfilment of a particular be-goal" but beyond this, there has been no attempt to integrate into mainstream UX thinking.

6.2 Two Modes of Experience

Returning to our main discussion, we would argue that our trio of involvement, affect and aesthetics are all cognitive faculties. This is not the small "c" version of cognition involving rule-driven symbol manipulation but the new treatments of cognition which recognise the importance of our embodiment, and the role of the external world in how we think. Further, this is not cognition as information processing which for many is seen as a largely an outmoded legacy from the computer metaphor for the brain.

As we have seen, involvement is very inclusive. It encompasses the means by which we engage with and make sense of the world (which necessarily includes digital technology). In addition to making our stance concernful towards technology, it provides us with the means to use, and even form relationships with digital products.

Affect is cognitive because it is how we make sense of the world. Affect tells us about good and bad and much of affect, as emotion, relies on appraisals such as these. An appraisal is not based on carefully weighing options one by one but may take the form of "thoughtless thoughts" or feelings which have been described as "embodied appraisals".

Finally, aesthetics is cognitive, as in addition to being a source of pleasure, as it serves to guide our decision making. Aesthetics prompt us to be oriented towards the attractive form because attractive things are easier to use.

All three place the experiencer at the centre of the world of his or her making. All three are the result of the interaction between the brain, the body of the organism and its environment (or digital product). All three could, very naturally, be described from an Enactive perspective (Valera et al. 1991). UX is unmistakably cognitive.

Two ways of thinking
Having recognised UX as cognitive, we should also see that cognition is modal, manifesting in at least two different forms. Kahneman, for example, in his *Fast Thinking, Slow Thinking* (2011) distinguishes between System 1 and System 2 thinking. While this is fairly traditional cognitive psychology in its origins, it is not being limited to the laboratory.

Kahneman describes System 1 thinking as occurring "automatically and quickly, with little or no effort and no sense of voluntary control" (*ibid*, p. 20) and he contrasts this with System 2 thinking which involves the "allocation of attention to the effortful mental activities that demand it, including complex computations. The operations of System 2 are also associated with the subjective experience of agency, choice, and concentration" (p. 21). System 2 may also be described, in more familiar terms, as reasoning or deliberation while System 1 is more perception-like, that is, seamless, immediate and unmediated. So, we can see that UX appears to rely on both systems.

6.3   A Third Form of Experience: Killing Time

We use digital products to get practical stuff done but, for some of the time, or perhaps even most of the time, we just idle with them. Here we do not mean playing a digital game which requires some effort to set up, but that often we simply use digital products to pass the time. This is not well understood but all we need do to find evidence of it is to travel on any public transport system. There, many of us can be seen distracting ourselves with our mobile digital products. People are flicking between screens on their devices, not reading or searching, just letting images pass before their eyes and waiting for time to pass. We can even see people out on dates ("romantic liaisons"), filling in the awkward silences and pauses in the conversation with "fiddling with their phones" or at the cinema, during the dull scenes in the second act checking for messages, even though they know that the notification system is more than capable of handling this for them or rather ineptly in the back row of a lecture theatre while attending class. We are inveterate fiddlers and there is a restless energy about us (which may have a little to do with the caffeine content of soft drinks). While this fiddling does not appear to be purposive, as we will see, it may not be entirely useless or pointless.

It is a fact of everyday life, even before we invented the mobile phone, that we all day-dreamed and idled. We spend inordinate amounts of time thinking of others, or the movie we watched last night or how the cat is feeling, or where to take a holiday next year—none of which could be described as being particularly purposive much less problem solving, yet the study of cognition (including the modern varieties) seems to be almost exclusively concerned with the serious use of our wits. And if our formal study of psychological processes does not appear to match how we spend our time, this is made doubly more mysterious when we realise that there is substantial neurological evidence that there is a "default circuit" in the brain devoted to just these kinds of apparently pointless activities. In the literature, these pointless activities are usually described as "mind wandering" and we should note that this is not usually associated with digital technology. However, we might describe web surfing (as opposed to web browsing which may be unplanned but purposive) as killing time with a browser. Various technology surveys tell us that browsing has gone mobile (that is, the web is more usually accessed from a phone rather than a personal computer) and that teenagers, in particular, much to our surprise spend an alarming amount of time web surfing.

Digital products mediate idling. It is evident that some of the current generation of digital products in addition to offering all manner of user experiences also actively promotes idling or killing time. If this seems to be something of an exaggeration, at least it is fair to say that they certainly support and scaffold time wasting. Books are still read, of course, but more and more people prefer to spend their quiet time (commuting to work or college; lounging on the holiday beach and, increasingly, while out with friends—even while sitting with them at the same table) idling with their smart phones rather than reading from bound sheets of paper. This clearly cannot be regarded as purposive in the usual sense (in that there are no goals or targets) and it does not appear to be a source of enjoyment in the same way playing a digital game is fun, but there is something compelling about it as lots of people spend lots of time killing time.

The neural basis of killing time

Before an fMRI can be used, the rest state of the person being examined needs to be established and Ingvar (refs) was the first to note the presence and importance of consistent and specific pattern of activity in the resting brain. To explain this unexpected phenomenon, Ingvar (1974, 1979, 1985) proposed that the "hyper-frontal" pattern of activity corresponded "to undirected, spontaneous, conscious mentation, the 'brain work' which we carry out when left alone undisturbed". Thus, what came to be known as the *default network* was identified. It is a network of highly correlated, interacting regions of the brain. The default network is most commonly shown to be active when a person is not focused on the outside world and the brain is at wakeful rest, such as during daydreaming but it is also active when the individual is thinking about others, thinking about themselves (retrieving autobiographical memories), remembering the past, and planning for the future (e.g., Buckner et al. 2008; Raichle et al. 2001). Since its identification, this default circuit has been of interest to those who were concerned to know why the brain was consuming more oxygen and glucose when it was at rest than when it was apparently busy (e.g., Raichle et al. 2001; Buckner et al. 2008).

The default network is a distinct neural system that is active when we are not focused on a particular task and on the basis of this evidence, Buckner et al. (2008) have proposed that it may be the source of internally directed cognition. It is implicated in the production of internal mentation, which itself is grounded in autobiographical memories, speculations about the future, but separate from the real world. Pace-Schott (2013, p. 1), writes that "dreams create new stories out of nothing. Although dreams contain themes, concerns, dream figures, objects, etc., that correspond closely to waking life, these are only story elements." Pace-Schott suggests that a credible source for these (night time) dreams is the default network. He then goes on to argue that this story-like structure found in dreams may have become integrated into existing belief systems, or even to create new beliefs and legends.

As the mental state resulting from the operation of this default network is by definition is our default condition, it follows that it must have a role in the everyday things we do including planning and prospective thought and our social relationships with others, and possibly creativity including storytelling (e.g., Bar et al. 2007; Buckner et al. 2008; Klinger 1971; McVay and Kane 2010; Mooneyham and Schooler 2013). The role in planning, for example, may prepare an individual for expected or forthcoming events, and visualising potential outcomes serves to improve our readiness in otherwise unpredictable situations. This also suggests that the default network may be active when we are idling with our mobile phones and the like. And Binky adds an empirical dimension to this argument.

Binky

Binky is a social network app that is available for Apple and Android mobile phones and offers "an infinite feed of random things to look at. These images are binks and all the user needs do is pay attention. It is a content-free services with no network or socializing but Binky may more satisfying than real social media services.[2] Its posts are innocuous and comprise images of a variety of fairly ordinary things which have been quite nicely photographed. Users are free to comment on the images without consequence and the likes or "re-binks" are not tallied.

The creator of Binky claims that the idea for it came to him while waiting for a train, telling us that he did not want to engage cognitively with anything but felt that he should be looking at his phone, which he describes as his "default state of being". His aim was to provide a service which allowed people to interact with it but without consequences. To this end he has created something with affords the repetitive actions of touching and tapping a glass rectangle with purpose and seeing it "nod in response". It may be that Binky offers something for our "default network" to do.

6.4   The Three Dimensions of UX

In this final section, we offer a reprise of our account of UX which we have constructed on a number of philosophical, psychological and empirical premises. Our first step was to observe, un-controversially, that our use of digital products is diverse. We still, of course, interact with them but the definitions of UX have not been up to the task despite being occasionally verbose or resorting to multiple footnotes.

We proposed that *involvement* is a better term as with it comes the recognition that we are "enfolded" by technology—etymologically, it is derived from the Latin and means to enfold (Skeat 1910). Thus, our account of user experience is based on our relationship with digital products rather than our interaction. Using the term

---

[2]The following section has been adapted from an interview in the Atlantic magazine. https://www.theatlantic.com/technology/archive/2017/06/the-app-that-does-nothing/529764/.

involvement, aside from its etymological appeal, also allows us to include its many forms and expressions, not least to recognise that we often treat technology as though it were another social agent and we also appropriate technology to ensure that it more closely meet our needs. Thus, our involvement with digital products also provides the background, (though *backdrop* introduces a suitably theatrical note), against which we have experiences.

The term involvement, of course, is not quite right if we follow Heidegger as he tells us that this is no involvement but involvements. As we discussed much earlier, Heidegger recognizes that tools, in addition to being in-order-to, are also associated with a broader set of purposes which he calls "for-the-sake-of-which". This underlines the fundamental interconnected-ness of the tools as equipment which make up the world. He writes, making reference to his favourite example, hammering …, as follows: "With hammering, there is an involvement in making something fast; with making something fast there is an involvement in protection against bad weather; and this protection "is" for the sake of providing shelter". We use a hammer to make something fast (secure) for the sake of making it weather-proof, for the sake of protecting one's home, for the sake of the health and happiness of one's family for the sake of … and so on. The nature of these involvements only being revealed within the broader context. An involvement[3] is itself revealed only on the basis of the prior disclosure of an involvement-whole. This network of involvements is not a simple series of dependencies but ultimately relies on who we are (that is, the role we have adopted).

So, for example, I am currently using my computer in my study in order to complete this chapter, which is intended to demonstrate the usefulness of Heidegger's definition of the involvement, for the sake of completing this book. The final involvement here, the for-the-sake-of-which, is crucial, because according to Heidegger all involvements rely a "link" of this type. Thus, every for-the-sake-of-which provides the base structure of all (subsequent and dependent) involvements and offers a possible way for *Dasein*[4] to be, to be an academic, or a writer or polemist (Wheeler 2011). Thus, I write (compose text, meet deadlines and so forth), if and only if, I understand myself as a writer, and I engage in writing acts for-the-sake-of my being a writer. (*If appears to be self-referential and circular, then you have read it correctly*).

---

[3]A final note on involvement. Heidegger tells us that care is the fundamental basis of our being-in-the-world and reveals itself in a variety of ways, for example: (and here we borrow freely from Wheeler 2011) as having to do something, producing something, attending to something and looking after it, making use of something, undertaking, accomplishing, considering, determining and so forth. In short, because we care, we are involved. However, we have chosen to base this account of UX on involvement rather than care, as the former is more manageable and familiar to the HCI professional for whom this book is written. However, we do recognise that a fuller treatment of human computer interaction is possible but would require care.

[4]Heidegger's usually untranslated word for "human-being".

The second component in our account is affect which, it is claimed, is the most important attribute of an experience. Dewey (1934) told us that affect is not separate from experiences but provides them with "colour", good, bad or indifferent and we might call this something like valence. Ortony et al. (1988) in their cognitive account of affect also regard it as being central to experience. Despite being widely regarded as being a cognitive faculty, affect is still treated by many as the complement to cognition (assuming that we are limiting cognition to thinking). Prinz tells us that the most popular (or probably the most researched) aspect of affect is emotion which is best thought of as "unthought thoughts" which is a particularly appealing description. From another perspective, UX researchers who would agree as numerous surveys have found that it is the most frequently cited attributes of UX. And, of course, from the doyen of user experience we have his endorsement for affectivity in *Emotional Design* (Norman 2004).

Finally, we included aesthetics, as in many respects, this is the most obvious attribute for the consumer, user and artist as it "speaks" directly to them. This refers to how a digital product looks, how it feels to the touch, and having purchased the "right" product, it may be a source of the ideologically pleasure which sensitive souls crave (Tiger 1992). Although aesthetics is elusive and difficult to define, we should recognise that it may be responsible for ensuring that we are paying attention to the "right things". Dutton described beauty as nature working at a distance and we can see this in action every time we are drawn to a new, shiny smart phone, with its attractiveness promising a "good design" and a "good experience" and astonishing price tag.

In proposing this tripartite model of UX, we wanted to ensure that it captured that digital products matter to us. UX is not a detached scientific phenomenon, as Heidegger might have put it, UX is ready-to-hand and our involvement with digital technology, and our affective and aesthetics responses to it are all expressions of this relationship.

Final words
After having reviewed a significant amount of published UX research, it has become clear that we care for digital technology and products in a manner which is not unlike other social beings. This is hardly a novel finding but it is an irresistible one. The fact that we do is unavoidable, but we should recognise that we have no other way to treat it, there is simple no other choice than to treat it like ourselves. It may be that our repertoire is limited to this kind of involvement (or care as Heidegger would have preferred), so, while they are not fellow human-beings, they are nonetheless social beings to us.

Interestingly, Turkle in a recent interview said that, "people use digital life to flee what they find messy and complex in human conversation" (Turkle et al. 2017). We might speculate that we are fleeing messiness and complexity, but not conversation. This might also answer a question for Mitcham (1994), who asked whether we are best described as Homo faber ("Man the Maker") or are Homo loquax ("Chattering man")? And perhaps "the greatest artefact" is language after all.

References

Bar M, Aminoff E, Mason M, Fenske M (2007) The units of thought. Hippocampus 17(6):420–428

Buckner RL, Andrews-Hanna JR, Schacter DL (2008) The brain's default network. Ann N Y Acad Sci 1124(1):1–38

Crosby B, Bendix W, Hardwicke C (1949) Busy doing nothing. Music by Jimmy Van Heusen. Lyrics by Johnny Burke. Paramount Pictures.

Csikszentmihalyi M (1992) Flow: the psychology of happiness. Rider, London

Csikszentmihalyi M (1996) Flow and the psychology of discovery and invention. Harper Collins, New York

Csikszentmihalyi M (1997) Finding flow: the psychology of engagement with everyday life. Basic Books

Csikszentmihalyi M (2014) Toward a psychology of optimal experience. In: Flow and the foundations of positive psychology. Springer Netherlands, pp 209–226

Csikszentmihalyi M, Abuhamdeh S, Nakamura J (2014) Flow. In: Flow and the foundations of positive psychology. Springer Netherlands, pp 227–238

Dewey J (1934/1980) (reprint) Art as experience. Perigee Books, New York

Hassenzahl M (2008) User experience (UX): towards an experiential perspective on product quality. In: Proceedings of the 20th Conference on l'Interaction Homme-Machine. ACM, pp 11–15

Ingvar DH (1974) Patterns of brain activity revealed by measurements of regional cerebral blood flow. Alfred Benzon Symposium VIII, Copenhagen

Ingvar DH (1979) "Hyperfrontal" distribution of the cerebral grey matter flow in resting wakefulness: on the functional anatomy of the conscious state. Acta Neurol Scand 60:12–25

Ingvar DH (1985) "Memory of the future": an essay on the temporal organization of conscious awareness. Hum Neurobiol 4:127–136

Kahneman D (2011) Fast Thinking, Slow Thinking

Klinger E (1971) Structure and functions of fantasy. Wiley, New York

McVay JC, Kane MJ (2010) Does mind wandering reflect executive function or executive failure? Comment on Smallwood and Schooler (2006) and Watkins (2008). Psychol Bull 136(2):188–207

Mitcham C (1994) Thinking through Technology: the Path between Engineering and Philosophy. Chicago University Press, Chicago

Mooneyham BW, Schooler JW (2013) The costs and benefits of mind-wandering: a review. Canadian Journal of Experimental Psychology/Revue canadienne de psychologie expérimentale 67(1):11–18

Norman DA (2004) Emotional design: why we love or hate everyday objects. Basic Books, New York

Ortony A, Clore GL, Collins A (1988) The cognitive structure of emotions. Cambridge university press

Pace-Schott EF (2013) Dreaming as a story-telling instinct. Front Psychol 4:159

Raichle ME, MacLeod AM, Snyder AZ, Powers WJ, Gusnard DA, Shulman GL (2001) A default mode of brain function. Proc Natl Acad Sci 98(2):676–682

Skeat WW (1910) An etymological dictionary of the English language. Clarendon Press, Oxford

Tiger L (1992) The pursuit of pleasure. Transaction Publishers, New Brunswick

Turkle S, Essig T, Russell GI (2017) Afterword: reclaiming psychoanalysis: Sherry Turkle in conversation with the editors. Psychoanal Perspect 14(2):237–248

Valera FJ, Thompson E, Rosch E (1991) The embodied mind: cognitive science and human experience. MIT Press, Cambridge, MA

Wheeler M (2011) "Martin Heidegger", The Stanford Encyclopedia of Philosophy (Winter 2011 edn) In: Zalta EN (ed) http://plato.stanford.edu/archives/win2011/entries/heidegger. Last accessed 1 Sept 2017

Bibliography

Akah B, Bardzell S (2010) Empowering products: personal identity through the act of appropriation. In: CHI'10 Extended Abstracts on Human Factors in Computing Systems. pp 4021–4026

Aly A, Tapus A (2013, March) A model for synthesizing a combined verbal and nonverbal behavior based on personality traits in human-robot interaction. In: Proceedings of the 8th ACM/IEEE international conference on Human-robot interaction. IEEE Press, pp 325–332

Andrews S, Ellis DA, Shaw H, Piwek L (2015) Beyond self-report: tools to compare estimated and real-world smartphone use. PloS One 10(10):e0139004

Augustin MD, Wagemans J, Carbon CC (2012) All is beautiful? Generality versus specificity of word usage in visual aesthetics. Acta Psychologica 139:1187–1201

Bailenson JN, Beall AC, Blascovich J, Raimundo M, Weisbuch M (2001) Intelligent agents who wear your face: users' reactions to the virtual self. Int Workshop Intell Virtual Agents. Springer, Berlin Heidelberg, pp 86–99

Baird B, Smallwood J, Mrazek MD, Kam JWY, Franklin MS, Schooler JW (2012) Inspired by distraction: mind-wandering facilitates creative incubation. Psychol Sci 23(10):1117–1122

Baron-Cohen S (2004) The essential difference. Penguin UK

Barsalou LW (1987) The instability of graded structure: implications for the nature of concepts. In: Neiser U (ed) Concepts and conceptual development: ecological and intellectual factors in categorization, Cambridge University Press, Cambridge, MA, pp 101–40

Barsalou LW (1999) Perceptual symbol systems. Behav Brain Sci 22:577–660

Barsalou, L. W. (2003a). Abstraction in perceptual symbol systems. Philos Trans R Soc London B Biol Sci, 358(1435):1177–1187

Barsalou LW (2003b) Situated simulation in the human conceptual system. Lang Cogn Process 18:513–62

Bartholow BD, Anderson CA (2002) Effects of violent digital games on aggressive behavior: potential sex differences. J Exp Soc Psychol 38(3):283–290

Bartholow BD, Sestir MA, Davis EB (2005) Correlates and consequences of exposure to digital game violence: hostile personality, empathy, and aggressive behavior. Pers Soc Psychol Bull 31(11):1573–1586

Bartholow BD, Bushman BJ, Sestir MA (2006) Chronic violent digital game exposure and desensitization to violence: behavioral and event-related brain potential data. J Exp Soc Psychol 42(4):532–539

Beaty RE, Silvia PJ, Nusbaum EC, Jauk E, Benedek M (2014) The roles of associative and executive processes in creative cognition. Mem Cogn 42(7):1186–1197

Ben-Bassat T, Meyer J, Tractinsky N (2006) Economic and subjective measures of the perceived value of aesthetics and usability. ACM Trans Comp Hum Inter 13(2):210–234

Benson JE, Sabbagh MA, Carlson SM, Zelazo PD (2013) Individual differences in executive functioning predict preschoolers' improvement from theory-of-mind training. Dev Psychol 49 (9):1615

Bickmore TW, Caruso L, Clough-Gorr K, Heeren T (2005) 'It's just like you talk to a friend' relational agents for older adults. Interact Comp 17(6):711–735

Biswal B, Zerrin Yetkin F, Haughton VM, Hyde JS (1995) Functional connectivity in the motor cortex of resting human brain using echoplanar MRI. Magn Reson Med 34(4):537–541

Blevis E, Stolterman E (2007) Ensoulment and sustainable interaction design. In: Proceedings of the International Association of Societies of Design Research. The Honk Kong Polytechnic University, 12th–15th November 2007

Blythe MA, Hassenzahl M, Law E, Vermeeren A (2007) An analysis framework for user experience (UX) studies: a green paper. Towards a UX Manifesto, p 1

Bødker S (1991) Through the interface—a human activity approach to user interface design. Lawrence Erlbaum Associates, Hillsdale, NJ

Bødker S, Lyle P, Saad-Sulonen J (2017) Untangling the mess of technological artifacts: investigating community artifact ecologies. In: Proceedings of the 8th International Conference on Communities and Technologies. ACM, pp 246–255

Boehner K, Sengers P, Warner S (2008) Interfaces with the ineffable: meeting aesthetic experience on its own terms. ACM Trans Comp Hum Interact 15(3):12

Borgmann A (1984) Technology and the character of contemporary life. The University of Chicago Press, Chicago

Borgmann A (2000) Reply to My Critics. In: Higgs E, Light A, Strong D (eds) Technology and the good life?. University of Chicago Press, Chicago

Bornstein RF (1992) Subliminal mere exposure effects. In: Bornstein RF, Pittman TS (eds) Perception without awareness. Guilford Press, NY

Brockmyer JH, Fox CM, Curtiss KA, McBroom E, Burkhart KM, Pidruzny JN (2009) The development of the game engagement questionnaire: a measure of engagement in video game-playing. J Exp Soc Psychol 45(4):624–634

Broekens J, Heerink M, Rosendal H (2009) Assistive social robots in elderly care: a review. Gerontechnology 8(2):94–103

Cafaro A, Vilhjálmsson HH, Bickmore T, Heylen D, Jóhannsdóttir KR, Valgarðsson GS (2012, September) First impressions: users' judgments of virtual agents' personality and interpersonal attitude in first encounters. In: International Conference on Intelligent Virtual Agents. Springer Berlin Heidelberg, pp 67–80

Card SK, Moran TP, Newell A (1983) The psychology of human-computer interaction. Hillsdale, New Jersey

Cech CJ, Shoben EJ, Love M (1990) Multiple congruity effects in judgments of magnitude. J Exp Psychol Learn Mem Cogn 16:1142–1152

Cesta A, Cortellessa G, Giuliani V, Pecora F, Scopelliti M, Tiberio L (2007) Psychological implications of domestic assistive technology for the elderly. PsychNol J 5(3):229–252

Chatterjee A (2014) Scientific aesthetics: three steps forward. Br J Psychol 105(4):465–467

Christoff K, Ream JM, Gabrieli JD (2004) Neural basis of spontaneous thought processes. Cortex 40:623–630

Churchland PM (1991) Folk psychology and the explanation of human behavior. In: Greenwood JD (ed) The future of folk psychology. Cambridge University Press, Cambridge, pp 51–69

Churchland PM (1992) Matter and consciousness. MIT Press, Cambridge, AM

Cinzia DD, Vittorio G (2009) Neuroaesthetics: a review. Curr Opin Neurobiol 19(6):682–687

Clark A (2009) Spreading the joy? why the machinery of consciousness is (probably) still in the head. Mind 118(472):963–993

Clark A, Chalmers DJ (1998) The extended mind. Analysis 58:10–23

Clavel C, Caroline F, Martin JC, Pesty S, Duhaut D (2013) Artificial companions with personality and social role. In: CICAC 2013—Symposium on Computational Intelligence for Creativity and Affective Computing, Singapore. IEEE, pp 87–95

Clavel C, Faur C, Martin J-C, Pesty AS, Duhaut D (2013) Artificial companions with personality and social role. In: CICAC 2013—Symposium on Computational Intelligence for Creativity and Affective Computing, Apr 2013, Singapore. IEEE, pp 87–95, 2013, Symposium Series on Computational Intelligence (SSCI)

Colombetti G (2005) Appraising valence. In: Colombetti G, Thompson E (eds) Emotion experience. Imprint Academic, Thorverton, UK, pp 103–126. Also published in Journal of Consciousness Studies 12:103–126

Colombetti G (2007a) Enactive appraisal. Phenomenol Cogn Sci 6:527–546

Colombetti G (2007b) Enactive appraisal. Phenomenol Cogn Sci 6(4):527–546

Colombetti G (2010a) Enaction, sense-making and emotion. In: Stewart J, Gapenne O, Di Paolo E (eds) Enaction: towards a new paradigm for cognitive science. MIT Press, Cambridge MA, pp 145–164

Colombetti G (2010b) Enaction, sense-making and emotion. sToward a new paradigm for cognitive science, Enaction, pp 145–164

Colombetti G (2014) The feeling body: affective science meets the enactive mind. MIT Press

Conway MA (2001) Sensory-perceptual episodic memory. Philos Trans R Soc B 356:1375–1384

Cosmides L, Tooby J (2000) Consider the source: the evolution of adaptations for decoupling and metarepresentation. In: Sperber D (ed) Metarepresentations: a multidisciplinary perspective. Oxford University Press, Oxford, UK

Csikszentmihalyi M (1990) Flow: the psychology of optimal experience. Harper and Row, New York

Cupchik GC, Gebotys RJ (1988) The search for meaning in art: interpretive styles and judgments of quality. Vis Arts Res, 38–50

Desmet PMA (2011) Nine sources of product emotion. In: Proceedings of the Conference: Interfejs użytkownika—Kansei w praktyce, Warszawa, pp 8–16

Desmet PMA, Dijkhuis E (2003) A wheelchair can be fun: a case of emotion-derived design. In: Proceedings of DPPI'03. ACM Press, pp 22–27

Dickey MD (2005) Engaging by design: how engagement strategies in popular computer and digital games can inform instructional design. Educ Technol Res Dev 53(2):67–83

Dijksterhuis A, Meurs T (2006) Where creativity resides: the generative power of unconscious thought. Conscious Cogn 15:135–146

DiSalvo C, Sengers P, Brynjarsdóttir H (2010, April) Mapping the landscape of sustainable HCI. In: Proceedings of the SIGCHI Conference on Human Factors in Computing Systems. ACM, pp 1975–1984

Dittmar A, Dardar L (2015) Personal ecologies of calendar artefacts. J Interact Sci 3(2). Available from: http://dx.doi.org/10.1186/s40166-015-0007-x

Djamasbi S, Siegel M, Skorinko J, Tullis T (2011) Online viewing and aesthetic preferences of generation Y and the baby boom generation: testing user web site experience through eye tracking. Int J Electron Commer 15:4121–4158

Duffy BR (2006) Fundamental issues in social robotics. Int Rev Inf Ethics 6(12):2006

Edmonds E, Muller L, Connell M (2006) Visual communication. 5(3):307–322, Effects of facial expression on responsibility attribution by groups and individuals. Pers Soc Psychol Bull 9:587–59

Eisenberger R, Jones JR, Stinglhamber F, Shanock L, Randall AT (2005) Flow experiences at work: for high need achievers alone? J Organ Behav 26:755–775

Ekman P (1992) An argument for basic emotions. Cogn Emot 6(3–4):169–200

Engelhardt CR, Bartholow BD, Kerr GT, Bushman BJ (2011) This is your brain on violent digital games: neural desensitization to violence predicts increased aggression following violent digital game exposure. J Exp Soc Psychol 47(5):1033–1036

Engeser S, Rheinberg F (2008) Flow, performance and moderators of challenge-skill balance. Motivation and Emotion 32:158–172

Fasola F, Matarić MJ (2013) A socially assistive robot exercise coach for the elderly. J Hum Rob Interact 2(2):3

Feil-Seifer DJ, Matarić MJ (2011) Ethical principles for socially assistive robotics. IEEE Robot Automat Mag 18(1):24–31

Ferguson CJ (2007) The good, the bad and the ugly: a meta-analytic review of positive and negative effects of violent digital games. Psychiatr Q 78(4):309–316

Fernaeus Y, Håkansson M, Jacobsson M, Ljungblad S (2010, June) How do you play with a robotic toy animal? a long-term study of pleo. In: Proceedings of the 9th International Conference on Interaction Design and Children. ACM, pp 39–48

Gácsi M, Kis A, Faragó T, Janiak M, Muszyński R, Miklósi A (2016) Humans attribute emotions to a robot that shows simple behavioural patterns borrowed from dog behaviour. Comp Hum Behav 59(June):411–419

Galloway A, Brucker-Cohen J, Gaye L, Goodman E, Hill D (2004) Design for hackability. In: Proceeding DIS'04. ACM Press, New York, NY, pp 363–366

Garrison J (2003) Dewey's Theory of emotions: the unity of thought and emotion in naturalistic functional "co-ordination" of behavior. Trans Charles S Peirce Soc 39(3):405–443

Gendlin ET (2006) Befindlichkeit: Heidegger and the philosophy of psychology. Rev Existential Psychol Psychiatry 16(3):1–27

Giambra LM (1979) Sex differences in daydreaming and related mental activity from the late teens to the early nineties. Int J Aging Hum Dev 10:1–34

Giambra LM, Grodsky A (1989) Task-unrelated images and thoughts while reading. Imagery Curr Perspect, 26–31

Govers PCM, HekkertP, Schoormans JPL (2004) Happy, cute and tough: can designers create a product personality that consumers understand?. In MacDonagh D, Hekkert P, Van Erp J, Gyi D (eds) Design and emotion, the experience of everyday things, Taylor & Francis, London, pp 345–349

Green C, Bavelier D (2003) Action digital game modifies visual selective attention. Nature 423:534–537

Gruberger M, Simon EB, Levkovitz Y, Zangen A, Hendler T (2011) Towards a neuroscience of mind-wandering. Front Hum Neurosci 5:56

Guthrie SE (1997) Anthropomorphism: a definition and a theory. In: Mitchell RW, Thompson NS, Miles HL (eds) Anthropomorphism, anecdotes, and animals. State University of New York Press, Albany, New York, pp 50–58

Han S, Song Y, Ding Y, Yund EW, Woods DL (2001) Neural substrates for visual perceptual grouping in humans. Psychophysiology 38(6):926–935

Hassenzahl M, Ullrich D (2007) To do or not to do: differences in user experience and retrospective judgments depending on the presence or absence of instrumental goals. Interact Comp 19(4):429–437

Heidegger M (1992) History of the concept of time: Prolegomena (vol 717). Indiana university press

Hekkert P, Wieringen PCW (1990) Complexity and prototypicality as determinants of the appraisal of cubist paintings. Br J Psychol 81(4):483–495

Hsu Ming-Chieh (2013) Annotation of dynamic identities in interactive aesthetics. Adv J Commun 01:441–449

Hsu S-H, Chou C-Y, Chen F-C, Wang Y-K, Chan T-W (2007) An investigation of the differences between robot and virtual learning companions' influences on students' engagement. The First IEEE International Workshop on Digital Game and Intelligent Toy Enhanced Learning, pp 41–48

Huang L, Morency LP, Gratch J (2011) Virtual Rapport 2.0[C]//International Workshop on Intelligent Virtual Agents. Springer Berlin Heidelberg, pp 68–79

Iacoboni M, Molnar-Szakacs I, Gallese V, Buccino G, Mazziotta JC, Rizzolatti G (2005) Grasping the intentions of others with one's own mirror neuron system. PLoS Biol 3(3):e79

Johnson RD, Marakas GM, Palmer JW (2008) Beliefs about the social roles and capabilities of computing technology: development of the computing technology continuum of perspective. Behav Inf Technol 27(2):169–181

Kahn PH Jr, Ishiguro H, Friedman B, Kanda T, Freier NG, Severson RL, Miller J (2007) What is a human? toward psychological benchmarks in the field of human–robot interaction. Interact Stud 8(3):363–390

Kätsyri J, Förger K, Mäkäräinen M, Takala T (2015) A review of empirical evidence on different uncanny valley hypotheses: support for perceptual mismatch as one road to the valley of eeriness. Front Psychol 6:390. https://doi.org/10.3389/fpsyg.2015.00390

Keller J, Bless H (2008) Flow and regulatory compatibility: an experimental approach to flow model of intrinsic motivation. Pers Soc Psychol Bull 34:196–209

Keller J, Blomann F (2008) Locus of control and the flow experience. An experimental analysis. Eur J Pers 22:589–607

Kiesler S, Hinds P (2004) Introduction to this special issue on human-robot interaction. Hum Comp Interact 19(1–2):1–8

Killingsworth MA, Gilbert DT (2010) A wandering mind is an unhappy mind. Science 330 (6006):932

Kim J, Lee J, Choi D (2003) Designing emotionally evocative homepages: an empirical study of the quantitative relations between design factors and emotional dimensions. Int J Hum Comp Stud 59(6):899–940

Kujala S, Miron-Shatz T (2015) The evolving role of expectations in long-term user experience. In: Proceedings of the 19th International Academic Mindtrek Conference. ACM, pp 167–174

Lankes M, Riegler S, Weiss A, Mirlacher T, Pirker M, Tscheligi M (2008) Facial expressions as game input with different emotional feedback conditions. In: Proceeding ACE '08, ACM, pp 253–256

Leakey LSB, Tobias PV, Napier JR (1964) A new species of the genus Homo from Olduvai Gorge. Nature 202:7–9

Lee S, Sundar SS (2015) Cosmetic customization of mobile phones: cultural antecedents, psychological correlates. Media Psychol 18(1):1–23

Lee YK, Chang CT, Lin Y, Cheng ZH (2014) The dark side of smartphone usage: psychological traits, compulsive behavior and technostress. Comp Hum Behav 31:373–383

Lewis MD (2005) Bridging emotion theory and neurobiology through dynamic systems modeling. Behav Brain Sci 28(2):169–194

Li DD, Liau AK, Khoo A (2013) Player-avatar identification in digital gaming: concept and measurement. Comp Hum Behav 29(1):257–263

Liu W, Pasman G, Taal-Fokker J, Stappers P (2013) Exploring 'Generation Y' interaction qualities at home and at work. Cogn Technol Work 16(3):405–415

Locher PJ, Nodine CF (1987) Symmetry catches the eye. Eye movements: from physiology to cognition. In: O'Regan J, Levy-Schoen A (eds), Elsevier Science Publishers BV

Lodge M, McGraw KM, Stroh P (1989) An impression-driven model of candidate evaluation. Am Polit Sci Rev 83(2):399–419

Loftus GR, Loftus EF (1983) Mind at play: the psychology of digital games. Basic Books, New York

Looser CE, Wheatley T (2010) The tipping point of animacy how, when, and where we perceive life in a face. Psychol Sci 21(12):1854–1862. http://journals.sagepub.com/doi/abs/10.1177/0956797610388044 // lots of face-based references

Low SM, Altman I (1992) Place attachment. In: Place attachment. Springer US, pp 1–12

Ludvigsen M, Petersen MG, Iversen O, Krogh P (2004) Aesthetic interaction: a pragmatists aesthetics of interactive systems

Lutz C, White GM (1986) The anthropology of emotions. Ann Rev Anthropol 15:405–436

MacDorman KF, Ishiguro H (2006) The uncanny advantage of using androids in cognitive and social science research. Interact Stud 7:297–337

MacDorman KF, Green RD, Ho C, Koch CT (2009) Too real for comfort? uncanny responses to computer generated faces. Comp Hum Behav 25:695–710. https://doi.org/10.1016/j.chb.2008.12.026

MacLean A, Carter K, Lövstrand L, Moran T (1990) User-tailorable systems: pressing the issues with buttons. Proceedings CHI '90. ACM Press, pp 175–182

Mahlke M, Thüring M (2006) Measuring multiple components of emotions in interactive contexts. CHI'06 extended abstracts on Human factors in computing systems. ACM

Mandler JM (1978) A code in the node: the use of a story schema in retrieval. Discourse Process 1(1):14–35

Margolin V (1997) Getting to know the user. Des Stud 18(3):227–234

Marin MM, Leder H (2016) Effects of presentation duration on measures of complexity in affective environmental scenes and representational paintings. Acta Psychologica, 16338–16358

Mayes DK, Cotton JE (2001) Measuring engagement in digital games: a questionnaire. In: Proceedings of the Human Factors and Ergonomics Society 45th Annual Meeting, pp 692–696

Medin DL, Lynch EB, Coley JD, Atran S (1997) Categorization and reasoning among tree experts: do all roads lead to Rome? Cogn Psychol 32(1):49–96

Milgram S (1967) The small world problem. Psychol Today 2:60–67

Morrison AJ, Mitchell P, Brereton M (2007) The lens of ludic engagement: evaluating participation in interactive art installations. In: Proceedings of the 15th International Conference on Multimedia. ACM New York, NY, USA

Mrazek MD, Smallwood J, Schooler JW (2012) Mindfulness and mind-wandering: finding convergence through opposing constructs. Emotion 12:442–448

Mukherjee S (2015) Digital games and storytelling: reading games and playing books. Palgrave MacMillan, London

Nass C, Isbister K, Lee EJ (2000) Truth is beauty: researching embodied conversational agents. Embodied Conversational Agents, 374–402

Neisser U (2014) Cognitive psychology: Classic edition. Psychology Press

Newman MW, Sedivy JZ, Neuwirth CM, Edwards WK, Hong JI, Izadi S, Marcelo K, Smith TF (2002) Designing for serendipity: supporting end-user configuration of ubiquitous computing environments. In: Proceedings of DIS '02, pp 147–156

Nichols S, Stich S (2005) Mindreading: a cognitive theory of pretense. Oxford University Press

Nielsen M, Dissanayake C (2000) An investigation of pretend play, mental state terms and false belief understanding: in search of a metarepresentational link. Br J Dev Psychol 18(4):609–624

Norman DA (2002) Emotion & design: attractive things work better. Interactions 9(4):36–42

Norman D, Miller J, Henderson A (1995) What you see, some of what's in the future, and how we go about doing it: HI at Apple Computer. In: Conference companion, CHI 1995. ACM, p 155

Overbeeke K, Wensveen S (2004) Beauty in use. Hum Comput Interact 19(4):367–369

Overbeeke K, Wensveen S (2003) From perception to experience, from affordances to irresistibles. In Proceedings of the 2003 international conference on Designing pleasurable products and interfaces, pp 92–97

Papert S (1980) Mindstorms: children, computers and powerful ideas. Basic Books, New York, NY

Pelowski M, Markey PS, Lauring JO, Leder H (2016) Visualizing the impact of art: an update and comparison of current psychological models of art experience. Front Hum Neurosci 10

Raichle ME, Snyder AZ (2007) A default mode of brain function: a brief history of an evolving idea. Neuroimage 37(4):1083–1090

Ratan R (2012) Self-presence, explicated: body, emotion, and identity extension into the virtual self. In: Handbook of Research on Technoself: Identity in a Technological Society. IGI Global, pp 321–335

Ratan R, Hasler BS (2010) Exploring self-presence in collaborative virtual teams

Ratcliffe M (2002) Heidegger's attunement and the neuropsychology of emotion. Phenomenol Cogn Sci 1:287–312

Reinecke K, Yeh T, Miratrix L, Mardiko R, Zhao Y, Liu J, Gajos KZ (2013, April) Predicting users' first impressions of website aesthetics with a quantification of perceived visual complexity and colorfulness. In: Proceedings of the SIGCHI Conference on Human Factors in Computing Systems. ACM, pp 2049–2058

Reisenzein R (2015) A short history of psychological perspective of emotion. In: Calvo RA, D'Mello S, Gratch J, Kappas A (eds) The Oxford handbook of affective computing. Oxford University Press, USA, pp 21–37

Rezasyah E, Mariane N, Toyong P, Binti Mokhtar S (2012) Redefining needs. In: 2012 IEEE Symposium on Business, Engineering and Industrial Applications, pp 579–584

Rozendaal MC, Keyson DV, de Ridder H (2007) Product behavior and appearance effects on experienced engagement during experiential and goal-directed tasks. In: Proceedings of the Conference on Designing Pleasurable Products and Interfaces, Helsinki, Finland, pp 181–193

Russell JA, Pratt G (1980) A description of the affective quality attributed to environments. J Pers Soc Psychol 38(2):1259–1283

Sabanovic S, Michalowski M, Simmons R (2006) Robots in the wild: observing human-robot social interaction outside the lab. In: Proceedings of AMC'06, Istanbul, pp 596–601

Sable P (1995) Pets, attachment, and well-being across the life cycle. Soc Work 40(3):334–341

Sageng JR, Fossheim HJ, Larsen TM (eds) (2012) The philosophy of computer games (vol 7). Springer Science & Business Media

Schachter S, Singer J (1962) Cognitive, social, and physiological determinants of emotional state. Psychol Rev 69(5):379

Scherer KR, Bänziger T, Roesch E (2010) A blueprint for affective computing: a sourcebook and manual. Oxford University Press

Schmajuk N, Aziz DR, Bates MJB (2009) Attentional-associative interactions in creativity. Creat Res J 21(1):92–103

Sestir MA, Bartholow BD (2010) Violent and nonviolent digital games produce opposing effects on aggressive and prosocial outcomes. J Exp Soc Psychol 46(6):934–942

Seyama J, Nagayama RS (2007) The uncanny valley: effect of realism on the impression of artificial human faces. Pres Teleoperators Virtual Env 16:337–351. https://doi.org/10.1162/pres.16.4.337

Sio UN, Ormerod TC (2009) Does incubation enhance problem solving? a meta-analytic review. Psychol Bull 135(1):94–120

Smallwood J, Schooler JW (2006) The restless mind. Psychol Bull 132(6):946

Spinosa C, Flores F, Dreyfus H (2001) Disclosing new worlds. MIT Press, Cambridge, MA

Steinfeld A, Fong T, Kaber D, Lewis M, Scholtz J, Schultz A, Goodrich M (2006, March) Common metrics for human-robot interaction. In: Proceedings of the 1st ACM SIGCHI/SIGART conference on Human-robot interaction. ACM, pp 33–40

Thorsteinsson G, Page T (2014) User attachment to smartphones and design guidelines. Int J Mob Learn Organ 8(3–4):201–215

Tractinsky N, Shoval-Katz A, Ikar D (2000) What is beautiful is usable. Interact Comp 13:127–145

Turkle S (2008) Always-on/always-on-you: the tethered self. Handbook of mobile communication studies, p 121

Turkle S, Breazeal C, Dasté O, Scassellati B (2006) Encounters with kismet and cog: children respond to relational artifacts. Digital media: transformations in human communication, p 120

Turner P (2016) HCI Redux: the promise of post-cognitive interaction. Springer

Turner P, Wilson L, Turner S (2009) Do web pages have personalities? In: Proceedings European Conference on Cognitive Ergonomics. Helsinki

Wang W (2017) Smartphones as social actors? social dispositional factors in assessing anthropomorphism. Comp Hum Behav 68:334–344

Watson D, Clark AL, Tellegen A (1988) Development and validation of brief measures of positive and negative affect: the PANAS scales. J Pers Soc Psychol 6:1063–1070

Werbach K, Hunter D (2012) For the win: how game thinking can revolutionize your business. Wharton Digital Press

Whiteside J, Wixon D (1987, January) Improving human-computer interaction—a quest for cognitive science. In: Interfacing thought: Cognitive aspects of human-computer interaction. MIT Press, pp 353–365

Whiteside J, Wixon D (1987) The dialectic of usability engineering. Proc INTERACT 87:17–20

Woolley A, Kostopoulou O (2013) Clinical intuition in family medicine: more than first impressions. Ann Fam Med 11(1):60–66

Xenakis I, Arnellos A, Darzentas J (2012) The functional role of emotions in aesthetic judgement. New Ideas Psychol 30(2):212–226

Złotowski JA, Sumioka H, Nishio S, Glas DF, Bartneck C, Ishiguro H (2015) Persistence of the uncanny valley: the influence of repeated interactions and a robot's attitude on its perception. Front Psychol 6(883):1–13

Web References

Cinzia DD, Ardizzi M, Massaro D, Di Cesare G, Gilli G, Marchetti A, Gallese V (2016) Human, nature, dynamism: the effects of content and movement perception on brain activations during the aesthetic judgment of representational paintings. Front Hum Neurosci 9

Design council http://www.designcouncil.org.uk/resources/report/value-good-design

Dewey (1934) https://www.marxists.org/reference/subject/philosophy/works/us/an-experience.htm

Google survey (2014) http://www.prnewswire.com/news-releases/teens-use-voice-search-most-even-in-bathroom-googles-mobile-voice-study-finds-279106351.html

http://news.bbc.co.uk/1/hi/health/8630588.stm

http://www.telegraph.co.uk/technology/facebook/7879656/One-third-of-young-women-check-Facebook-when-they-first-wake-up.html

http://www.telegraph.co.uk/technology/facebook/7985985/Facebook-hits-exam-results-by-20-per-cent.html

https://www.fastcodesign.com/1669924/steve-jobs-almost-named-the-imac-the-macman-until-this-guy-stopped-him. Last accessed 30 Aug 2017

https://www.technologyreview.com/s/542921/robot-toddler-learns-to-stand-by-imagining-how-to-do-it/1/

iPAD reference http://www.softwareadvice.com/resources/top-5-medical-devices-ipad-iphone/

Jones MG (1998) Creating electronic learning environments: games, flow, and the user interface. In: Proceedings of Selected Research and Development Presentations at the National Convention of the Association for Educational Communications and Technology (AECT), pp 205–214. http://eric.ed.gov/ERICWebPortal/detail?accno=ED423842. Last retrieved 4th Nov 2012

Knefel J (2015, August 24). The air force wants you to trust robots. Should you? Reprinted in Scientific American, August 25, 2015. Retrieved from http://www.scientificamerican.com/article/the-air-force-wants-you-totrust-robots-should-you/

Kubrick S, Clarke AC (1968) Screenplay for 2001: a space Odyssey, available via http://www.visual-memory.co.uk/amk/doc/0057.html. Last accessed 24 Aug 2017

Lenhart A (2007) Social networking websites and teens: an overview. Pew Research Center, Washington, DC, USA. Available online: http://www.pewinternet.org/~/media//Files/Reports/2007/PIP_SNS_Data_Memo_Jan_2007.pdf. Last accessed on 27 Nov 2015

Lawson JF (2016) Psychology and sexuality Published Online: 13 Oct 2016

Li L Exploration of adolescents' Internet addiction. Psychol Dev Educ, 20:26. Available online http://en.cnki.com.cn/Article_en/CJFDTOTAL-XLFZ2005019.htm. Accessed on Feb 20

Mac naming site: https://apple.stackexchange.com/questions/39477/what-started-the-whole-i-movement

MIT (n.d.) Cog Project. http://www.ai.mit.edu/projects/humanoid-robotics-group/cog/overview.html. Last accessed 09 Aug 2017

MIT (n.d.) http://www.ai.mit.edu/projects/humanoid-robotics-group/cog/overview.html. Last accessed 09 Aug 2017

New scientist (2008) https://www.newscientist.com/article/dn14147-mirror-neurons-control-erection-response-to-porn/

Norman (TED talk) https://www.ted.com/talks/don_norman_on_design_and_emotion/transcript?language=en

SciAm (1859, July) https://www.scientificamerican.com/article/100-years-ago-baseballs/

SoftBank Robotics (n.d.(a)) Nao www.ald.softbankrobotics.com/en/robots/nao. Last accessed 20 Aug 2017

SoftBank Robotics (n.d.(a)) www.ald.softbankrobotics.com/en/robots/nao. Last accessed 20 Aug 2017

SoftBank Robotics (n.d.(b)) Pepper www.ald.softbankrobotics.com/en/robots/pepper. Last accessed 20 Aug 2017

Steward M (2017) Empathy and the role of mirror neurons. All Regis University Theses. 820. http://epublications.regis.edu/theses/820. Last accessed 1 Sept 2017

Taggart W, Turkle S, Kidd CD (2005, July) An interactive robot in a nursing home: preliminary remarks. In: Towards social mechanisms of android science: A COGSCI workshop

The Cog Interview. http://www.youtube.com/watch?v=olvHuifsI7I. Last accessed 1 Sept 2017

The Nielsen Company (2009) Global faces and networked places. The Nielsen Company, New York, NY, USA. Available online: http://blog.nielsen.com/nielsenwire/wpcontent/uploads/2009/03/nielsen_globalfaces_mar09.pdf. Last accessed 1 Sept 2017

The Telegraph (2015) My weekend with Pepper http://www.telegraph.co.uk/news/worldnews/asia/japan/12022795/My-weekend-with-Pepper-the-worlds-first-humanoid-robot-with-emotions.html. Last accessed 21 Aug 2017

The Times (2017) https://www.thetimes.co.uk/edition/news/robots-learn-about-tea-and-sympathy-to-care-for-elderly-plz7kzzn7. Last accessed 1 Sept 2017

Times newspaper (2017a,February) http://www.thetimes.co.uk/edition/news/with-this-vr-set-i-thee-couple-to-wed-virtually-909hb2m9w. Last accessed 1 Sept 2017

Times newspaper (2017b, February) http://www.thetimes.co.uk/article/woohoo-amazon-s-digital-assistant-gets-excitable-qbd6j03p9. Last accessed 1 Sept 2017

Wundt WM (1897) Outlines of psychology (trans: Judd CH). Available from http://psychclassics.yorku.ca/Wundt/Outlines/sec15.htm. Last retrieved 29 Aug 2017

Printed in the United States
By Bookmasters